1977

how
PROGRESSIVE ROCK
defied punk

Kevan Furbank

sonicbondpublishing.com

Sonicbond Publishing Limited
www.sonicbondpublishing.co.uk
Email: info@sonicbondpublishing.co.uk

First Published in the United Kingdom 2025
First Published in the United States 2025

British Library Cataloguing in Publication Data:
A Catalogue record for this book is available from the British Library

Copyright Kevan Furbank 2025

ISBN 978-1-78952-367-6

The right of Kevan Furbank to be identified as the author of this work has been asserted by him in accordance with the Copyright, Designs and Patents Act 1988. All rights reserved. No part of this publication may be reproduced, stored in a retrieval system or transmitted in any form or by any means, electronic, mechanical, photocopying, recording or otherwise, without prior permission in writing from Sonicbond Publishing Limited

Typeset in ITC Garamond Std & ITC Avant Garde Gothic
Printed and bound in England

Graphic design and typesetting: Full Moon Media

1977

how
PROGRESSIVE ROCK
defied punk

Kevan Furbank

sonicbondpublishing.com

Would you like to write for Sonicbond Publishing?

At Sonicbond Publishing we are always on the look-out for authors, particularly for our two main series:

On Track. Mixing fact with in depth analysis, the On Track series examines the work of a particular musical artist or group. All genres are considered from easy listening and jazz to 60s soul to 90s pop, via rock and metal.

On Screen. This series looks at the world of film and television. Subjects considered include directors, actors and writers, as well as entire television and film series. As with the On Track series, we balance fact with analysis.

While professional writing experience would, of course, be an advantage the most important qualification is to have real enthusiasm and knowledge of your subject. First-time authors are welcomed, but the ability to write well in English is essential.

Sonicbond Publishing has distribution throughout Europe and North America, and all books are also published in E-book form. Authors will be paid a royalty based on sales of their book.

Further details are available from www.sonicbondpublishing.co.uk. To contact us, complete the contact form there or
email info@sonicbondpublishing.co.uk

Acknowledgements
I would like to thank John Greaves and Stanley Whitaker for
giving up their time to talk about their music. Thanks also
to Stephen Lambe and his team at Sonicbond for making sense
of my scribbles. Most of all, I would like to thank my wife,
Elizabeth, for her endless patience, love and support, and my
children, Sarah and Emily, for constructive criticism. Oh, and my
new granddaughter, Maeve – please grow up to be a prog fan!

1977
how
PROGRESSIVE ROCK
defied punk

Contents

Introduction

The prevailing wisdom is that punk rock killed prog in the late 1970s – presumably by drowning it in spittle. Like the asteroid that wiped out the dinosaurs 66 million years ago, punk smashed into our planet with its snarling three-chord rebellion and creative use of safety pins, obliterating some of the bigger prog behemoths and forcing others to take shelter underground. Punk's victory in this cataclysmic musical revolution was summed up by a T-shirt worn by Sex Pistols lead singer Johnny Rotten that defiantly proclaimed I HATE PINK FLOYD.

But is this really true? By heck, it isn't! Prog didn't just survive what turned out to be the short-lived rule of the barbarians, it prospered and evolved. In 1977 – the year punk supposedly conquered the world (well, the UK, anyway) – many of our most well-established progressive rock bands released some of their best albums.

There was *Going For The One* by Yes, arguably the last of their great classic albums (and the first Yes album I heard, giving it a special place in my musical heart). Jethro Tull's *Songs From The Wood* was a return to form after the disappointment of 1976's *Too Old To Rock 'N' Roll, Too Young To Die*, and is surely one of the top five best albums from one-legged flute warbler Ian Anderson. Rush's *A Farewell To Kings* is a personal favourite of mine, and Steven Wilson's, apparently, as is *Animals* from Mr Rotten's hated Pink Floyd.

It is undoubtedly true that a few prog bands were close to extinction at this point. Emerson, Lake & Palmer released no fewer than six sides of vinyl in 1977, plus a hit single in 'Fanfare For The Common Man' – two years later, they were practically history. Gentle Giant's *The Missing Piece* showed a band in a state of schizophrenic uncertainty – they struggled on for two more albums before being cut down to size. King Crimson were on an extended hiatus after breaking up in 1974, Genesis were about to transform into a world-conquering pop beast with the departure of guitarist Steve Hackett and Gong had lost main man Daevid Allen and were heading into the world of bland jazz fusion under percussionist Pierre Moerlen.

But the year also saw debut albums from defiantly uncommercial prog bands such as Happy the Man and Univers Zero, and from former Genesis frontman Peter Gabriel. Meanwhile, Godley & Creme's bizarre first solo release was to have serious *Consequences* for 10cc.

In this book, I have picked a bunch of albums and artists that I think represent the pinnacle of the genre's achievement in 1977. Some may be obvious choices, and I have already mentioned a few of them above. Others may be new to you, even if you consider yourself a bit of a prog cognoscente, and will hopefully encourage you to explore some new, hopefully ear-opening, sounds. All are studio albums released in 1977 – live albums don't count, so no *Seconds Out* by Genesis or *Livestock* by Brand X.

This is obviously a subjective list, and you may find some of your own favourites given the cold shoulder. That's why I include a section on albums that merit a mention in despatches, the ones that also served to make the year a little more colourful than it might otherwise have been. I have also tried to avoid making the list too UK-centric, although that is difficult because progressive rock has been (and still is) a very British preoccupation. So, you will find bands and artists from countries including the US and Italy within these pages.

Join me on a trip back to 1977. To mangle a quote penned by the immortal Bard of Avon, lend me your eyes and ears. I come to praise progressive rock, not to bury it. As for Mr Rotten Esq., he later admitted he loved *The Dark Side Of The Moon*. Cheeky little proghead he is.

Memories Of Old Days

They say if you can remember the 1960s, you weren't there. If you can remember the 1970s, however, you may wish you hadn't been there.

The decade is generally regarded as a grim nightmare, foreshadowed perhaps by the fatal stabbing of a fan at the Altamont festival in California in 1969 and the break-up of The Beatles in 1970 – events that signalled the 1960s dream was well and truly over.

It was a decade of strife, with energy crises, soaring inflation and political upheaval. In the UK, power cuts caused by striking coal miners and railway workers forced a Tory government to bring in a three-day working week before TWO general elections in one year – 1974 – kicked them out of office until 1979.

The nation was rocked by repeated IRA and loyalist massacres that spread from Northern Ireland to mainland Britain, the most notorious outrages being the Birmingham pub bombings in 1975 that killed 21 innocent people and injured 182, and the Dublin and Monaghan bombings a year earlier that slaughtered 34 people and an unborn child. Then there was Bloody Sunday in 1972 when British paratroopers shot dead 14 unarmed civilians – an act of State terrorism that has impacted Northern Ireland ever since.

In the US, the Watergate scandal in 1974 and the defeat in Vietnam the following year shook America's view of its country as the 'greatest in the world'. The racial conflict that had exploded during the 1960s spilt over into the following decade and the nation was wracked with riots and protests as people fought for long-demanded freedoms. Political instability continued throughout the 1970s with two one-term presidents, Jimmy Carter and Gerald Ford (actually a three-quarters of a term president as he failed to be elected after replacing the disgraced Richard Nixon). Carter's presidency ended in chaos thanks to the Iran hostage crisis, the Soviet invasion of Afghanistan and another energy crisis.

The key events of 1977 include the death of the King of Rock 'n' Roll, Elvis Presley, notoriously while on the toilet at his Memphis, Tennessee, home, Graceland, after months of constipation. He had performed his final concert just eight weeks previously. The year also saw the deaths of three members of rock band Lynyrd Skynyrd in a plane crash near Mississippi, while another flight disaster in Indiana claimed the lives of 15 members of the University of Evansville basketball team. Marc Bolan was killed in a car crash in London at the very tender age of 29.

Amid the doom and destruction, it's no wonder that people wanted to escape not just their miserable environments but the very planet itself – the big films of the year were the first *Star Wars* instalment and *Close Encounters Of The Third Kind*. If intergalactic travel was just a pipe dream, then perhaps we could dance our way to happiness with *Saturday Night Fever*, a film that not only established John Travolta as a star but also lit the blue touchpaper under disco music. The soundtrack, featuring songs by the Bee Gees, became one of the biggest-selling albums of the 1970s.

Indeed, we can join ABBA in saying 'Thank You For The Music' in 1977. The all-conquering Swedish combo released their second-best album, *Arrival*, in that year (the best was *ABBA: The Album* in 1978), while Fleetwood Mac's *Rumours* eventually became the bestselling LP of the year. Other bands dominating the album charts included: 1960s legends The Shadows, who hit the UK number one twice in 1977, once with Cliff Richard; The Beatles with *Live At Hollywood Bowl*; Frank Sinatra with *Portrait Of Sinatra – Forty Songs From The Life Of A Man*; and, believe it or not, Connie Francis's *20 All Time Greats*. It was the same story in the US, where the *Billboard* 200 was topped by The Eagles, Fleetwood Mac, Barbra Streisand and Kris Kristofferson. Then, there was Wings' 'Mull Of Kintyre' – nine weeks at number one in the UK, outselling anything The Beatles did.

It was also the year that saw the Electric Light Orchestra become an all-conquering beast with the release of *Out Of The Blue*, an album that, like *Rumours*, was packed with so many hit singles that critics complained it was TOO good. ELO were almost prog – their melding of pop and classical music was surely inspired by The Moody Blues' *Days Of Future Passed*, the first album that can claim to be progressive rock, in my view. Earlier ELO releases, such as the second album and 1974's *Eldorado*, certainly deserve the tag. In 1977, the pop content had certainly taken over, but there were still moments when ELO allowed their proggy side to come to the fore on tracks such as 'The Whale' and the four-song suite 'Concerto For A Rainy Day'.

All this may come as a surprise to those who thought 1977 was Year Zero for punk rock, such as the music press, who gave the genre far more publicity than it merited. In reality, few punk artists came within spitting distance of the number-one spot in the album or even the singles charts, which were dominated by disco, soft pop and bloody 'Mull Of Kintyre'. It is true that The Ramones, The Stranglers, The Buzzcocks and The Clash released albums that were later seen as important punk milestones, but, apart from The Stranglers, who were really too good to be punk, they rarely troubled the top ten in the charts.

The Sex Pistols were the real exception. Their controversial 1977 single 'God Save The Queen' – timed to coincide with Queen Elizabeth II's silver jubilee – was kept off the top spot by some industry jiggery-pokery, while their album *Never Mind The Bollocks, Here's The Sex Pistols* hit number one for two weeks (during which time, a court ruled the word 'bollocks' not obscene. So, bollocks, bollocks, bollocks). But then, so did Yes with *Going For The One* – a progressive rock album that topped the chart in 1977! Clearly, rumours of prog's death had been greatly exaggerated.

Closer To The Heart

It is true that the first great progressive rock era, which we can say started in about 1969, was coming to an end. In that time, we saw prog evolve out of the psychedelic rock of the mid to late 1960s to reach its peak in 1972/73, with groundbreaking albums such as Jethro Tull's *Thick As A Brick*, Yes's *Close To The Edge*, Pink Floyd's *The Dark Side Of The Moon* and Emerson, Lake & Palmer's *Trilogy* and *Brain Salad Surgery*. These were albums that were both commercially and critically successful, released during a time when you could walk down the street with a prog album under your arm and not be subjected to ridicule and contempt.

What was – and is – prog? Greater minds than mine have wrestled with this question and still are. But we can identify a few key elements. One is the gumbo of genres – prog combined the compositional and structural ambition of classical music, the instrumental and improvisational flair of jazz and the storytelling of folk, plus a smattering of non-Western influences, particularly from the Middle East and India.

The three-minute pop song, with its rigid structure of verses and choruses, gave way to lengthy compositions that sometimes spanned entire albums. An almost obsessive dedication to technical skill meant players could treat their instruments as part of intricately arranged electric orchestras. Lyrical content developed from simple rhymes about boy meets girl to discourses on life, death, money, power, science, religion and the antics of little Pothead Pixies with propellers on their heads from the Planet Gong.

Thanks to the success of The Beatles, who showed record companies they could let the artists take creative control and still make money, prog bands used the recording studio as another instrument to piece together their creations. Thanks also to ever-developing technology, musicians had an armoury of new instruments and machinery to realise their visions. The Beatles recorded *Revolver* in 1966 on a four-track tape machine; by 1977, bands had at least 24 tracks to play with – even more if they linked two or more machines together. The first digital recordings were released in that year.

If you wanted an orchestra in the 1960s, you had to hire one. Then, the Mellotron, which played short tape loops of sound, was introduced and became a must-have instrument for prog bands in the early 1970s. By 1977, there was the Polymoog synthesiser, the Synclavier and the Yamaha CS-80, which had true eight-voice polyphony (that's eight notes sounding at the same time) and touch-sensitive keys just like a piano.

As the 1970s wore on, some prog bands began to sink under the weight of their own excesses or found their artistic visions were out of sync with commercial reality. Take Yes, for example. *Close To The Edge*, with its side-long title track, achieved the perfect balance of artistic ambition and melodic accessibility. But 1973's *Tales From Topographic Oceans*, a double album of four side-long tracks inspired by Hindu guru Paramahansa Yogananda's Autobiography of A Yogi, became almost a symbol of self-indulgent over-reach. Some fans love it, but even Yes keyboardist Rick Wakeman hated it, dubbing it 'Tales from Toby's Graphic Go-Kart' and quitting the band in disgust (he came back in 1977).

But he can talk. For didn't Mr Wakeman release an album about King Arthur and his knights of the round table and then perform it ON ICE? Wearing A CAPE! Yes, he did, in 1975, losing bucketloads of money in the process. Perhaps he should have staged it in Toby's go-kart.

So, by 1977, progressive rock artists were scrabbling about for ways to remain relevant. For most of them, the songs had become shorter and a bit more accessible, and the subject matter a little less esoteric. That doesn't mean they were reflecting any of the political and social issues of the time. What is fascinating about prog is the way it pretty much ignored the musical and political landscape of 1977 and stuck to what it did best. For most prog bands, disco and punk weren't even on the radar.

Part of the reason is that most of the prog albums of the year were recorded in 1976 before punk had really taken off. However, even if you fast-forward to 1978, you will struggle to find much prog that even acknowledged the musical landscape was changing. It remained in its little cape-wearing bubble.

I remember 1977 as the year I discovered prog. Until then, I was a rabid Beatles fan who had transferred his affections to Wings, a band who were later considered a bit naff – in Brett Easton Ellis's 1991 book *American Psycho*, his disturbed protagonist prefers Wings to the Fab Four, clearly a sign of a deranged mind. Nevertheless, I will arm-wrestle anyone who doesn't think *Wings Over America*, released at the tail end of 1976, is one of the greatest live albums of all time.

My revelation came when I heard the title track of *Going For The One*. I was hooked and immediately rushed out to scoop up every Yes album I could afford on my wages from a part-time job as an assistant chef at a Wimpey bar. Then, someone lent me *In The Land Of Grey And Pink* by Caravan, sending me down the labyrinthine rabbit hole of Canterbury music, helped along by a Christmas present of a 1977 live album by Aussie-Anglo-French space rockers Gong. In the next few years, I soaked up prog like a little soundwave sponge until, in 2024, I'm sitting in front of a computer writing books about a musical genre that has soundtracked my life for nearly 50 years.

The 1977 albums that follow in this book are some of my favourites, the ones I still listen to today. For those readers who also know and love these albums, perhaps this will inspire you to get them out, dust them off and play them again. For those who know nothing about them – well, what a wonderful world of musical joy you are about to discover.

Pink Floyd – Animals

Personnel:
David Gilmour: lead vocals, lead guitar, bass guitar, acoustic guitar, talk box
Nick Mason: drums, percussion, tape effects
Roger Waters: lead vocals, harmony vocals, acoustic guitar, rhythm guitar, bass guitar, tape effects
Richard Wright: Hammond organ, ARP string synthesiser, Fender Rhodes, Minimoog, Farfisa organ, piano, clavinet, EMS VCS 3, harmony vocals
Recorded at Britannia Row Studios, London, between April and December 1976
Produced by Pink Floyd
Engineered by Brian Humphries
Label: Harvest (UK), Columbia (US)
Release date: 21 January 1977
Chart places: Holland: 1, Germany: 1, Italy: 1, New Zealand: 1, Spain: 1, Austria: 2, Norway: 2, UK: 2, Australia: 3, Sweden: 3, US: 3, Finland: 9
Tracks: 'Pigs On The Wing (Part One)', 'Dogs', 'Pigs (Three Different Kinds)', 'Sheep', 'Pigs On The Wing (Part Two)'
All tracks composed by Waters except Dogs by Waters/Gilmour

The Story So Far...

London architecture students Roger Waters, Nick Mason and Richard Wright joined Sigma 6 in 1963 before changing the name to The Tea Set in 1964, rebranding themselves a year later as The Pink Floyd Sound after the addition of Syd Barrett. A performance at the Marquee Club in London interested economics lecturer Peter Jenner and business partner Andrew King, who became their managers.

Signed by EMI, their first singles, 'Arnold Layne' and 'See Emily Play', hit number 20 and number six in the UK singles chart, respectively (despite radio stations banning 'Arnold' over cross-dressing references), and their debut album, *Piper At The Gates Of Dawn,* was a top-ten UK psychedelic hit. Concerns over Barrett's mental health resulted in the recruitment of Cambridge-born guitarist David Gilmour. Barrett was dumped in early 1968 before their second album, *A Saucerful Of Secrets*, which signalled a more space-rock direction. Subsequent singles failed to register, and the band went through a period of uncertain and patchy albums: *More* (1969), *Ummagumma* (1969) and *Atom Heart Mother* (1970). *Meddle* in 1971, with side-long epic 'Echoes', was critically well-received and commercially successful in the UK, Netherlands and Italy but failed to break the US. *Obscured By Clouds* (1972) was a patchy but interesting soundtrack album. Then, in 1973, Pink Floyd released *The Dark Side Of The Moon*, catapulting the band to megastar status. *Wish You Were Here* in 1975 was an inevitable disappointment in comparison, but still reached number one in the UK and US.

The Album

The punks were not the only ones to gob on their audience. Roger Waters did it in July 1977 at the Montreal Olympic Stadium on the final date of the *In The Flesh* tour. After weeks of playing cavernous arenas to stoned fans screaming for 'Money', Waters had become increasingly depressed and disillusioned. He was also unwell, suffering from stomach cramps from hepatitis, and relying on muscle relaxants to make him comfortably numb enough to get through the shows.

He was also highly irritated by some fans setting off fireworks, particularly through part two of the gentle acoustic number 'Pigs On The Wing'. 'Oh, for fuck's sake,' he exploded, 'stop all that fireworks and shouting and screaming! I'm trying to sing a song!' Then, incensed, it was said, by a fan at the front constantly demanding 'Careful With That Axe, Eugene', Waters stepped forward and spat directly into his face. Other reports suggested the fan threw a beer bottle on stage.

Afterwards, Waters was disgusted with himself. 'Oh my God, what have I been reduced to?' he said. David Gilmour was also mortified and sat out the encore behind the sound desk. In the massive stadium, with the band just tiny stick figures on a distant stage to most of the audience, no-one noticed he wasn't there.

How had it all come to this for the Floyd, just a few years after their commercial and critical breakthrough? In many ways, *The Dark Side Of The Moon* had become a millstone around their necks. It had brought them fame and fortune, which sometimes can be as destructive to a band as penury and failure. They bought big houses, travelled separately to gigs, brought their bickering wives on tour and lost money in dodgy financial deals. The band were also under pressure to create equally successful follow-ups to *The Dark Side Of The Moon*, which most critics believe they never managed to do (although, as stated before, I rate *Animals* more highly). In fact, Pink Floyd always seemed on the verge of breaking up every time they went into a studio as their personal relationships began to deteriorate.

These days, Roger Waters likes to paint himself as the sole creative force in Pink Floyd and the rest of the band as lucky passengers just along for the ride. He told *The Telegraph* recently: 'They can't write songs, they've nothing to say. They are not artists! They have no ideas, not a single one between them. They never have, and that drives them crazy.' Of course, it wasn't true – Pink Floyd would have been nothing without David Gilmour's languid, lyrical guitar solos and distinctive vocals, Richard Wright's atmospheric, slightly jazzy keyboards and Nick Mason's gentle, laidback drumming. Every band member contributes something to the recording and performance of a song, no matter whose name is on the credits – including Gilmour, who wrote or co-wrote at least a third of the tracks officially issued when he and Waters were in the band together.

However, it is true that Waters had started to take creative control of the music, deciding the themes and concepts around which he would pen most of the songs, culminating, of course, in *The Wall* (1979) and its spin-off, *The Final Cut* (1983). The ego had landed. So, it was he who decided on the concept of *Animals*, loosely based on George Orwell's 1945 political fable *Animal Farm*, although with its anger directed towards capitalism rather than Stalinism (then again, all extremist 'isms' look the same in the end). It was Waters' increasing sense of isolation and frustration – and his bitter cynicism towards the record industry and, sometimes, the fans themselves – that brought a harder, darker, more aggressive mood to the music.

In his highly readable biography *Inside Out: A Personal History Of Pink Floyd*, Nick Mason suggests the band may have been subconsciously influenced by the punk zeitgeist of the time. However, a look at the history of the songs on *Animals* doesn't quite bear this out. Two of the three main tracks were actually composed in early 1974 when punk was but a twinkle in Malcolm McLaren's eye, during writing sessions for the follow-up to *The Dark Side Of The Moon*.

The story of the band's struggle to create *Wish You Were Here* is for another book, but it impinges on our little tale because, among the many start-stop attempts to produce something that was as successful but nothing like *Dark Side…*, there was a song called 'Raving And Drooling'. Based on an insistent, pounding bass rhythm not unlike the one that underpinned 'One Of These Days' on *Meddle*, it had Waters yelling out lines such as 'How does it feel to be empty and angry and spaced/Split up the middle between the illusion of safety in numbers/And the fist in your face'. It seems to be a song about a homicidal maniac, raving and drooling while he 'fell on his neck with a scream'. On the recording of the track's live debut in Paris on 24 June 1974, Waters does indeed scream, although it's more of a long, drawn-out howl of pain and anger, while Gilmour supplies vicious slabs of guitar chords and Mason beats the hell out of his drum kit.

There was a slower, slightly less manic instrumental section in the middle that once again harked back to the same device used in 'One Of These Days', with Gilmour playing piercing guitar licks that would be repeated on the final recorded version. Then, we gradually go back into the screaming, the raving and the drooling, followed by a fantastic descending chord sequence by Gilmour that also made it onto the vinyl record three years later.

It has been suggested that 'Raving And Drooling' was a reaction to the breakup of Waters' marriage to childhood sweetheart Judith Trim – although he admits it was HIS fault. Perhaps it was the feeling that the band themselves had become prey to the wolves of the record industry, feasting on Pink Floyd's success, and a reaction to the press accusations of a sellout following a misguided decision to take part in an advertising campaign with French drinks company Gini. Perhaps it was an attempt to recreate some of the more disturbing music they used to make earlier in their career. Or maybe it was a wider comment on the 'violent social disorder' of the 1970s, as suggested in the (eventually withdrawn) sleeve notes for the new 2021

Animals remix (although most of the 'disorder' referenced there occurred later in the decade).

Whatever the reason, 'Raving And Drooling' wasn't the only disturbing song to come out of Pink Floyd's 1974 jam sessions. In November, another exercise in social cynicism was unveiled during a live concert at Wembley. 'You've Got To Be Crazy' was based on a four-chord acoustic guitar sequence in the key of E minor devised by Gilmour, with lyrics that seemed to foretell the sentiments of *Wish You Were Here*'s 'Have A Cigar' and 'Welcome To The Machine' – how we are all trapped in the straitjacket of social convention ('You gotta keep your shoes and your car clean/You gotta keep climbing, you gotta keep fit/You gotta keep smiling, you gotta eat shit') and how miserable life is for the poor successful, megarich rock star ('Gotta be sure you look good on TV/Gotta resemble a human being … You gotta keep everyone buying this shit').

Apart from the higher key and the tsunami of lyrics that tested Gilmour's singing abilities, 'You've Gotta Be Crazy' has most of the musical and lyrical elements that became 'Dogs' on *Animals*. There's the slightly yearning intro chords, played in a surprisingly jaunty, syncopated strum; the slow loping middle section with the emphasis on being 'dragged down by the stone'; Gilmour's lead guitar licks that seem to weep and howl like a wounded animal; the final slow chant and the repetition of 'Who was' at the beginning of each line ('Who was born in a house of pain … Who was ground down in the end … Who was dragged down by the stone').

Nevertheless, at this time, there were no animals in sight – no dogs, no sheep, no pigs – but there was one more new song, unveiled in Paris in June, that pointed the band in the direction of their next album. 'Shine On' was supposedly about Syd Barrett, Floyd's original singer, guitarist, vocalist and guru-type leader who had descended into drug-fuelled schizophrenia; the band decided that this track and a few others penned during 1974 and early 1975 worked together as an album about alienation and the demands of the music industry. 'Raving And Drooling' and 'You've Got To Be Crazy' didn't fit and were shelved … for the time being.

Whoosh! Hear that? It's the sound of us fast-forwarding to 1976. *Wish You Were Here*, the follow-up to *The Dark Side Of The Moon*, was released to inevitable disappointment. The tours got longer, and the venues, stage effects, financial rewards and egos got bigger. The band bought a three-storey block of church halls in Britannia Row, Islington, in inner London and converted them into a recording studio, reasoning they could spend as much time as they wanted tinkering with their latest album. Perversely, the making of *Animals* was probably quicker and more straightforward than any of the post-*Dark Side…* releases before the big split.

After all, they already had two songs sitting on the shelf, one of which was about 18 minutes long. They didn't need much more to finish two sides of vinyl, about 40 minutes of music. They also had the inspiration for a concept

– George Orwell's *Animal Farm*. Written between November 1943 and February 1944, Orwell's novel was itself inspired by another book – a manual issued by the UK government's wartime Ministry of Information on how the BBC should be nice to the Soviets because they were Britain's allies at the time.

Orwell's experiences in the Spanish Civil War left him deeply opposed to Stalinism, and *Animal Farm* was intended as a satirical tale ripping apart Stalin's brutal Communist ideology. He used the allegory of a farm after seeing a ten-year-old boy driving a huge carthorse, whipping it to keep it in line. He wrote: 'It struck me that if only such animals became aware of their strength, we should have no power over them and that men exploit animals in much the same way as the rich exploit the proletariat.'

So, the book imagines a group of animals who rebel against their human farmer in the hope they can create a society in which everyone is equal. The farm stands for Russia, the farmer Tsar Nicholas II, the pigs the revolutionaries and the dogs the secret police. The horses are the loyal, hard-working proletariat, and the sheep are the mindless conformist masses. However, there is no socialist utopia in the end – instead, the revolution fails and the pig Napoleon, who represents Stalin, becomes dictator. The pigs learn to walk on two legs, so they become indistinguishable from humans.

The book became a set subject for study in school English classes, so every child read it (or was supposed to if they had done their homework) and discussed its meaning. It is not surprising, therefore, that Waters saw some of the issues it explored reflected in 1970s British society as striking workers took on authoritarian governments in increasingly bitter battles. In the 'banned' sleeve notes published on his website, Waters 'portrays the human race as three sub-species trapped in a violent, vicious cycle, with sheep serving despotic pigs and authoritarian dogs.' It's almost as if *Animals*, the album, is *Animal Farm Part Two: What Happened Next*.

As the recording sessions stretched from April 1976 into the following year, the two 1974 songs were taken out of storage and dusted off. 'Raving And Drooling' became 'Sheep', only these are ruminants who bite back. New lyrics depict them 'harmlessly passing your time in the grassland away', unaware they are about to end up as Sunday lunch until they are driven to turn on the dogs and fall on their necks with a scream. A rejigged centre section ups the resemblance to 'One Of These Days', with the bassline (played by Gilmour, not Waters, because the latter wasn't good enough) sounding uncannily like the theme music to long-running BBC TV science fiction series *Doctor Who*, and an anonymous roadie's voice put through a vocoder for a satirical take on Psalm 23, The Lord Is My Shepherd. In this version, the Lord 'made me to hang on hooks in high places/He converteth me to lamb cutlets'. But these sheep, 'through quiet reflection and great dedication, master the art of karate/ Lo, we shall rise up and then we'll make the bugger's eyes water'. The final major key guitar chords are like a triumphant release.

'Sheep' was also given a new introduction by Richard Wright, who was clashing with Waters over his lack of any writing contribution to the album. Wright admitted to *Melody Maker* in 1978: 'I, in fact, didn't contribute anything, and that was partly because there was enough material from Roger and also because I wasn't feeling very creative anyway.' Like Waters a few years earlier, Wright was having marriage problems that appeared to have sapped his energy. But he made his mark on the album with the improvised jazzy Fender Rhodes solo that opens 'Sheep', even though he didn't get a writing credit.

'You've Got To Be Crazy' became 'Dogs' and was recorded with two major changes: the key was lowered from E minor to D minor and the lyrics thinned out to make them easier to sing. This allowed Gilmour to put much more emotion and feeling into the words now that he was able to draw breath occasionally. He also provides some gorgeous trademark solos that soar over the song like an inflatable pig over a power station. Waters then takes over on lead vocals for a calmer section in which he appears to realise that even dogs can be manipulated and misled by the pigs in charge and, by the end, it's the dog who is 'broken by trained personnel … fitted with collar and chain … dragged down by the stone'.

During the recording sessions, Waters came up with two new songs, both with very similar titles. 'Pigs (Three Different Ones)' is clearly a song written to the conceptual brief – each verse highlights someone Waters believed fitted the 'pig' profile, who had wealth and power and was feeding on the rest of society. One is a 'big man' with a 'pig stain on your fat chin', a general reference to fat cat (or fat pig) businessmen. The second is a 'rat bag' who is 'hot stuff with a hatpin', believed to refer to British politician Margaret Thatcher, who, in 1976, was the new leader of the Conservative Party and became Britain's first female prime minister three years later.

The third 'pig' is clearly named as anti-smut campaigner Mary Whitehouse, head of the National Viewers and Listeners Association. A devout Christian and teacher who was shocked by the 'immoral' beliefs of her pupils, she spent most of the 1960s, 1970s and 1980s campaigning against what she saw as declining moral standards in the media, particularly within the BBC. She objected to homosexuality – writing a pamphlet for parents on how to help their sons avoid being gay – *Opportunity Knocks* presenter Hughie Greene, coverage of the Vietnam War, the TV comedy *Til Death Us Do Part*, 'horrific' plots on *Doctor Who*, Benny Hill, Dave Allen and Chuck Berry's song 'My Ding-A-Ling'.

She was a frequent cultural target, lampooned as 'Mary Long' on Deep Purple's 1973 album *Who Do We Think We Are* (a mash-up of Whitehouse and the like-minded Lord Longford) and by publisher David Sullivan, who used her surname for a porn magazine. Waters blasts her as a 'house proud town mouse' who wants to 'keep our feelings off the street' – she considered suing him as a result. Speaking later to *Mojo* magazine, Waters said: 'Oh, she was everywhere pontificating on TV. Interfering in everybody's life, making a nuisance of herself and trying to drag English society back to an age of Victorian propriety.'

Musically, 'Pigs (Three Different Ones)' is a relatively simple song. The key is E minor and there are just three other chords. The three verses all follow the same chord pattern, and each verse repeats the line 'Ha ha, charade you are' and ends with the same refrain of 'you're nearly a laugh (a treat in the case of Mary Whitehouse) but you're really a cry'. An instrumental section after verse two that alternates between the chords Em and C sees Gilmour using a 'talk box' on his guitar to mimic the sound of grunting pigs.

What lifts this song into a different realm is Wright's simple but menacing keyboard intro, the short bass guitar solos played by Gilmour, the chopping guitar chords from Waters and Mason's slightly swinging drum pattern and hypnotic cowbell. The song fades out on a suitably dramatic guitar solo from Gilmour.

The performances on these three tracks, which make up 95% of the album, belie Waters' ridiculous claim that the rest of the band had 'no ideas'. This is the sound of a band working together, each providing the musical elements and textures that were required to create something powerful and dramatic. They were also having fun – or about as much fun as four uptight Englishmen who didn't like each other very much could have – by sprinkling the songs with sound effects of baa-ing sheep and barking dogs.

The final track to be written and recorded – 'Pigs On The Wing', which opens and ends the album – is a solo Roger Waters effort on acoustic guitar. A simple ballad in G major, it is a love song for Waters' then-new wife Carolyne, daughter of aristocrats Hector Lorenzo Christie and Lady Jean Agatha Dundas. Its purpose is to provide a sunnier contrast to the dark, menacing nature of the other songs, although it is not without its own gentle sense of paranoia – Waters sings of 'watching for pigs on the wing', British pilots' slang during World War 2 for enemy planes. So, even while he is expressing his love for his new wife (they divorced in 1992), he's looking about him for signs of attack.

There is another version of this song on the eight-track format of *Animals* (a housebrick-sized tape cartridge once used in cars, kiddies) featuring future Thin Lizzy guitarist Terence Charles 'Snowy' White, who joined the band for their tour later that year. He turned up at the studio and was invited to overdub a Gilmour-like guitar solo between the two verses, probably as a subtle audition. The solo was cut when the track was split to bookend the album, but Snowy got the job.

As with many progressive rock albums in the 1970s, the album cover tells as much of a story as the music. In fact, most people are probably more aware of what's on the outside of the LP than the inside, and the tale of the runaway inflatable pig over London has been told many times in print, TV and in a movie documentary, 2022's *Squaring The Circle* (see it, it's brilliant).

So, we will give a brief resume of the surreal events of December 1976 when pigs – or a pig, at least – did indeed fly.

The job of designing the *Animals* cover went to design trailblazers Hipgnosis, run by Aubrey 'Po' Powell and the late Storm Thorgerson. They had a long association with Pink Floyd – in fact, they founded the company after designing the cover of the band's second album, *A Saucerful Of Secrets*, in 1968, and were responsible for the cow on *Atom Heart Mother*, the prism on *The Dark Side Of The Moon* and the burning man on *Wish You Were Here*.

But their suggestions, which included a child watching his parents copulating like animals, were dismissed in favour of Waters' idea of an inflatable pig flying over Battersea Power Station, which he drove past regularly on his way from his home to the studio. A 40ft pig was constructed, and on 2 December, it was filled with helium and attached by a line to the imposing building known for its four iconic white chimneys. A marksman stood by in case the pig, named Algie, broke free and had to be shot down.

Unfortunately, bad weather stopped photography, so the crew returned the following day – but the band's manager, Steve O'Rourke, forgot to book the marksman. The pig broke free and floated over Heathrow Airport, alarming pilots and forcing flights to be cancelled, before crashing into a farm in Kent and scaring the cows. Learning nothing from this, a THIRD attempt was made to get the shot until it was decided to do what they should have done in the first place, which was to superimpose the pig on the power station back in the design studio.

The cover has become so iconic that it was referenced in the opening ceremony of the 2012 Summer Olympics in London, as well as in several movies, including *Nanny McPhee Returns* (2012) and *Children Of Men* (2006). In 1993, The Orb put a sheep over the power station for the cover of a live album.

Animals was released to mixed reviews. *New Musical Express* called it 'extreme, relentless, harrowing and downright iconoclastic', while *Melody Maker* hailed an 'uncomfortable dose of reality'. *Rolling Stone*, however, accused Pink Floyd of turning 'bitter and morose' and 'pointless and tedious'. That didn't stop it from reaching number one in five countries, peaking at number two in the UK and number three in the US. It has been reassessed over the last nearly 50 years and is seen as a strange, dark but compelling album that 'surges with bold blues-rock guitar lines and hypnotic space-rock textures', according to website Allmusic. *Animals* thrills and amazes me every time I play it, while its two predecessors are a little too laidback and sometimes ponderous.

Whether by accident or design, but mostly by accident, the ultimate dinosaur prog rock band had managed to create something as angry, immediate and relevant as any two-minute punk song. The fractured psyche of a multi-millionaire rock star somehow chimed with the general atmosphere of social desperation and violent upheaval that made the 1970s such a miserable decade.

As for the animals, they haven't changed. The pigs still dictate to the sheep while gorging themselves on the world's wealth, and the sheep continue to stupidly vote for them, while the dogs enforce increasingly draconian laws that, inch by inch, rob us of our freedoms, our dignity and our right to 'march cheerfully out of obscurity into the dream'. All I can say to the pigs is, watch your necks.

Yes – Going For The One

Personnel:

Jon Anderson: lead vocals, harp

Steve Howe: steel guitar, acoustic and electric guitars, vachalia (12-string Portuguese guitar), pedal steel guitar, vocals

Chris Squire: bass guitar, fretless bass, 8-string bass, vocals

Rick Wakeman: piano, electric keyboards, church organ at St Martin's church in Vevey, Polymoog synthesiser, choral arrangement on 'Awaken'

Alan White: drums, percussion, tuned percussion

With

Ars Laeta of Lausanne: choir on 'Awaken'

Richard Williams Singers: choir on 'Awaken'

Recorded at Mountain Studios, Montreux, Switzerland, between October 1976 and April 1977

Produced by Yes

Executive producer: Brian Lane

Engineered by John Timperley & David Richards

Sleeve design: Hipgnosis

Label: Atlantic

Release date: 15 July 1977

Chart places: UK: 1, Germany: 6, Norway: 7, US: 8, Canada: 8, Holland: 9, Sweden: 10, France: 10

Tracks: 'Going For The One' (Anderson), 'Turn Of The Century' (Anderson, Steve Howe, Alan White), 'Parallels' (Chris Squire), 'Wonderous Stories' (Anderson), 'Awaken' (Anderson, Howe)

The Story So Far...

Formed in London in 1968 by Lancashire singer Jon Anderson, London bassist Chris Squire, guitarist Peter Banks, drummer Bill Bruford and keyboard player Tony Kaye, it took Yes three albums and a change of guitarist to Londoner Steve Howe to hone their distinctive sound. *The Yes Album* (1971), *Fragile* (1971) – which saw the departure of Kaye and the arrival of Middlesex-born Rick Wakeman – and *Close To The Edge* (1972) established them as the UK's premier prog band. Bruford left and was replaced by Alan White from County Durham for 1973's *Tales From Topographic Oceans*. Wakeman was briefly replaced by Patrick Moraz for *Relayer* (1974).

The Album

I WAS a Wings fan in 1977. Please don't hold it against me. It seemed a natural progression from my Beatles obsession. But my schoolmates were into more progressive things, and one day, a friend showed me a record with a man's bare arse on the cover and said: 'Listen to this.'

The opening strains of 'Going For The One' burst out of the speakers, and I was instantly converted. The squealing slide guitar! The jumping basslines! The sweet falsetto vocals! The pounding, unapologetic repetition! The sheer balls of it all!

From that moment on, I was a Yes fan, although they were soon to be replaced as top dogs by Jethro Tull. However, I devoured every previous album, even those two early attempts before Howe arrived. Hey, I can even sit through *Tales...* without napping. I adore *Close To The Edge* and *Relayer*, but *Going For The One* will always hold a special place in my heart as my gateway to their world of fantasy, spiritual gibberish and crazily good musicianship.

It's the classic lineup, of course. Anderson, Howe, Squire, Wakeman and White, back together again after Rick's brief absence (in a previous book, on the progressive rock of 1972, I pointed out that the keyboard wizard joined, left, rejoined, left, rejoined, left, rejoined, left, rejoined and, finally, left. I say finally – both Rick and Yes are still recording and performing, so there's time for one last reunion).

His first departure came after *Tales...* – he felt he had little to offer to both the album and the band, famously eating a curry onstage during a particularly boring bit, so he quit and was replaced by Swiss musician and film composer Patrick Moraz for the jazzier *Relayer* in 1974. However, after touring the US, Canada and the UK to support the album, the band decided to take a break so various members could do their own thing for a while.

Anderson released *Olias Of Sunhillow*, a concept album about an alien race journeying to a new planet. Chris Squire recorded *Fish Out Of Water* with the help of former Yes drummer Bill Bruford. Howe put together *Beginnings* with the help of, yes, that Bruford fella again, while White produced his only solo effort, *Ramshackled*. Meanwhile, new boy Moraz released *The Story Of I*, a concept album about a tower in which people could experience their wildest desires. Oooerr, missus! They regrouped in 1976 for the *Solo Albums* tour, in which their individual compositions were mixed up with classic Yes tracks.

By this time, the members of Yes had become so wealthy that they were advised to leave the UK to avoid the punitive tax rates imposed by the Labour government at the time – a top rate of 83% on earned income and an eye-watering 98% on investment income. Like Emerson, Lake & Palmer and, later, Queen, Yes decided to record their next album in Switzerland, where the rate was a more bearable 44%, and where there was a studio within a casino complex in Montreux on the shores of the beautiful Lake Geneva. It was also Patrick Moraz's country of birth, although he was living in Brazil at the time.

So, in September 1976, Yes decamped to Montreux, along with their family, the band's management and recording team – with new engineer John Timperley replacing Yes stalwart Eddy Offord – and a film crew. Any money saved by avoiding UK tax was promptly splashed out on accommodation and travel – Steve Howe famously bought a first-class seat on Concorde just for his guitar, and he and his family rented NINE rooms in a luxury hotel. Substantial sums of money were also splashed out on renting hire cars and then trying to wreck them as quickly as possible by racing them around Lake Geneva. Later, Anderson would sing on an outtake: 'Money high, money low/ Money come, money go/Don't worry me'. Clearly not.

When they arrived, they discovered the studio was still being used by Emerson, Lake & Palmer, who had overrun their recording sessions for the *Works* albums. The wait meant they could work further on the songs they had written, but it also added to the already inflated costs of their Swiss sojourn – the delay proved fatal for Patrick Moraz's time in the band.

The cracks supposedly started to show during the rehearsals. Moraz was a talented player, but he never really fitted into the band, partly because of his nationality – Yes always saw themselves as British through and through. According to Dan Hedges's *Yes: An Authorized Biography*, Anderson thought Moraz 'just wasn't playing like he was involved … it was obvious that he just wasn't getting off on what we were doing.' He also claims that the rest of the band were waiting weeks for Moraz to join them from Brazil.

Moraz disputes that, saying he had helped to write a lot of material on *Going For The One*, particularly for 'Awaken', 'Wonderous Stories' and 'Parallels', which, he told the Let It Rock website in 2000, 'were as much part my composition as anyone else in the band at that time. The fact that I was not credited as a writer of the songs does not mean I did not compose for the group. As a member of the band, I composed as much as I could, as much as I was allowed to compose by the others.'

The final split came in a particularly brutal fashion – a headline in *Melody Maker* saying 'Wakeman Rejoins Yes'. This came as a surprise to both Moraz and Wakeman – the latter hadn't even been asked before the issue had gone to print. Luckily, he said yes to Yes the night before he saw the paper. As for Moraz, the split left a certain bitter taste in his mouth and, he claims, a large hole in his wallet, although it didn't stop him from trying to rejoin the band some years later. In the Let It Rock interview, he said:

Unfortunately, I was forced to leave, and even though, at the time, the split was not made to appear acrimonious, I suffered extremely and extensively. To be asked to leave so suddenly put me in a lot of turmoil and disturbance. The fact is, I was never compensated for anything. I never ever got paid for any of my tour participation in the extremely successful and extensive Yes tour of 1976, which comprised about 65 concerts, many of them in front of sold-out audiences of more than 100,000 people. After all, as a member of the band, I was entitled to a 20% cut from what the band were getting. In addition, it was an extremely complicated and difficult situation for me to be stranded on the street with my baby daughter and her mother without any transport or money in the cold winter of Switzerland. Then, the fight for survival to stay alive – it all became surreal.

Moraz sees the hand of Yes manager Brian Lane in the decision. Wakeman had released four solo albums by the time he rejoined, some of them selling more than the band's. But all the money he earned was being lost on lavish live shows, particularly when staging *The Myths And Legends Of King Arthur And The Knights Of The Round Table* on ice. Recent albums, including soundtracks for the films *Lisztomania* and *White Rock*, had failed to set the charts alight, so Wakeman needed a cash injection. Moraz says that's why Lane wanted Rick back in Yes.

So far as Wakeman was concerned, he liked the songs the band were rehearsing. In the beginning, he was there as a guest session player but was convinced by Claude Nobs, founder of the Montreux Jazz Festival, to take a full-time role. He'd got his own job back. The move certainly seemed to rejuvenate the band. In Chris Welch's book *Close To The Edge: The Story Of Yes*, personal manager Jim Halley revealed:

We spent the whole winter in Switzerland and the band were getting on really well with each other. There was a lot of rehearsing and writing in the recording studio itself. People would come along with ideas and be in the studio, composing and writing the songs. Jon and Rick wrote together. But one of the best tunes, 'Turn Of The Century', Alan White was instrumental in writing. It was a joint effort, though, and they'd all gather in the studio at one o'clock in the afternoon and say, 'Right, what do you think of this?' Someone would play a riff and Alan would start playing along, and that's how they created in those days. People would come in with little ideas and the others would augment them to develop the songs. My impression was that they would all contribute to each song. It seemed to be a very happy time.

The happy vibe seems to have seeped into the resulting album, which is full of joy and overflowing with musical ideas. The opening title track bursts out of the grooves like a thoroughbred racing chaser, propelled by the banshee squeal of Howe's bluesy pedal steel guitar, Squire's stabbing bass and White's pounding drums. In an interview with the Sound Opinions podcast, Anderson recalled:

I was singing away on the song, thrashing away on my acoustic guitar, and Steve suggested a steel guitar, and I thought, 'Are you sure? You're going to play it on that?' I didn't say anything until Alan counted it in and then dooer-did, dooer-did, dooer-did, it was like, oh my God! We are rocking and rolling here. It was a very exciting day when we recorded that song.

Anderson sings lyrics that seem to have a sporting reference, suggesting it's a song about personal achievement, about going for gold, but there's also an element of self-deprecation, as he admits: 'Now the verses I've sung don't add much weight to the story in my head.' There's a lengthy coda that cycles almost endlessly through the chords of Bb and Am7, during which Anderson repeats phrases such as 'listen in time/taken so high/too tough to move/travel twilight' and, most cryptically, 'turnstile to one'. Yes, a turnstile. And there's a 'roundabout' to add a bit of conceptual continuity.

Look, Anderson's lyrics are not intended to be studied too deeply – it's the sound that's important, not necessarily the meaning. Even Anderson probably didn't know what he was singing about. He fully admits he was making light of himself and of the idea that he might be a bit too cosmic, man!

Anderson's other solo contribution is the short but delightful 'Wonderous Stories', written during 'a beautiful day' in Montreux in what Anderson called his 'Renaissance period'. The song has an unusual chord sequence in the verse that takes it from B major to B minor, then up to D minor. Howe plays a Portuguese 12-string guitar, while White scored the bass and drums. It was released as a single, backed with 'Parallels', and was promoted by Yes's first-ever music video.

'Awaken', which closes the album, is nearly 16 minutes of pure, transcendent Yes music, cramming in virtually everything the band learned to do over the preceding three albums, yet in a concise, controlled way that never outstays its welcome. In the Sound Opinions podcast, Anderson said he saw Awaken as getting to 'the top of the mountain' after *Fragile*, *Close To The Edge* and *Tales....* He recalled how the song started life during the *Solo Albums* tour:

I was in the Hilton Hotel and I was heading to the breakfast table at about 8.30. I was walking past Steve Howe's room and there was smoke coming from underneath the door, so I knew he was stoking up on a joint. So, I had a quick joint with him. He was playing this riff – dung, dung, dung-dung, dyee-dyee-dyee-dyee. I went to breakfast and came back an hour later and he was still playing it! I said Steve, can you change the key? And he went dung, dung, dung-dung, dyee-dyee-dyee-dyee in a different key, so I said, 'Put on my tape recorder.' He started playing it, and I started singing this line against the rhythm he was playing. Then I said to him, 'Okay, we've got that as the beginning of the verse; now, how many chords can you play at the same time without repeating?' So, he started playing them – still recording, dunga, dunga, dunga, dunga, dunga, dunga, dunga, dunga, probably about eight or nine chords, and I started singing 'Workings of man set to ply out historical life/ Reregaining the flower of the fruit of his tree/All awakening, all restoring you'.

In Montreux, Anderson remembered the recording and the band started rehearsing it, adding a new middle section in which he played two simple, repetitive notes on his harp, Howe added slide steel guitar and Chris a bassline. Then, Anderson said:

Rick was getting ready to do a solo in the middle of 'Awaken', and he would play it on his keyboard, and I just felt it wasn't the right thing. I just turned round out of the blue and said, 'Rick, would you like to record in a church on a church organ, a real one?' And he said, 'Of course, yeah, that would be so cool.' So, we found out from the engineer at the studio that there was a town called Vevey about ten miles away and they had a most beautiful church and a great church organ, and that's where we recorded the organ for the middle of 'Awaken' – the best part, the most wonderful part, I think, where it lifted the whole piece up.

Initially, the plan was to set up a mobile studio at St Martin's church until it was discovered that Swiss telephone lines were so good the organ and Anderson's harp could be recorded together and fed down the cable back to Mountain Studios, where the rest of the band could play along. It was one of the first examples of remote recording that has now become commonplace, but at the time, it could only be attempted thanks to superior Swiss telecommunications – and, of course, the keyboard skills of the massively talented Mr Wakeman.

It was also Rick who wrote the choral part in 'Awaken' that was performed by the Richard Williams Singers, a Welsh group who were frequent visitors to Montreux for the International Choral Festival, and the Ars Laeta choir of Lausanne. Rick again used the St Martin's pipe organ to play the powerful opening chords for Chris Squire's song 'Parallels', originally composed for his solo album *Fish Out Of Water*, but he ran out of space on the vinyl. The track rocks like anything, driven along by Wakeman with Howe sprinkling guitar droplets all over it and Anderson singing 'making love towards perfection', which, of course, is what we all strive for, whatever my wife says.

Wakeman is all over the album, from the fast piano arpeggios that open 'Awaken' to his exquisitely sensitive, lyrical playing on 'Turn Of The Century'. Yet, that song began life thanks to drummer Alan White's surprise keyboard skills. One day, Anderson walked into the studio early and there was White fingering gentle piano chords – a C6, then a Dm and a G with a C bass. Anderson immediately started singing and sketching down some lyrics about an artist making a sculpture of 'his lady', who eventually passes away within the song. Then, Howe arrived and he started playing the chords before Anderson suggested he play solo acoustic guitar all around the chords. The result is another magical Yes composition that builds in intensity and instrumentation, coupled with deeply felt lyrics that carry real meaning and emotional punch.

In fact, 'Turn Of The Century' is one of Anderson's most effective lyrics – for once, he is actually telling a story rather than just stringing airy-fairy phrases together. The artist 'works to mould his passion into clay'. His lady is ill, and 'in the still light of dawn she dies'. But the artist works on, and in his lifelike creation, he remembers their time together – 'We walk hands in the sun/ Memories when we're young love lingers so'.

Howe's acoustic guitar – so beautifully played, with ghostly reverb making each phrase shimmer – gives way to Wakeman's piano, then electric guitar, bass and drums come in for the big finish and the evocative line 'like leaves we touch' before the lone acoustic guitar takes us gently out. For me, this is the true masterpiece of *Going For The One*.

There are some who see in the album's shorter, punchier songs a reaction to punk rock as if Yes were rising to the musical challenge posed by the gobbing brigade. Even Jon Anderson seems to have bought into the myth – because myth it surely is. We should remember that punk didn't really make much impact in the UK until the end of 1976 – the first single released in Britain was 'New Rose' by The Damned in October, while the Sex Pistols' debut, 'Anarchy In The UK', came out on 26 November, by which time, Yes were well into their recording sessions.

More likely, Yes were reacting to the muted response to *Tales…* and coming out of a period when they were writing shorter songs for their solo albums. Anderson had also dialled down his musical ambitions after a frank and open chat with Wakeman, in which he apologised for going over the top. That didn't stop *Going For The One* from being fully Yes, but with a slightly simpler approach that harked back to *The Yes Album*.

That simplification also extended to the cover, which, for the first time since *Fragile*, was NOT designed by Roger Dean, whose name is synonymous with Yes. It seems there were early discussions with Dean about the cover, but these seemed to flounder for several reasons, many of them conflicting. In any event, the band turned to Pink Floyd-inspired design gurus Hipgnosis, who came up with the naked torso of a man, shot from the rear, looking up at the Century Plaza Towers in Century City, California – designed by Minoru Yamasaki, who also created the old World Trade Center in New York. Spread across a triple gatefold, the combination of the silver towers against the unnaturally blue sky gave the album a slick, modern look.

Going For The One did indeed go for number one in the UK and was top ten in practically every other country on the planet – not bad for a bunch of dinosaurs. Critics hailed its back-to-basics approach and relative melodic simplicity, with *Record Mirror* saying 'they're back stronger than ever' and *Billboard* describing it as their 'most ambitious and awesome work yet'. It still stands up as a great progressive rock album from any year, let alone from 1977. We'll leave the last word (or many words, as is his wont) to Anderson from the podcast mentioned earlier:

> We were still on the same path; we got to the top of the mountain of musical ideas we'd done over the years and we'd finished up with that wonderful work and it was done with love … towards the end of the 1970s, to finish up with an album like *Going For The One* was such a relief on many levels for everybody.

Jethro Tull – Songs From The Wood

Personnel:

Ian Anderson: lead vocals, flute, acoustic guitar, mandolin, cymbals, whistles, all instruments (on track 2)

Martin Barre: electric guitar, lute

John Glascock: backing vocals, bass guitar

John Evan: piano, organ, synthesisers

Dee Palmer: piano, portative pipe organ, synthesisers

Barriemore Barlow: drums, percussion, marimba, glockenspiel, bells, nakers, tabor

Recorded at Morgan Studios, London, between 14 September and 16 November 1976

Produced by Ian Anderson

Engineered by Robin Black

Label: Chrysalis

Release date: 11 February 1977

Chart places: Denmark: 8, Norway: 9, US: 9, Canada: 9, Germany: 10, UK: 13

Tracks on original LP release: 'Songs From The Wood', 'Jack-In-The-Green', 'Cup Of Wonder', 'Hunting Girl', 'Ring Out, Solstice Bells', 'Velvet Green', 'The Whistler', 'Pibroch (Cap In Hand)', 'Fire At Midnight'

All tracks composed by Ian Anderson, with additional material by Martin Barre and Dee Palmer

The Story So Far...

Originally called the John Evan Band/Smash, formed by Blackpool schoolmates Ian Anderson, Jeffrey Hammond and John Evans (the 's' came and went) in 1964. They recruited drummer Barriemore Barlow and guitarist Chris Riley, playing blue-eyed soul. Hammond was replaced on bass by Glenn Cornick and Riley by Mick Abrahams. By 1967, they were a four-piece blues band with Clive Bunker on drums. The new name, Jethro Tull, came from a booking agent's staff member, who was a history buff (Mr Tull invented the horse-drawn seed drill in 1700), and first single 'Aeroplane' – originally recorded by the John Evan Smash – was released in 1968 on MGM Records (and famously mistakenly credited to 'Jethro Toe'). Signed to Island Records, the band recorded a blues album heavily influenced by Abrahams, who left soon after (or was pushed). The title, *This Was*, suggested changes to come. Recruiting new guitarist Martin Barre, leader Anderson took Jethro Tull in the direction of progressive blues and folk, releasing the UK number-one album *Stand Up* in 1968 and the number-three single 'Living In The Past'. The follow-up, *Benefit,* in 1970 fared less well despite the return of John Evan(s) on keyboards, but 1971's *Aqualung* was a million-seller, cracking the US top ten. Bunker left in May 1971 and was replaced by Barrie Barlow. 1972's single-track opus, *Thick As A Brick,* was a number-one record in many countries, while the denser *A Passion Play* (1973) received such hostile reviews from some quarters that it was announced the band had split up. They hadn't really, but Anderson concentrated on albums of shorter songs with *War Child* (1974), *Minstrel In The Gallery* (1975) and the disappointing *Too Old To Rock 'N' Roll, Too Young To Die* (1976).

The Album

Here is Squire Anderson, striding across the velvet green of his Buckinghamshire estate, backdropped by the woods, hills and valleys of Albion's bucolic countryside. The social and industrial strife and unrest of 1970s Britain is not for him; his England is a land of rosy-cheeked villagers supping cups of wonder and dancing galliards (a 16th-century dance with lots of leaping) in the forest, robust hunting girls with healthy appetites hopping off their horses to roger a local so-and-so senseless in the bracken, fields of waving golden corn ripening under a heavy, yellow sun, cows lowing in the meadows and birds tweeting happily in the bushes. Then, at night, find him in his study, a roaring fire in the grate, a pair of golden retrievers at his feet, leafing through a copy of *Folklore Myths And Legends Of Britain*, a glass of chilled ale on the mahogany side table and nothing to disturb his mildly inebriated reverie, not even a pinching codpiece.

This is the man who many think IS Jethro Tull, the one-legged flute warbler who turned a small, four-piece blues outfit into one of the most successful progressive rock bands of the 1970s, with albums such as *Stand Up*, *Aqualung* and *Thick As A Brick* becoming classics of the genre. But in 1976, he was nearly 30 and had transformed himself from a bug-eyed, hyperactive frontman wearing his father's shabby coat into a country gent with a new home and a new wife. Indeed, the Buckinghamshire pile – a 16th-century farmhouse on a 500-acre estate – was his first real home since he left Blackpool in the mid-1960s to become an impoverished musician, although he was on to wife number two, Shona Learoyd, a ballet dancer and press officer at Chrysalis Records. They are still together nearly 50 years later.

Few progressive rock bands took any notice of what was happening in Britain in 1977, and Jethro Tull are probably a prime example. In fact, I think there's just one other album in this book that was even more out of touch than *Songs From The Wood*. But that didn't stop JT from hitting the top ten in most parts of the world, along with a Christmas single that's now played every year. In fact, see those three albums I mentioned above? Add *Songs From The Wood* and 1987's *Crest Of A Knave* and you have the five JT albums that are an essential part of every discerning music lover's collection.

There may have been rioting amid mountains of rotting rubbish in the big cities, but in the English countryside, all was ripe fruitfulness and misty myths. The book Anderson was reading – published by Reader's Digest, a US magazine turned publishing company – had been passed on to him by Tull's new manager, New Yorker Jo Lustig. It covered all kinds of ancient superstitions and folklore across Britain, including the origins of traditional festivals and stories of fairies, giants, dragons and ghouls. There were also woodcut illustrations of such fantasy figures as Herne the Hunter, the antler-sporting spirit who haunts the woods of Berkshire. Some of these tales and characters were to find their way into Anderson's songs, particularly Jack-in-the-green, a pre-Christmas nature spirit who looks after all things that grow in the long, cold winter months. In the liner notes for the *Songs From The Wood* 40th anniversary box set, he said:

> When I read it, it certainly gave me thoughts about the elements of characters and stories that played out in the songwriting for the *Songs From The Wood* album, which then carried on over to the *Heavy Horses* album and even beyond that into the *Stormwatch* album. It wasn't the only reference I had; it was just something new for me to learn from. Other than a smattering of knowledge from history lessons or hearsay, I didn't really have a definitive literary guide to that world until Jo gave me this book.

Another influence on the album was Anderson's connection with the folk-rock fraternity. He knew Fairport Convention, who had started life as Jefferson Airplane clones before embracing the concept of performing traditional songs with untraditional electric instruments, and would later invite that band's bass player, Dave Pegg, to join Tull (as did, briefly, Fairport's Maartin Allcock and Dave Mattacks). Anderson had also produced *Now We Are Six*, a studio album by Fairport offshoot Steeleye Span that included traditional songs such as 'Thomas The Rhymer' and 'Two Magicians'.

So, he was no stranger to rocking up traditional music – and, of course, no stranger to using acoustic and folk instruments on Tull's albums. See 'Fat Man' on *Stand Up*, 'Wond'ring Aloud' on *Aqualung*, the opening to *Thick As A Brick* and most of *Minstrel In The Gallery*. But he had no interest in going down the traditional route, which he regarded as rather twee, and the songs he composed in 1976 still contained generous dollops of his trademark humour and cynicism.

But first, the band said hello to a new member who wasn't really that new. David – now Dee – Palmer had been involved with Jethro Tull from the very first album in 1968. As a freelance arranger and conductor, he (now she) came up with the horn and string arrangements for original guitarist Mick Abrahams' track 'Move On Alone', and then worked on every subsequent album. By March 1976, he was part of the touring outfit, playing orchestral parts on a bank of synthesisers, and became a de facto band member. There was no formal announcement, just a gradual absorption. Now, there were two keyboard players – the other was John Evan(s), who had joined in 1970 for the *Benefit* album. Luckily, there were few clashes between the ivory tinklers. Guitarist Martin Barre said:

We really welcomed David Palmer into the band because he was such a great character. He brought warmth and humour and musicality, and it was a real injection of the type of musicality that wasn't there before. He was a fantastic person to have in the band, and he made everything really pleasurable. Obviously, with both David and John playing keyboards, they had to have a connection, and happily, they got on really well.

Palmer also introduced the band to the portative pipe organ, and it became a signature sound on the album, particularly on the track 'Velvet Green'. He had found one in Morgan Studios and discovered it had a lovely, woody sound reminiscent of the instrument in the Walt Disney film *Snow White And The Seven Dwarfs*. He had two made by Mander Brothers in London, and their 'woody' sound fitted perfectly with the 'woodiness' of the album.

Most of the songs were written on the road – Tull were one of the busiest bands in the business and, in 1976, were touring almost non-stop across Europe and the US from the beginning of May until the end of August. In the 40th-anniversary booklet, Palmer recalls writing out the vocal harmonies for the title track 'backstage at the shittiest theatre that I've ever been in, in Buffalo'. Sorry, Buffalo! He was also writing out music in tearooms before gigs. In fact, it was Palmer's job to come up with most of the introductions and 'incidental' music for the songs, which he would then teach to the rest of the band. Palmer said:

Ian would come into the studio, get into the biggest flight case, pull the lid down to perhaps half an inch gap, and go to sleep in it – during which time, I would teach the guys the material I'd written so that by the time Ian woke up and was ready to join in, the band had learned what I'd written and we could play it.

The studio was Morgan in Willesden, north London – the first time Tull had recorded an album in the UK since early 1974. Both *Minstrel In The Gallery* and *Too Old To Rock 'N' Roll...* were made in Monte Carlo with a mobile studio, with the idea that the band could concentrate on the music without the distraction of families and homes. In fact, the opposite happened – there was just too much fun to be had, swimming, skiing and playing at racing drivers. Being back in Blighty seemed to improve things, and all the band remember the *Songs From The Wood* sessions as happy and productive, particularly as relationships began to deteriorate over the next few albums until a big split in 1980. Working in the capital, the band weren't insulated from what else was going on in 20th-century Britain – Ian Anderson told *Classic Rock* magazine that he remembered checking under Martin Barre's car for bombs amid fears that rock and pop stars could be the next targets of the IRA.

Through late 1976, Tull recorded more than a dozen tracks, some of which were early versions of songs that would appear on later albums, others destined to be B-sides or simply left in the can until the wallet-emptying box set 40 years later. One was recorded twice. 'Ring Out, Solstice Bells' was intended to be a Christmas single, but the record company had reservations about its unusual 7/8 time signature, so it was redone with Steeleye Span and Wombles band producer Mike Batt in straight, no-nonsense 4/4. In the end, however, it was the 7/8 version that was released as a limited edition EP – too late to do much in the charts for Christmas 1976 but destined to become a staple of the festive season soundtrack for the next 50 years.

What both versions had in common was an 'infinite canon' at the end written and played by Palmer on Victorian handbells – the notes follow each other in what is known as a 'round' and seem never-ending until they fade out, accompanied by powerful drumming from Barriemore Barlow. The EP release gave the band an opportunity to perform on *Top Of The Pops*, replacing Rod Stewart, who had pulled out.

We have already seen that Palmer had a strong input into the album's title track harmonies – he also wrote the instrumental section in the middle that is punctuated by the repetition of the song title. A complex piece that opens with acapella vocals suggesting that the singer brings you 'songs from the wood, to make you feel much better than you could know', it jumps around from 4/4 to 3/4 to 2/4 in a dazzling display of musical dexterity, ending with a sequence of 11 fanfare-like chords. It serves as a powerful and impressive opening to the album – a kind of 'calling-on' song, the sort of thing Morris groups would play to summon their dancers together – and has become an evergreen part of Tull's setlist.

Palmer also provided the distinctive keyboard intro to 'Hunting Girl', a saucy, whip-cracking rocker about a 'high-born huntress' seducing a 'local so-and-so' during a hunt (inspired by a riding school near Anderson's home), and the pipe-organ opening for 'Velvet Green', a similarly cheeky ditty about a young maiden being seduced in the long grass. 'Won't you have my company', sings Anderson, 'yes, take it in your hands'. Fnarr, fnarr.

Other songs on the album gave the rest of the band a chance to shine. On 'Pibroch (Cap In Hand)', Martin Barre created a bagpipe sound with his guitar, using backwards tapes, echo and plenty of reverb. Again, Palmer had a hand in composing the very folky middle section. 'The Whistler', the second single released from the album (backed with 'Strip Cartoon', recorded earlier in 1976), required Anderson to switch between two tin whistles in different keys. He recalls being too ill with shingles to stand up while recording the video for it.

'Jack-In-The-Green', another hardy staple of the live set, was composed by Anderson one morning and recorded and mixed by the evening of the very same day, with the talented chap playing every instrument, including bass and drums. Finally, closing track 'Fire At Midnight' harks back to the image I described earlier of Squire Anderson with his feet up in the farmhouse, enjoying a 'golden toddy', otherwise a warm whisky.

The album – fully titled *Jethro Tull With Kitchen Prose, Gutter Rhymes And Divers Songs From The Wood* – was released to mixed reviews from the press, although there was a tendency among some critics to dismiss any music that didn't consist of just three chords and a sneer. *New Musical Express*, surprisingly, called it 'one hell of a record', while the UK rock magazine *Cream* said it was 'a genuinely brilliant album'. However, *Sounds* dismissed it as 'like background music to TV's Robin Hood' and *Melody Maker* could only mumble that it was 'fairly good'.

Of course, the only critic worth listening to is the record-buying public, who thought well enough of it to put it in the top 20 in most countries around the globe. These days, it is regarded as a welcome return to form, and even the band like it. Barre called it 'hard work but rewarding' and Anderson, like me, puts it in his top five Tull treats. It also showed the band at the peak of their powers, working together in perfect unison like a team of heavy horses. Sadly, like the 1970s themselves, it was pretty much downhill from now on. A Stormwatch was gathering…

Emerson, Lake & Palmer – Works Volume 1 & Works Volume 2

Personnel:
Keith Emerson: keyboards
Greg Lake: vocals, guitars, bass
Carl Palmer: drums, percussion
Works Volume 1 recorded at Mountain Studios, Montreux; De Lane Lea Studios, London, and Pathe-Marconi EMI Studios, Paris in 1976
Produced by Keith Emerson (side 1), Greg Lake (sides 2 & 4), Carl Palmer (side 3), Peter Sinfield (side 2)
Engineered by John Timperley & Roger Cameron
Label: Atlantic
Release date: 25 March 1977
Chart places: Italy: 5, Australia: 6, UK: 9, Germany: 10, Austria: 11, Norway: 11, US: 12. Certified gold in US, UK and Canada
Tracks: 'Piano Concerto No.1' – 'First Movement: Allegro Giojoso'; 'Second Movement: Andante Molto Cantabile'; 'Third Movement: Toccata Con Fuoco' (Keith Emerson), 'Lend Your Love To Me Tonight' (Greg Lake, Peter Sinfield), 'C'est La Vie' (Lake, Sinfield), 'Hallowed Be Thy Name' (Lake, Sinfield), 'Nobody Loves You Like I Do' (Lake, Sinfield), 'Closer To Believing' (Lake, Sinfield), 'The Enemy God Dances With The Black Spirits' (Sergei Prokofiev, arr Emerson, Lake, Carl Palmer), 'LA Nights' (Palmer), 'New Orleans' (Palmer), 'Two Part Invention In D Minor' (JS Bach, arr Palmer), 'Food For Your Soul' (Palmer, Harry South), 'Tank' (Emerson, Palmer), 'Fanfare For The Common Man' (Aaron Copland, arr Emerson, Lake, Palmer), 'Pirates' (Emerson, Lake, Sinfield)
Works Volume 2 recorded at various locations over the years between 1973 and 1976
Produced by Keith Emerson, Greg Lake, Carl Palmer
Engineered by various people over the years
Label: Atlantic, Shout! Factory
Release date: November 1977
Chart places: UK: 20, Canada: 34, US: 37. Certified gold in US
Tracks: 'Tiger In A Spotlight' (Keith Emerson, Greg Lake, Carl Palmer, Peter Sinfield), 'When The Apple Blossoms Bloom In The Windmills Of Your Mind I'll Be Your Valentine' (Emerson, Lake, Palmer), 'Bullfrog' (Ron Aspery, Colin Hodgkinson, Palmer), 'Brain Salad Surgery' (Emerson, Lake, Sinfield), 'Barrelhouse Shake-Down (Emerson), 'Watching Over You (Lake, Sinfield), 'So Far To Fall' (Emerson, Lake, Sinfield), 'Maple Leaf Rag' (Scott Joplin, arr Emerson), 'I Believe In Father Christmas' (Lake, Sinfield, Sergio Prokofiev), 'Close But Not Touching' (Palmer), 'Honky Tonk Train Blues' (Meade Lux Lewis, arr Emerson), 'Show Me The Way To Go Home' (James Campbell, Reginald Connelly)

The Story So Far...

Yorkshire-born Keith Emerson played in a variety of bands before achieving commercial and critical success with The Nice in 1968. Greg Lake, from Dorset, played in several bands before being invited to join King Crimson, appearing on their influential debut *In The Court Of The Crimson King*. The two met each other when The Nice and KC played at the Fillmore West in San Francisco in 1969. Deciding to form a band, they chose Brummie Carl Palmer, who had played in the Crazy World of Arthur Brown before forming Atomic Rooster, for drum duties. Their second gig was at the Isle of Wight Festival in front of a 600,000-strong crowd that ended with the band firing off two cannons. Signed by EG Records (who distributed through Island in the UK and Atlantic in the US), their self-titled debut reached number four in the UK and number 18 in the US, almost immediately establishing the band as a prog rock supergroup. Follow-up *Tarkus*, released in 1971, hit number one in the UK. Their third album, a live performance of Modest Mussorgsky's *Pictures At An Exhibition,* followed just four months later and peaked at number three in the UK and number ten in the US. *Trilogy* (1972) was a top-ten triumph across most of planet Earth, a feat almost equalled by *Brain Salad Surgery* the following year. Live album *Welcome Back, My Friends, To The Show That Never Ends – Ladies And Gentlemen* followed in 1974 before the band took an extensive break from recording and touring.

The Albums

Emerson, Lake and Palmer picked a bad time to make a comeback. The punks were spitting out two-minute blasts of raw, ragged anger, revelling in their musical incompetence, and how did prog's supergroup respond? With three LPs of big band jazz, syrupy love songs, novelty numbers deemed not worthy of inclusion on previous albums and an 18-minute piano concerto. Oh, and they went on tour with a 110-piece orchestra and choir, 63 roadies, secretaries, personal assistants and a doctor, losing bucketloads of money in the process despite taking TWO accountants with them. 'Teenage Kicks' it wasn't.

Yet, in the biggest irony of ironies, this most pretentious and overblown of prog bands – so hated by John Peel that he called them 'a complete waste of time, talent and electricity' – scored their biggest ever UK hit single in 1977, reaching number two with the fantastic 'Fanfare For The Common Man'. All together now, bumba, bumba, bumba, bumba, bumba, bumba, bumba, bumba...

Some of what they produced that year was great, even the piano concerto, the ultimate keyboard player's artistic statement. However, like The Beatles' *White Album, Works Volume 1* was the sound of individual musicians doing their own thing and only coming together for a couple of tracks. The problem with ELP was that, after 1974, the band had really run its course. The three members just didn't know it yet. Instead, they took an extended break, feeling they had been 'milked dry' by five years of incessant recording and touring. Emerson told *Melody Maker* in 1977:

We'd all been working non-stop since we started in 1970, and we'd been working continuously before that. It was pretty strenuous all the way through, and I guess it reached a point where we said: 'We've got to this stage; what are we going to do next?' Speaking for myself, I wanted to do something more meaningful. I wanted time to think, 'Where do you go from here?' rather than just keep on recording.

Greg Lake added: 'We really wanted to make a break in the basic direction we were going in. We had flogged it to death from every standpoint.' But the break wasn't as restful as they may have hoped – certainly not for Keith Emerson. He suffered a major fire at his Sussex home that destroyed many of his musical scores and recordings, leaving him so depressed that he briefly sought solace in drink and drugs.

Despite his trials and tribulations, Emerson still managed to have a solo hit single in the shape of a 1927 song written by US boogie-woogie pianist Anderson Meade 'Lux' Lewis. He played 'Honky Tonk Train Blues' with jazz legend Oscar Peterson on the latter's TV show in January 1976 and, luckily, his own recording of the piece survived the fire. Released later that year, it reached number 21 in the UK charts, backed with a self-penned tune he had played on the show, 'Barrelhouse Shake-Down'.

Lake also managed to bag himself a hit single during the break, one that is much better remembered than Emerson's effort. The seasonal smash 'I Believe In Father Christmas' started life as a little acoustic guitar ditty, but with orchestral accompaniment and slightly cynical lyrics from Peter Sinfield of King Crimson and Bucks Fizz fame (he wrote 'The Land Of Make Believe'), it turned into a UK number-two festive hit in December 1975 and is still played in tinsel-strewn shopping malls and supermarkets everywhere to this day.

Meanwhile, Palmer kept a lower profile, moving to Tenerife with his future wife, playing big band jazz with pianist and composer Harry South and taking lessons in tuned percussion and karate.

With the singles under their belts, it was inevitable that Emerson and Lake began thinking about releasing solo albums, beavering away almost secretly on their own musical projects. For Emerson, that meant achieving his long-held ambition to write a piano concerto, this being the thing you do if you want to be viewed as a 'proper' pianist rather than just someone who sticks knives into Hammond organs. He began by consulting John Mayer, a Calcutta-born composer and conductor known for combining jazz and Indian music in his group Indo-Jazz Fusions – the pair met during work on the third album by Emerson's previous band, The Nice. Keith told *Contemporary Keyboard* magazine in 1977:

He'd tell me what I needed here and there and this is what has to come next to make it work. It's all instinctive with me. Often, there were times he'd say, 'Well, look, it's stuck. You have to make a movement there that's fast.' And I'd invariably come up with something on the spot. We always worked together, either at my house or at his. Then I'd be listening to it, and it just seemed to work.

Recorded in 1976 with the London Philharmonic Orchestra, Emerson's concerto is divided into three movements. 'Allegro Giojoso' is mostly fast and playful, with a frenetic intro reminiscent of George Gershwin's 'An American In Paris'. In fact, there's a lot of Gershwin in Emerson's jazzy piano style. 'Andante Molto Cantabile' acts as a short, two-minute interlude, mostly piano with gentle strings and flute backing, almost Tudor-like in its rhythm and simple melody.

Then, we reach the third movement, 'Toccata Con Fuoco'. The previous two movements were said to have been inspired by Emerson's peaceful existence at his Sussex home – the third seems to mirror his panic and anger as the fire consumed his belongings. In fact, 'con fuoco' means 'with fire'. Heavy, low, pounding piano notes create a sense of disorder and foreboding, punctuated by dramatic bursts from the orchestra. You can almost see those violin bows leaping up and down. However, it ends with triumphant chords that rise to a powerful major chord finish. The fire may have wreaked havoc, but everything is going to be all right once the insurance payment arrives.

The classical critics sneered a bit, but then they always do when a 'non-classical' composer dares to invade their territory. All I can say is that Emerson's concerto is always entertaining and, in its third movement, heart-pounding and emotional. It is said that Emerson's wife cried when she first heard it. Taken as a whole, 'Piano Concerto No.1' is a fine work that, according to those who know these things, also shows influences from Aaron Copland, Alberto Ginastera and Leonard Bernstein.

What was Greg Lake doing during this time? He was working on a clutch of mostly acoustic guitar songs he had hanging around that he couldn't fit onto previous ELP albums, all of which were intended for a solo album. His co-writer on all the tracks that ended up occupying side two of *Works Volume 1* was Peter Sinfield, an English poet and songwriter who, like Lake, was a former member of King Crimson, albeit in a non-playing capacity. Lake sang Sinfield's lyrics on KC's influential debut album, *In The Court Of The Crimson King*, and the follow-up, *In The Wake Of Poseidon*. The pair started writing together again in 1974, and Sinfield penned the lyrics for 'Benny The Bouncer' and 'Karn Evil 9: 3rd Impression' on *Brain Salad Surgery*.

Most of the songs they produced for *Works* are … well, they're okay – a bit cheesy and cliched, typical singer-songwriter fare mostly based on strummed or fingerpicked acoustic guitars with the occasional dodgy lyric. Impassioned ballad 'Lend Your Love To Me Tonight' contains a string of howlers that were no doubt meant to be deep and meaningful but come across as utterly ludicrous. My personal favourite is "The lamp of laughter dies too soon/To live reflected in a spoon'. Yes, a spoon.

On the downbeat 'C'est La Vie', Lake needed French café-style accordion but turned down Emerson's offer to provide it, using a session player instead, such was the atmosphere of secrecy and suspicion surrounding the solo projects.

The angry 'Hallowed Be Thy Name' was initially considered for *Brain Salad Surgery*, so both Emerson and Palmer play on it, while string players offer harsh, stabbing glissandos. 'Nobody Loves You Like I Do' also features Emerson on ragtime piano, but it's buried deep in the mix, and Lake plays harmonica and restrained electric guitar.

Finally, 'Closer To Believing' is another ballad so drenched with slushy orchestral strings that it's like drowning in syrup. It apparently took Lake and Sinfield two years to perfect, which is about as long as it feels like to listen to.

For me, Carl Palmer's contributions fare a little better. They show an artist striving to do something a bit different – in this case, mostly big-band jazz. Like Emerson and Lake, Palmer's recordings started as a solo album, and by 1976, he had produced nearly an hour of music that could easily have been trimmed down to the 40-odd minutes required for a vinyl release. Instead, the majority of the tracks were spread across the two *Works* albums, while his brilliant 22-minute 'Concerto For Percussion' didn't see the light of day until a 2001 retrospective.

Palmer's side opens with an arrangement of 'The Enemy God Dances With The Black Spirits' from Sergei Prokofiev's 1917 ballet *Ala And Lolly*. Dramatic and driving, it's as close to classic ELP as any of the band have managed to come so far, so you won't be surprised when I tell you that it was originally tried out with the group but sounded better with an orchestra. It certainly is a powerful piece of music, and Palmer's drums seem to spur the orchestra on without being intrusive.

'LA Nights' is one of the earliest recorded pieces on the album. Credited to both Palmer and Emerson, the backing track was put together in early 1974 with the help of Eagles guitarist Steve Walsh. Fast, furious and funky, it is clearly mostly improvised and doesn't really go anywhere, although the jazz horns at the end are enjoyably frenzied.

'New Orleans' is, frankly, a waste of everyone's time, a slightly greasy bit of plodding funk based on a boringly repetitive guitar riff by Snuffy Walden. Johann Sebastian Bach's 'Two Part Invention In D Minor' was scored by Harry South for strings and tuned percussion, played by Palmer and classical musician James Blades. It is short and sweet because it is short. 'Food For Your Soul' is bright and brash big band jazz written by Palmer for Harry South, whom he described as 'England's Quincy Jones' – South scored the horns and Emerson provided the Moog parts.

Finally, Palmer took one of the band's classic tracks, 'Tank', from the first album, and rescored it for orchestra and soprano sax. Some fans don't like it, but personally, I think it's an improvement on the original. In any case, the final two minutes consist of the original track grafted onto the end.

All three members of the band could have gathered up enough material to release three solo albums, but in 1976, things changed. For a start, they realised they had all used orchestras, which seemed serendipitous, to say the least. Then, there was the fear that if they didn't create a band album, it might be the end of the road for ELP.

In his autobiography *Lucky Man*, Lake said:

> Instead, we tried to have it both ways. I cannot remember who came up with the idea, but there was a proposal that we could make a double album that embodied both the solo and orchestral concepts and a joint effort from the band. This eventually became *Works Volume 1* – three sides of solo material (one from each of us) and just one side from the three of us working together as a band … I went against my gut instinct and committed to making the new album a success. In hindsight, this was a critical moment.

The band decamped to Switzerland to use Mountain Studios in Montreux and escape the ruinous 83% income tax rate imposed by James Callaghan's Labour government. Tax the rich until they squeak, he said. ELP were beginning to do mouse impressions. The trouble was, no-one really wanted to leave Blighty and, despite the peaceful and idyllic location, they felt bored and isolated. They also had unlimited time at the studio (now a museum dedicated to Queen) and swiftly ran up a bill of more than $1 million.

They also clashed with the Swiss orchestra. Thirty seconds from the end of recording the accompaniment to 'Pirates', the orchestra leader stood up, pointed to his watch and said time was up. Understandably, Lake told the departing musicians to 'fuck off' and the piece was instead recorded in Paris with members of the city's much more professional symphony orchestra.

'Pirates' has an interesting history. It was originally composed by Emerson for a movie adaptation of author Frederick Forsyth's book *Dogs Of War*, about mercenary soldiers attempting to depose the leader of a fictional African country. The film was delayed (it was eventually made in 1980), so Emerson considered it for his solo side of *Works*, asking Lake to pen some lyrics. The adventurous, swashbuckling music – part ELP, part Erich Korngold, who scored such films as *Captain Blood* and *The Sea Hawk* – inspired Lake and Sinfield to pen lines about pirates, using it as a metaphor for the band's relationship with its fans. As Gorge Forrester, Martyn Hanson and Frank Askew wrote in their book *Emerson Lake & Palmer: The Show That Never Ends*:

> It's all there – the adventuring, intrepid, devil-may-care spirit, setting out on brave voyages, seeking fortune, fighting, conquering all in sight, looting money and treasure, indulging in as much wine, women, song and gambling

as possible along the way. In its sometimes ironic discourse of loyalty and heroism, 'Pirates' is as much about ELP and their relationship with their fans as it is about seafaring outlaws of old.

I couldn't have put it better myself. But then, it did take three of them to write it. One of the first people to hear the track outside the band and the crew was the composer and conductor Leonard Bernstein of *West Side Story* fame. He was working across the road from the Paris studio and popped in wearing a red polka-dot neckerchief and waving a stick of French bread. His response? 'Singer's not bad', he said, which must have undoubtedly made Lake's head swell. Then, he listened to Emerson's piano concerto, cryptically suggesting it reminded him of 'Grandma Moses'. Later, the band discovered 'Grandma Moses' was an American painter famous for simple, naïve folk art. The cheek.

So, we come to 'Fanfare For The Common Man'. Bumba, bumba, bumba (that's enough). Aaron Copland's most famous musical work was written in 1942, inspired by then-US vice-president Henry Wallace's claim that the world had entered the 'century of the common man'. Emerson was a Copland fan – he had previously adapted the composer's 'Hoedown' for the band's *Trilogy* album. He claimed he first heard it at the office of the band's record label, Manticore – Lake says HE had introduced it to the group by playing it repeatedly in the studio.

One day in Montreux, Keith started playing the main theme on his new Yamaha GX1 keyboard, Lake added a pounding, shuffling bassline (bumba!) and Palmer joined in on drums. Jamming together for the first time in nearly two years, laying down what Lake called a 'dirty r&b sound', the band turned Copland's elegant, restrained fanfare into a locomotive engine thundering down the musical tracks. With a lengthy, spontaneous, improvised middle section, they created a ten-minute epic that captured the quintessential ELP sound – that combination of rocking up the classics with no-holds-barred instrumental chutzpah.

An edited version, without the improv, was released as a single and hit number two in the UK, held off the top spot by 'Bohemian Rhapsody' – two great prog masterpieces that the punk fraternity could only dream of being able to hum along to, let alone play. Even Copland himself loved it … eventually. The band needed his permission to use his music, so they sent him the edited version, worried that Copland wouldn't like the improvisation. The composer responded by saying he could see no reason why he should give his permission because it sounded just like the original. So, he was sent the full version. His response was: 'This is brilliant, this is fantastic. This is doing something to my music.'

The single was helped up the charts by a video shot while ELP were in the underground car park at the Montreal Olympic stadium, rehearsing for the *Works* tour. Initially, the band said they were too busy to make a video. Then,

Lake went upstairs for some fresh air and saw the stadium covered in untouched snow. It proved to be a perfect setting for the band to shoot the video, despite the fact they could only film 30 seconds at a time before their fingers started freezing.

Works Volume 1 was released in March 1977 to mixed reviews, with some critics being particularly sniffy about the solo sides. However, all seemed to agree that side four showed the band at the top of their game. What they didn't know, of course, was that this was to be the last decent album ELP would produce – it was downhill from now on.

Works Volume 2, released in November to critical and commercial indifference, was a disappointment, containing cast-offs from previous albums such as 1973's 'Tiger In A Spotlight', various single B-sides, a reworking of Lake's holiday hit and a few leftovers from the individual solo sessions. To give you some idea of the quality on offer, the closer is the 1925 pub sing-along 'Show Me The Way To Go Home', which the group used to play to end their live shows.

By this time, Emerson, Lake & Palmer were almost on the ropes. Their big 1977 US tour may have set records for its size and ambition, but it left them almost bankrupt. The decision to take an orchestra on tour required three buses for the performers and seven 45-foot articulated trucks for the equipment, the construction of a purpose-built stage with more than 300 lights and a 72,000-watt PA system feeding to a complex mixing desk under the stage. The bill reached more than a million dollars before a single live note had been played – and it cost $300,000 a week to keep the show on the road.

An added challenge was a musicians' union ruling that the orchestra could not travel more than 100 miles a day, which, in America, meant concerts were too close to each other to sell out. However, the only way the tour could break even was if every seat had a bum on it. When three of the dates were cancelled – one for poor ticket sales – it cost the band more than $2 million.

Eventually, they had to jettison the orchestra to save money – the musicians offered to play for free but were overruled by their union. This left ELP unable to play some of the set, including the third movement of Emerson's piano concerto and 'The Enemy God'. By the end of 1977 and into early 1978, ELP were a three-piece again – and it would be the last tour they ever played. There was one final studio album before the break-up, the ludicrous *Love Beach* that showed the three on the cover posing like the Bee Gees with big toothy grins and lots of exposed chest hair. Then, ELP were no more, killed off not by the punks but by their own overweening ambition.

Greg Lake said in *Lucky Man*:

I believe that the orchestral project ultimately led to the demise of ELP. Prior to the orchestra and *Works Volume 1*, ELP were a multiple platinum album-selling act, performing in stadiums and arenas all over the world, inspiring a new generation of musicians. After the orchestral project, we were supposed to pare back our stage show and the innovative recordings dried up. To me, it seemed that the flame of ELP that had ignited so many audiences throughout the world had begun to die.

Emerson begged to differ, claiming the orchestral project was one of the best things he had done. However, that didn't change the fact that it sank the band – the iceberg to ELP's Titanic.

Listening to *Works Volume 1* nearly 50 years later, there's a sense of regret that they didn't follow their initial instincts and release their solo albums as planned. Emerson could then have got his orchestral ambitions out of his system, and the band could have come together again to produce a single album to equal anything they had done in the past.

After all, they DID have their biggest UK hit in that year, and there is still something thrilling and magical about hearing that fanfare of notes from Emerson's Yamaha, then the rhythmic throb from Lake's bass and Palmer's steam engine drums. All together now … bumba, bumba, bumba, bumba, bumba…

Styx – The Grand Illusion

Personnel:

Dennis DeYoung: lead vocals, keyboards

James 'JY' Young: vocals, electric guitars, synthesiser on 'Come Sail Away'

Tommy Shaw: vocals, electric and acoustic guitars

Chuck Panozzo: bass guitar

John Panozzo: drums, percussion

Recorded at Paragon Recording Studios, Chicago, in early 1977

Produced by Styx and Barry Mraz

Production assistance/engineer: Barry Mraz

Engineered by Rob Kingsland

Mastered by Mike Reese at the Mastering Lab, Los Angeles, California

Label: A&M

Release date: 7 July 1977 on A&M Records.

Chart places: US: 6

Tracks: 'The Grand Illusion' (Dennis DeYoung), 'Fooling Yourself (The Angry Young Man)' (Tommy Shaw), 'Superstars' (James 'JY' Young, DeYoung, Shaw), 'Come Sail Away' (DeYoung), 'Miss America' (Young), 'Man In The Wilderness' (Shaw), 'Castle Walls' (DeYoung), 'The Grand Finale' (Young, DeYoung, Shaw)

The Story So Far...

Formed in Chicago in 1972 by Dennis DeYoung, James 'JY' Young, twin brothers Chuck and John Panozzo and John 'JC' Curulewski, the band name was chosen because it was the only one none of them hated (it's the river that runs through Hell in Greek mythology). They signed to Wooden Nickel Records after being spotted by a talent scout and released their debut album, *Styx*, that year, charting in the US with the single 'Best Thing'. *Styx II* (1973), *The Serpent Is Rising* (1973) and *Man Of Miracles* (1974) followed, without much impact. However, in 1975, the belated release of 'Lady' hit number six in the US and *Styx II* went gold. Signed to A&M Records, the band released *Equinox* that year, and then Tommy Shaw (born in Montgomery, Alabama, on 11 September 1953) replaced JC on guitar for *Crystal Ball* (1976). Both albums were moderately successful but failed to establish the band across the US. What Styx needed was the big breakthrough album...

The Album

Dennis DeYoung was depressed. His band Styx had released six albums in four years, scored a top-ten single with 'Lady' and signed to record label behemoths A&M. They were musical heroes in their home city of Chicago, Illinois. But national recognition eluded them. In fact, they seemed to be going backwards. It appeared Styx were destined to remain in the sticks.

In an interview with podcast In the Studio With Redbeard, he said: 'We'd done *Equinox*, which was a fantastic record. It had done respectably, but it had not been the success we thought it would be. Then *Crystal Ball* actually sold less than *Equinox*, so we were feeling, uh-oh, we're on that downward slide a little bit, and we couldn't understand it.'

It was tough for US bands that didn't hail from the East or West coasts. Illinois is known as one of the 'flyover states' – that huge swathe of America that people fly over to get to New York or Los Angeles. Without the internet to promote themselves, bands could easily get overlooked and ignored by a record industry that believed the M in Midwest also stood for 'mediocre'.

Styx's first four albums were on a local record label, Wooden Nickel, whose other acts included the Siegel-Schwall Band, James Lee Stanley and Jaggerz. No, I haven't heard of them either. Signing to A&M was supposed to be the first step in helping Styx break out of Chicago into the mainstream (Wooden Nickel sued them for breach of contract before folding). But it seemed the grand plan was failing.

Prone to becoming angry and depressed at setbacks in his life, DeYoung began to question his career choice and yearned for a simpler life. He also cast a cynical eye on the illusion of being a 'rock star', seen as somehow special and different when, only a few years earlier, he was just a fan in the audience. This broadened out into a general cynicism towards the false images served up by 1970s America and his debunking of the myth of success.

His musings led to two tracks that are the cornerstones of the album – the hit single 'Come Sail Away' and the title track 'The Grand Illusion'. On 'Come Sail Away', he told the podcast:

A lot of times, I write songs to remind myself of what I should be thinking rather than what it is I AM thinking. It's good therapy if the song gets played and people relate and they communicate and they say, you know what you say in that song, that's my life, that's the way I feel. 'Come Sail Away' was really about growing up and escaping. It was a time of total reflection: I decided I always wanted to be a rock musician and now here I am right in the middle of this thing, and I was saying to myself, why? Why do I do this? What was motivating me to be what I am? What was making me who I am? And 'Come Sail Away' is really about that feeling of saying, I wish a gathering of angels would appear somewhere and show me the way and let me just sail away.

Opening as a plaintive piano ballad in C major, the song grows in instrumentation until guitars and drums crash in, turning it into a driving rock number for the chorus, interspersed with a brief keyboard instrumental before it plays out on a repeat of the chorus under JY's soaring lead guitar. It is a bravado performance that took 'Come Sail Away' to number eight in the *Billboard* singles chart.

The title of the second track came to DeYoung during the recording of *Equinox* two years earlier, from the French 1937 anti-war film, but he forgot about it until a friend reminded him just before the band was due to go into the studio to make their seventh album. Here he is in that podcast again:

> I said, yeah, you know something, that's a good title and it really fits how I feel in my life right now, about what I do and about the whole atmosphere in America. It had something to do with the paradox of illusion versus reality in our culture, in that the things you see in advertisements and television and hear on the radio, they present lifestyles and images that are, by and large, false. It sets up disappointment in two ways: one, if you never achieve any amount of 'success', as it is viewed in our culture, then when you see all these images, you feel yourself a failure; you feel like you've missed out on something, that somebody else has the answers and somebody else is living the life that you're missing out on. You feel less because of it. On the other hand, if you are fortunate enough to succeed, you find out quite quickly that all those images are somebody else's imagination in the first place because even if you do succeed, those images, that lifestyle, that perception of reality, doesn't exist for anyone. 'The Grand Illusion' was, in part, my way of saying don't be fooled by all the things you see because that's not reality.

Kicking off with a fanfare in 4/4 marching rhythm, DeYoung sings, 'Welcome to the grand illusion/Come in and see what's happening/Pay the price, get your tickets for the show', punctuated by riffs from JY. But he warns, 'Don't be fooled by the radio/The TV or the magazines/They show you photographs of how your life should be/But they're just someone's fantasy'. With DeYoung on organ and JY playing dirty lead guitar, the track is not only regarded as Styx's greatest musical moment, but it also established a loose concept for the album that the rest of the band quickly bought into.

For example, JY woke up in the middle of the night with the idea that one of the grandest cultural illusions in the US was the Miss America beauty pageant, which started in 1921 as a bathing beauty revue and is still going more than 100 years later. These days, it tries to pretend it's about minds and character, but back in the 1970s, it was little more than an excuse to parade women about in bathing costumes. Astonishing, really, that men would want to watch such a thing.

He wrote a song based on a heavy guitar riff inspired by the one played by Martin Barre on Jethro Tull's 1975 track 'Minstrel In The Gallery', with snarling vocals that rip into 'your cage in the human zoo/They all stop to look at you/Next year, what will you do when you have been forgotten'. It resulted in the band being accused of 'misogynistic misdirection', but Tommy Shaw says the critics were wrong. He told the Redbeard podcast that it drew on 'a corollary between the Miss America contest and the way people in America seemed to look at things. It's a beauty pageant without much depth or substance beneath it. The title was a bit of a pun – don't you miss America? In other words, don't you remember the way things used to be? It looks at Miss America as an animal in a cage, to be admired as some sort of animal in a zoo'.

Shaw himself was inspired to come up with the power ballad 'Man In The Wilderness', which explored similar themes to 'The Grand Illusion' but on a more personal level – his feelings of confusion at being adored by thousands of fans every night at gigs but without any of those people caring about how he really feels. He also penned the most proggy track on the album, the pointed 'Fooling Yourself (The Angry Young Man)', which was aimed squarely at DeYoung and his tempestuous character. The song goes through a number of time signatures, including 6/8, 5/8 and 7/4, as well as the usual straight 4/4, with acoustic guitar and DeYoung's keyboards well to the fore. In fact, he gets to play a tempestuous solo at the end that sounds like Tony Banks on steroids.

Another track that fitted the concept nicely was 'Superstars', a fairly straightforward rocker with almost screaming vocals that lyrically took another jab at the fantasy of fame, saying: 'Step right this way, everyone's welcome/We want your dreams/The offer's simple – momentary immortality'. 'Castle Walls', written by DeYoung, is a power ballad about the barriers we put up to surround us that displays the writer's keyboard skills. The album ends with a 'Grand Finale' that repeats riffs and themes from the title track.

It's clear the band knew they had something special in the can, but, hoping a lucky number would help sales success, decided to release their seventh album on the seventh day of the seventh month of 1977. It worked even better than they could have hoped, helping to send the album up the US album chart to number six, one above seven. Its ascent was also propelled by the positive reviews, with *Rolling Stone* magazine hailing its 'strong sense of musical dramatics' and 'progressive, keyboard-oriented intellectualism of primitive Yes'. The normally difficult-to-please Allmusic gives the album four stars, with one of the site's reviewers praising the band's 'prog-rock orientation, melodic instincts, incredible harmonies, first-rate instrumentation and catchy chord progressions.'

With its surreal, mysterious cover inspired by Belgian surrealist artist Rene Magritte's 'The Blank Signature', the album went triple platinum and began a run of five successful releases that finally gave Styx the national recognition they hungered for. After *The Grand Illusion*, Styx went from being everyone's support band to the headliners, blowing the likes of Kiss and Aerosmith out of the water.

Were Styx really prog? They have been called 'pomp rock', even 'corporate rock', and it is true they cared more about catchy choruses and hit singles than most prog bands would admit. But their albums, particularly *The Grand Illusion* and its follow-up, *Pieces Of Eight*, had much more intellectual depth than most run-of-the-mill rock music, examining issues that few mainstream acts would even consider. Furthermore, they had a level of musical ability and compositional complexity to rival many prog bands, not least in the Rick Wakeman-inspired keyboard theatrics of DeYoung. He told *Prog* magazine in 2012:

> If you talk to a Gentle Giant fan, they'll tell you that Styx are not a prog rock band in the strictest sense of the term, and they'd be right. But a lot of our roots do come from the great British prog bands of the 1970s, in particular Yes and ELP. I was probably more responsible than any other member of the band for bringing in the progressive influences. As a keyboard player, I admired the way that Keith Emerson and Rick Wakeman made the instrument so important. I listened to them, and it gave me the inspiration to compete with show-off guitarists.

On *The Grand Illusion*, Styx took their prog influences and refashioned them into something more suited to the commercial realities of the late 1970s. A lot of our favourite prog bands followed them down the same path.

Peter Gabriel – Peter Gabriel I [Car]

Personnel:
Peter Gabriel: lead vocals, keyboards, flute, recorder
Robert Fripp: electric guitar, classical guitar, banjo on 'Excuse Me'
Steve Hunter: acoustic guitar on 'Solsbury Hill', 'Slowburn' and 'Waiting For The Big One', electric guitar, electric rhythm guitar, pedal steel
Dick Wagner: backing vocals, electric guitar on 'Here Comes The Flood'
Tony Levin: bass guitar, tuba, leader of the Barbershop Quartet on 'Excuse Me'
Jozef Chirowski: keyboards
Larry Fast: synthesiser, programming
Allan Schwartzberg: drums
Jimmy Maelen: percussion, synthibam, bones
London Symphony Orchestra: strings on 'Down The Dolce Vita' and 'Here Comes The Flood'
Michael Gibbs: orchestral arrangement
Recorded at The Soundstage, Toronto; Morgan Studios, London; Olympic Studios, London, in the autumn of 1976
Produced by Bob Ezrin and Peter Gabriel
Label: Charisma
Release date: 25 February 1977
Chart places: France: 5, Norway: 5, UK: 7, Sweden: 8, Holland: 9, Germany: 9, Austria: 10
Tracks: 'Moribund The Burgermeister', 'Solsbury Hill', 'Modern Love', 'Excuse Me', 'Humdrum', 'Slowburn', 'Waiting For The Big One', 'Down The Dolce Vita', 'Here Comes The Flood'
All tracks composed by Peter Gabriel, except 'Excuse Me' by Gabriel/Martin Hall

The Story So Far...

Born in Chobham, Surrey, in 1950, Peter Gabriel was one of the founders of progressive rock giants Genesis with Charterhouse School friends Tony Banks, Chris Stewart, Anthony Phillips and Mike Rutherford. Drummer Stewart was later replaced by John Silver, who was then replaced by John Mayhew. Early albums *From Genesis To Revelation* (1969) and *Trespass* (1970) flopped in the UK, although the latter did well in Europe. Guitarist Phillips quit and was replaced by Steve Hackett, while Phil Collins became the band's drummer. *Nursery Cryme* (1971) was again more successful in continental Europe than in the UK, but that changed with *Foxtrot* (1972), which included the 23-minute prog classic 'Supper's Ready'. *Selling England By The Pound* hit number three in the UK the following year and served up more classic prog songs in 'Firth Of Fifth' and 'The Cinema Show'. In 1974, Genesis embarked on their most ambitious album yet, *The Lamb Lies Down On Broadway*, which followed the surreal adventures of Puerto Rican youth Rael. Friction during this time, coupled with Gabriel's wife, Jill, having a difficult birth of their first child, resulted in him announcing he would leave the band after the 1974/75 tour.

The Album

Peter Gabriel left Genesis because he wanted to grow more cabbages. At least, that's what he claimed in a no-doubt tongue-in-cheek statement released when he finally quit the band in 1975. He said he couldn't expect the other members to sit around waiting while he tended his vegetables. Of course, there was more to it than that. In the press release, he added:

> The vehicle we had built as a co-op to serve our songwriting became our master and had cooped us up inside the success we had wanted. It affected the attitudes and the spirit of the whole band. The music had not dried up, and I still respect the other musicians, but our roles had set in hard. To get an idea through 'Genesis the Big' meant shifting a lot more concrete than before. For any band, transferring the heart from idealistic enthusiasm to professionalism is a difficult operation.

Or, putting it more succinctly in his first solo hit single, 'I was feeling part of the scenery/I walked right out of the machinery'. In subsequent interviews, he also blamed the band's lack of support when his then-wife, Jill, was dangerously ill during childbirth – in fact, doctors feared baby daughter Anna-Marie wouldn't survive – and their refusal to let him take time to explore writing a movie with William Friedkin, director of *The Exorcist*.

The last gig with Genesis was in the small French town of Besançon, near the Swiss border. At the end of the show, Gabriel played 'The Last Post' on his oboe. Then, he was on his own.

Nearly 50 years later, Gabriel is regarded as one of the world's most innovative and successful musicians, with a string of acclaimed albums, singles and soundtracks to his name, including 2023's number-one hit *i/o*. But back in 1975, the critics pretty much wrote off both him and his former band – and, in the case of Gabriel, it initially appeared they were right.

Far from leaping out of the traps with his own solo material, Gabriel withdrew from the music business to concentrate on other things – as he said in his press release: 'It was important to me to give space to my family, which I wanted to hold together, and to liberate the daddy in me.' He did yoga, took piano lessons and, yes, grew cabbages. He considered joining a French commune and took a course on 'mind control'. He also made more babies – his second daughter, Melanie, was born in August 1976. Meanwhile, Genesis showed they were quite capable of producing hit albums without their frontman, as *A Trick Of The Tail* gave them a number-one placing in France and a number-three in the UK. Peter who?

His first foray into the recording studio after making the decision to quit was hardly auspicious. Assembled in George Martin's Air Studios were some of the genre's most talented musicians: Genesis drummer Phil Collins, Brand X bassist Percy Jones, King Crimson guitarist Robert Fripp, virtuoso pianist Keith Tippet and Fairport Convention songbird Sandy Denny.

They were there to record the backing track for 'You Never Know', a composition by Peter Gabriel and his friend Martin Hall, a poet from Staffordshire. The lead vocalist, whose name and face would adorn the cover of the single, was none other than Charlie Drake. Who? For readers unfamiliar with British comedy stars of the 1950s and 1960s, Drake was a diminutive TV comic with a cherubic face and unruly red hair whose catchphrase 'Hello, my darlings!' was uttered in a child-like voice. Apart from a TV career that stretched from 1954 to the 1970s – and stage roles after that – he released a string of singles, mostly produced by George Martin, including 'Splish Splash' and 'My Boomerang Won't Come Back'.

By the 1970s, his recording career had become more sporadic, but here he was singing on a track composed by a member of Genesis, backed by a who's-who of prog stars. Chart success would surely follow. Or perhaps not. Despite the illustrious lineup, 'You Never Know' sank without a trace. 'Goodbye, my darling', said the record-buying public.

The following year, Gabriel recorded The Beatles classic 'Strawberry Fields Forever' for the universally derided documentary film *All This And World War II* (the *New York Times* said the PG rating stood for 'Positively Ghastly'). Taken too slow, with overbearing orchestral backing and 'strangled cat' harmonies, his first solo recording wasn't his finest hour. Gabriel needed to make his mark with his own material or disappear into relative obscurity like Anthony Phillips.

Eventually, the musical ideas started to come out in the shape of interesting piano chords and melodies. Perhaps there was a little bit of rivalry to spur him on. In an interview with Barbara Charone, published in *Sounds* in October 1976, he revealed he had seen his old band live and feared 'paranoia' would set in. It didn't, but the experience undoubtedly led him to question his own musical future. He said:

I knew they were gonna be able to carry on with strong music. It surprised me just how easily they did … Had I done an album straight away after leaving the band, it would have seemed like I'd quit just to run off to do my solo album, which wasn't the case at all. At the time, I thought *I* was the little guy breaking away from the establishment, but the way it was portrayed was that the little guys have kicked the establishment in the ass. I've shrunk again to the situation where the last shall be first, the first shall be last, when the original guy shall have another go at it.

By the end of 1975, he had about 20 songs, many written with his friend Hall, who met Gabriel at a recording session back in 1971. It was a strange pairing because both men were lyricists first and foremost, although Hall played guitar. They recorded demos at the Putney home of another Charterhouse friend, David Thomas, with Gabriel on piano and Hall on guitar. The demos included two songs – 'Excuse Me' and 'Here Comes The Flood' – that would eventually end up on Gabriel's solo debut. In the spring of 1976, he went into Trident Studios in London to make some more professionally recorded demos, this time with the help of Anthony Phillips, Collins, Mike Rutherford and Brand X guitarist John Goodsall. Those sessions produced another version of 'Here Comes The Flood' and the first demo of 'Slowburn'. Then, he went looking for a producer.

Various names appear to have been thrown around as a possible producer for Gabriel's first album, including Todd Rundgren, but he eventually settled on Bob Ezrin despite admitting he was an unlikely choice. At that time, Ezrin was best known as Alice Cooper's go-to producer and co-writer. He knew of Gabriel's work with Genesis and had seen them at Toronto's Massey Hall opening for Lou Reed – in fact, he told Reed's manager: 'I want to work with the kid with the flower on his head!'

Gabriel told British TV show *Pop Scene*: 'Neither I was interested in his track record, nor he in mine. But we got on very well. He was enthusiastic about the songs, and his criticism and suggestions were very much what I thought the album should be anyway. So, we tried some things and I thought it worked well, so we went ahead.'

For Ezrin, it was Gabriel's song 'Here Comes The Flood' that hooked him. He told *Prog* magazine:

If there's anything that made me work with Peter Gabriel in the first place, it was his natural sense of humility. Humility in the Christian sense of the word in that he is a humble guy. I was impressed that a person that brilliant can also hold himself on such a realistic level of esteem. All I know is that Peter played me 'Here Comes The Flood' in my living room on our first meeting. I was in the middle of producing albums for both Kiss and Alice Cooper, working on tight deadlines. In the midst of all that, I went to bed singing 'Here Comes The Flood' instead of my own records! There are not many songs I've heard fresh from the writer's mouth that are that great.

They agreed to co-produce the album – Ezrin would handle the straightforward 'rock' elements, while Gabriel would be responsible for the more proggy bits. It was Ezrin who gathered together most of the musicians who would not only help to bring Gabriel's compositions to life but would go on to tour and record with him for the next few decades. Many of them were seasoned US session musicians who had previously worked with Ezrin on Alice Cooper's albums or had graced such prog epics as, er, 'Tie A Yellow Ribbon Round The Old Oak Tree' by Dawn.

However, Gabriel ensured he had at least one fellow Brit in the lineup by persuading Robert Fripp to end his musical sabbatical following the disintegration of King Crimson. Fripp agreed but asked that he be credited under a pseudonym – which Ezrin overruled for the LP – and played any live performances in the wings or behind a curtain so he couldn't be seen by the public. On the tour, he was credited as 'Dusty Rhodes'.

In the autumn of 1976, the musicians met up at Ezrin's studio in Toronto, where the snow was deep and crisp, but the music was, in Gabriel's words, 'fast, exciting and hot'. The songs Gabriel chose for his debut solo album are eclectic, to say the least. There are the fairly straightforward pop sounds of 'Solsbury Hill' and 'Modern Love', the proggy 'Moribund The Burgermeister', 'Waiting For The Big One' and 'Down The Dolce Vita', the big power ballad 'Here Comes The Flood' and even a barbershop quartet on 'Excuse Me', the only Gabriel/Hall collaboration to survive the weeding-out process. Some have criticised the album for its variety of voices – for Gabriel, it was about the songwriting rather than trying to create a particular sound. When asked by Piccadilly Radio what his new direction was, he replied: 'North, south, east and west!'.

In fact, many of the startling and unusual approaches came about during the recording process. Ezrin told radio station Chom 97 that he wanted Gabriel 'to have a good time, to loosen up and really enjoy the process, and surrounded him with people who made it as much a celebration, to kind of create a party that was full of crazy ideas.'

One of those 'crazy ideas' came about after bassist Tony Levin revealed he used to be in a barbershop quartet. It was instantly decided to put a barbershop quartet opening on 'Excuse Me' – Levin wrote out the parts and the vocalists sang it. 'It was amazing!' said Ezrin. The song is notable for having Robert Fripp on banjo. The song also helped the band get through the West German border while on tour – they sang an acapella version to prove they really were the musicians they claimed to be after being suspected of being the terrorists who had murdered West German industrialist Dr Hanns-Martin Schleyer.

'Solsbury Hill' became Gabriel's first solo hit, reaching number 13 in the UK singles chart, despite being in the unusual time signature of 7/4. The jangly guitars are instantly recognisable, but the song was actually composed on piano – Gabriel had the Bb, Eb and F chords in the strange time signature, then added the rhythmic tritone bassline. Initially, the lyrics were about 'stress, you got me in a mess, is there nothing I can do', but soon Gabriel realised they were rubbish and the song deserved something a little deeper and less clichéd. Inspiration came from the geography near his hometown of Bath. He told Piccadilly Radio in 1977:

It's a hill just above where I live … where I would go to sit and think. Allegedly, the ninth king of England, called Bladud, went over to Greece to study under Pythagoras, then he came back to England and set up the first druid university nearby and built temples on the seven hills around the city to different gods, and there was one on Solsbury Hill built to Apollo. Supposedly, after his magical experiments, the hot springs of Bath came from under Solsbury Hill, and he died, some say, after he tried to fly like an eagle off the Temple of Apollo.

A lovely story – and, I'm afraid, total balderdash. Nevertheless, the hill and its legend provided the inspiration for Gabriel's lyrics, along with oblique references to his departure from Genesis (see quote above) and a general nod towards the importance of striving for what seems hopeless. What sounds like 12-string guitars on the song are actually a multi-tracked six-string played by Steve Hunter, while drummer Allan Schwartzburg plays a shaker and hits a telephone directory, and keyboardist Larry Fast provides syn-drums.

The success of the song came as a surprise to Gabriel, not least because it nearly didn't make the album. Ezrin told Chom 97 7:

We had a catchphrase at the end of the last line of the chorus that was not what it ended up being; it didn't do the song justice and it wasn't living up to the promise of the song. I was completely aware of what that song needed, so I said, 'No, we're not putting that song out with that last line.' We tried everything we could think of for the last line, and then one day, while we were in New York during mixing, Peter said, 'Grab your things, I've come to take you home'. I went, bingo, that's it. He sang it live there and then.

A more promising single, in Gabriel's eyes at least, was 'Modern Love', a satirical take on the complexities of romantic relationships, driven by a hard rock riff played by Fripp, who also provides wailing blues guitar on 'Waiting For The Big One' – almost Genesis-length at over seven minutes. 'Modern Love' was indeed released as the second single from the album, but didn't do well – perhaps record buyers were turned off by the accompanying video, which showed Gabriel thrusting his hips while clad in American football player's gear.

In a 2021 podcast interview with Booked on Rock, Ezrin recalled being unhappy with Gabriel's delivery of the line 'Oh, the pain! Modern love can be a strain'. It just wasn't painful enough! So, the singer was sent up a ladder and his armpits were duct-taped to a studio pillar. That worked.

The London Symphony Orchestra provided strings for the otherwise hard-rocking disco-funk of 'Down The Dolce Vita', the contemplative 'Humdrum' and for the song that both started the album, by getting Ezrin on board, and ends it – 'Here Comes The Flood'.

One of the first songs Gabriel wrote after leaving Genesis, it refers to a mental flood, not a watery one, inspired by a dream he had in which people could see each other's tsunami of thoughts. In a 1977 interview quoted in Mick St Michael's 1994 book, *Peter Gabriel In His Own Words*, he explained:

You know, a release, a wash over the mind, not necessarily the land. A downhill course which leads to disaster – an opening up, a telepathic society where people can read each other's minds. Of course, in such a situation, there'd be no real change for people who have been honest and open with whatever is in their minds, but those who have been rather two-faced and who have kept their thoughts hidden would find it very difficult.

A simple, atmospheric minor-key ballad, it has been a staple of Gabriel's setlists and is a song he keeps going back to time and time again. On the debut album, it is awash with strings, tinkling synths, acoustic guitars, various odd bits of percussion and crunching electric guitar from Dick Wagner. Later, he would record sparser versions for Robert Fripp's 1979 album *Exposure*, a Kate Bush TV show and on his 1990 compilation album *Shaking The Tree*. Ezrin admits there were things Gabriel wished he could try again, and 'Here Comes The Flood' is undoubtedly top of the list. Having said that, Gabriel's vocal performance is magnificent, chock-full of power and passion.

Genesis fans would have found opener 'Moribund The Burgermeister' reassuring as it is one of the proggiest tracks on the album, with its atmospheric keyboards, shifting keys and time signatures and thought-provoking lyrics, inspired by a story his grandmother told him about her Hungarian village. In the liner notes of his 2002 compilation, *Hit*, he explained: 'The story goes that the townspeople couldn't agree where to build the graveyard, so they had to put it in the middle of town. From then on, they had all sorts of strange happenings. People started turning into animals, things like that.' So, the lyrics depict a sort of St. Vitus's dance affecting the villages while Moribund the Burgermeister – German for a town mayor – tries to get to the bottom of the hysteria. 'I will find out', he says to the sound of a wooden school ruler being twanged on a desk.

Some of the songs had more down-to-earth inspirations. 'Humdrum' appears to be about the tensions between being a 'rock star' and a family man and how he needed to 'listen to my heart'. At the end, he mentions 'our amoeba, my little liebe schoen' (German for 'dear beauty'), believed to be a reference to his daughter Anna-Marie. Musically, 'Humdrum' opens with sedate keyboards and weary vocals before transitioning into an insanely catchy Latin rhythm. Gabriel opens his heart, but he's dancing the tango while doing it.

'Slowburn' is a great side-two opener, a rocking track powered along by excellent lead guitar solos from Steve Hunter. Gabriel's lyrics allow for at least two interpretations – this is either the story of a difficult human relationship or is perhaps a little dig at his former Genesis colleagues, with 'back telling me your apocalypse' possibly being a reference to a part of 'Supper's Ready' that Phil Collins was now singing on the band's tours. It ends with a soaring lead guitar over a slow, emotional coda, followed by spooky, rhythmic guitar chords. A longer version of Slowburn, with an extended intro, was later released on Gabriel's *Flotsam & Jetsam* compilation.

The seven-minute 'Waiting For The Big One' combines jazz and blues in what is said to be a tribute to songwriter Randy Newman – the lyrics read a little bit like a song from a musical, with clever wordplay such as 'Once I was a credit to my credit card' – but is also a reference to the pressure Gabriel felt under to produce a 'big' album, one that would establish him as a solo star and make him some much-needed money as he was surviving solely on Genesis royalties.

Finally, 'Down The Dolce Vita' is said to be part of a longer concept involving a central character called Mozo, who is referenced on Gabriel's second album. The lyrics tell of a journey across the sea by four men, including Aeron and Gorham – clearly a perilous journey as they are 'trying to find a way to make it alive'. Musically, it is a bizarre mixture of 1970s disco funk and movie soundtrack drama from the London Symphony Orchestra, with a strange interlude of ticking clocks and ringing bells. It is one of the tracks that perhaps justifies the criticism that Gabriel was trying to put too much into his songs.

The album was released with a deliberately understated cover – after all, this was about the songs, not the singer. Gabriel sits in a 1974 Lancia 2000 – owned by Hipgnosis founder Storm Thorgerson – sprayed with water, the singer's eyes almost closed and his face partly obscured. The picture was hand-coloured from a black-and-white original, making the car bonnet with its metallic-looking water droplets leap out while the star of the show sinks back into monochrome gloom. There was no title, the reasoning being that this was just one part of an ongoing piece of work, but it is generally known as *Peter Gabriel I* and sometimes as *Car* from the cover art. Gabriel saw his first four albums as 'chapters' in his musical stories or as a magazine like *Newsweek* that came out once a year rather than as separate, discrete products.

It was released to generally positive reviews, with *Rolling Stone* calling it 'impressively rich' and *NME* saying it was 'a fine record with at least one 24-carat irresistible classic'. Some critics found the variety of styles off-putting and lacking in depth, but they overlooked the fact that Gabriel was pointing the way to the future of progressive rock and how it could survive in a future of shorter attention spans and increasing commercial pressures.

For Gabriel himself, it was confirmation that he could survive and thrive outside of Genesis. As Bob Ezrin told Chom 97 7:

Peter is a really interesting character. He is a true artist in the sense that he is compelled by an inner fire and a vision of the things that he wants to do that is unrelenting, undeniable and that he cannot help but give in to. So, if he gets an idea that he's going to do something, that guy is going to do it. But at the same time, he also has a measure of self-doubt and a little bit of self-examination.

Today, we see a supremely successful, talented and visionary artist who is revered and respected by both music lovers and music-makers. That process from the quiet, tentative recluse wracked with self-doubt to the elder statesman of rock started here, with a debut solo album that was one of the defining prog statements of 1977.

The Alan Parsons Project – I Robot

Personnel:
David Paton: bass, acoustic guitar, backing vocals
Stuart Tosh: drums, percussion, backing vocals
Ian Bairnson: electric and acoustic guitars, backing vocals
Eric Woolfson: keyboards, vocoder, backing vocals
Alan Parsons: keyboards, vocoder, backing vocals, acoustic guitar
Duncan Mackay: keyboards
B.J. Cole: steel guitar
John Leach: cimbalom, kantele
Lenny Zakatek, Allan Clarke, Steve Harley, Jack Harris, Peter Straker, Jaki Whitren, Dave Townsend, the English Chorale, the New Philharmonia Chorus: vocals
Hilary Western: backing vocals
Smokey Parsons: backing vocals
Tony Rivers, John Perry and Stu Calver: backing vocals on 'Some Other Time'
Orchestra and choir arranged and conducted by Andrew Powell
Recorded at Abbey Road Studios, London, between December 1976 and March 1977
Produced and engineered by Alan Parsons
Executive producer: Eric Woolfson
Label: Arista
Release date: 8 July 1977
Chart places: Germany: 2, New Zealand: 2, Spain: 2, US: 9, Australia: 10, UK: 28
Tracks: 'I Robot', 'I Wouldn't Want To Be Like You', 'Some Other Time', 'Breakdown', 'Don't Let It Show', 'The Voice', 'Nucleus', 'Day After Day (The Show Must Go On)', 'Total Eclipse', 'Genesis Ch1 v32'.
All tracks by Alan Parsons and Eric Woolfson, except 'Total Eclipse' by Andrew Powell

The Story So Far…

Londoner Alan Parsons worked at the tape duplication department at EMI before moving to the company's recording studios in Abbey Road. He famously engineered The Beatles' last two albums, as well as Pink Floyd's *The Dark Side Of The Moon*. Glaswegian Eric Woolfson was a self-taught pianist who wrote songs for artists including Marianne Faithfull, Frank Ifield and The Tremeloes. He released an unsuccessful single in 1971 with the help of the future 10cc. He became a record producer before going into management with artists such as Carl Douglas of 'Kung Fu Fighting' fame. He met Parsons when they were working on projects at what had been renamed Abbey Road Studios and agreed to manage him as an independent producer. Woolfson had composed music for a concept album based on the macabre writings of author Edgar Allan Poe, and the pair worked together to record it, releasing *Tales Of Mystery And Imagination (Edgar Allan Poe)* in 1976 under the name of the Alan Parsons Project. It was a top-40 hit in the US and some parts of Europe.

The Album

'I took no notice of punk', said Alan Parsons gleefully in the liner notes for the 2007 reissue of *I Robot*. Indeed, he and Eric Woolfson paid scant attention to any changes in the musical landscape, unashamedly churning out their progressive rock concept albums for more than a decade. Along with Pink Floyd, their band name became synonymous with what some critics sneered at as 'dinosaur' music and they were the targets of frequent mockery. In the spy movie spoof *Austin Powers: The Spy Who Shagged Me* (1999), it was the name of Dr Evil's space laser, while in US TV sitcom *30 Rock*, the Pete Hornberger Alan Parsons Project Project was a short-lived tribute band.

It's true that few bands stuck so doggedly to the conceptual element of prog. Apart from *Tales…* and *I Robot,* there was *Pyramid* (about all things Egyptian), *Eve* (about women), *The Turn Of A Friendly Card* (gambling), *Eye In The Sky* (belief systems), *Ammonia Avenue* (scientific developments), *Vulture Culture* (the ruthlessness of Mankind), *Stereotomy* (pressures of the modern world), *Gaudi* (Antonio Gaudi and the work/life balance), *Freudiana* (Sigmund Freud) and *The Sicilian Defence* (chess moves).

I Robot was, as the name strongly suggests, inspired by Isaac Asimov's science-fiction stories collected in three volumes under the title *I, Robot*. It became their first smash hit, partly thanks to the serendipitous release of the first *Star Wars* movie, featuring lovable tin Laurel and Hardy in R2D2 and C-3PO. Furthermore, as world leaders warn of the dangers of artificial intelligence, it has come to be seen as remarkably prescient.

The original plan for the band's second album was to make 'Tales Of Mystery And Imagination Part 2' – after all, Woolfson and Parsons had barely scratched the surface of Poe's literary output. However, their first album had come out on 20th Century Fox Records in the US (Charisma in the UK), and by the end of 1976, they had been signed up to a nine-album deal by Arista, who didn't want a follow-up to another label's release.

So, it was back to the drawing board for Parsons and Woolfson, but not for long. Eric was a big fan of Asimov's *I, Robot* trilogy and thought the stories would make a great record. There were nine tales in all, written between 1940 and 1950, and they explored the moral issues of human and robot interaction, particularly how Mankind could protect itself from the possible malign actions of advanced technology.

Asimov came up with the Three Laws of Robotics: first, a robot may not injure a human being or, through inaction, allow a human being to come to harm; second, a robot must obey the orders given to it by human beings except where such orders would conflict with the first law; third, a robot must protect its own existence as long as such protection does not conflict with the first or second law. Simple yet powerful, the laws have helped influence the thinking around controlling artificial intelligence.

So far, so good. But there was a problem. In a 2013 interview on the band's YouTube channel, Woolfson revealed:

> When I started looking at the legalities of it, our lawyers got in touch with the Asimov representatives who said that, unfortunately, Mr Asimov had done a deal some ten years previously with a television company for a series based on *I, Robot* which included all kinds of recordings that might be related to the theme, so obviously we couldn't use the Asimov stories. I did have a very pleasant call with Dr Asimov; he was quite enthusiastic about the idea of us making an album … We were still able to do our own version – his book was I comma Robot, which was obviously inspired by the *I, Claudius* book of Robert Graves. I thought, well, to avoid confusion, I'll drop the comma and just make it The Alan Parsons Project's *I Robot*.

Mmm, don't know how they got THAT through the lawyers. Anyway, Parsons and Woolfson decided to make another, more obvious, change to further distance their work from Dr Asimov. The foolishly optimistic author believed his laws meant everything would turn out all right – robots would be tamed and become servants to the human race, not its masters. The music makers, on the other hand, decided to reverse the philosophy – the album suggests artificial intelligence will eventually destroy us, which, nearly 50 years later, seems a more likely scenario. Basically, said *I Robot* the album, we're screwed.

The tracks don't explicitly reference any of Asimov's stories – instead, they are more generally supposed to chart the rise of artificial intelligence and the inevitable decline of Man. In an interview with podcast In the Studio with Redbeard, Parsons explained: 'We're already approaching the age where machines are more intelligent than we are. I think there is a real danger that if we invent thinking machines, then they might ultimately destroy us.'

Woolfson wrote 95% of the music and all the lyrics on the APP albums, as well as playing keyboards on most of the tracks and handling the band's business side. Parsons' contribution was to shape the sound of the albums, choosing the musicians and singers. Thanks to his production contacts, he was able to persuade some big names to perform, but generally, Parsons and Woolfson opted for less high-profile vocalists, judging them on their voices rather than their level of audience recognition.

Occasionally, Parsons would play keyboards, particularly on the synth-based instrumental tracks that APP became famous for. In fact, four of the ten compositions on *I Robot* are instrumentals, and Parsons had a hand in composing three of them, frequently using a Yamaha CS-80, an eight-voice polyphonic synthesiser that was hot off the production line. It gave the album the 'sci-fi' feeling Parsons was after – he could create intricate sound loops that would mimic the pounding of machinery or the hum of an electronic brain.

The APP also helped pioneer the use of samplers by designing an instrument they called a Projectron. An early predecessor of the Fairlight, it involved putting sound and music loops onto a 24-track tape machine that was then controlled by a keyboard – each note was plugged into a key on the keyboard, enabling Parsons to create the backing ooohs and aaaahs. Indeed, the use of synths on APP albums became so ubiquitous that the band began to get an electronica tag, even though Parsons insisted it was more of a guitar group with real orchestras.

The electronic approach is evident on *I Robot* from the moment the needle hits the vinyl (or you click on the track on Spotify, ugh). There are shades of 'On The Run' from Pink Floyd's *The Dark Side Of The Moon* – engineered, of course, by Parsons – in the way the title track fades in on a bed of a bubbly synth loop. It began with Parsons improvising on a suitcase-sized EMS SynthiA, accidentally stumbling on the chord sequence that ended up in the track.

With the sequence going, he then came up with the clavinet melody to play over the top. With the rest of the musicians – mostly from the Scottish band Pilot – added to the mix, the English Chorale conducted by Andrew Powell and soprano Hilary Western providing wordless vocals, Parsons created a classic APP track and established the tradition of the band's albums opening with an instrumental. By the way, an early version of this track included the sound of metal spheres from the French game of boules being banged lightly together. Needless to say, the idea was scrapped!

The biggest hit from the album, reaching number 36 in the US singles chart, was the second track, 'I Wouldn't Want To Be Like You', with vocals by Anglo-Indian singer Lenny Zakatek, who is distantly related to Cliff Richard and Freddie Mercury. He was the lead singer for British funk band Gonzales – best known for their 1979 hit 'Haven't Stopped Dancing Yet' – who were managed by Woolfson, and he became an APP regular, singing on seven further albums.

His first APP song also featured a highly regarded lead guitar solo from Iain Bairnson, and was accompanied by a music video, the only one to feature Parsons himself. Lyrically, the song has only a vague connection to the album's concept, but the video establishes a stronger link by depicting Parsons chasing a mysterious humanoid that eventually spontaneously bursts into flames. The lyrics could then be read in two ways – either Parsons doesn't want to be like the humanoid, or it's the robot that is rejecting human characteristics.

'Some Other Time' was famously inspired by Paul McCartney – Parsons was chasing him to read a line of poetry for APP's first album, but McCartney replied: 'Some other time, Alan, some other time.' A powerful piano-based ballad with rich orchestration, the lyrics are once again a bit opaque, with references to someone or something 'looking into my mind'. As Woolfson reveals in an interview on the band's website, the song was recorded twice by two different vocalists, with the aim of choosing the best performance:

> One was an artist I'd heard in cabaret called Peter Straker, who was an electrifying performer to see live, and we got Peter in and he tried a vocal that worked in certain bits and didn't work in others. It was one of the problems that you often had in the studio because we often recorded the backing without any idea who was going to sing it. We had to take a guess at what the proper key would be and it didn't always work. Peter was a man who sang with a very soft, feminine tone in his voice … I remembered a singer I had met sometime before called Jaki Whitren, who was almost the exact opposite, a girl who sang with tones that were actually very busy and masculine in terms of the delivery. So, we tried it with Jaki and we had the same problem – some bits were good and some didn't work. But we realised that if you combined the two, you had this kind of androgynous lead singer made up of composite parts and many people never realised that the verse is sung by one and the chorus by another.

Only one vocalist was required for 'Breakdown', and that was Allan Clarke of The Hollies. Parsons had worked with the band for some years as an engineer and approached him to perform on *I Robot* (another Hollie, Terry Sylvester, had sung on *Tales Of Mystery And Imagination*). Clarke loved the idea as he had never worked on someone else's record before, and he paved the way for other, more well-known artists to lend their talents to the APP. A medium-paced rocker with a bass intro sounding like 'Under Pressure' in reverse, 'Breakdown' has a chord sequence by Parsons and lyrics by Woolfson that connect most strongly to the concept than any of the songs on the album. They are inspired by the fact that both humans and robots can 'break down', and there's a sense of ambiguity there about which of the two the song is talking about.

Woolfson comes close to a political statement towards the end of the song; with the Berlin Wall still dividing Germany (it would be torn down by Pink Floyd – sorry, by the German people – on 9 November 1989), he depicts robotic citizens finally rebelling against their masters, demanding that the wall be taken away.

Side one of *I Robot* ends with what sounds suspiciously like a Broadway musical number. In fact, Parsons is on record as saying that he believed much of Woolfson's work had a theatrical element to it, and this was proved to be so when 1990's 'unofficial' APP album *Freudiana* became a stage show. 'Don't Let It Show' features a stately pipe organ backing, played by Woolfson, with British songwriter Dave Townsend (he penned 'Miss You Nights' for Cliff Richard) starting off as gently plaintive before giving it the full showstopper treatment.

Right: Pink Floyd in 1977: David Gilmour, Roger Waters, Nick Mason and Richard Wright. But soon, the band would hit a 'Wall'. (*Getty*)

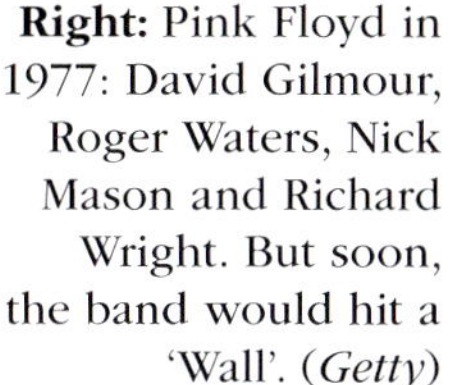

Left: The classic Yes lineup of Chris Squire, Rick Wakeman and Steve Howe at the back, Jon Anderson and Alan White at the front.

Below: Ian Anderson, centre, and the merry crew of Jethro Tull light a very dangerous fire in the middle of a wood. (*PRR Publicity Ltd*)

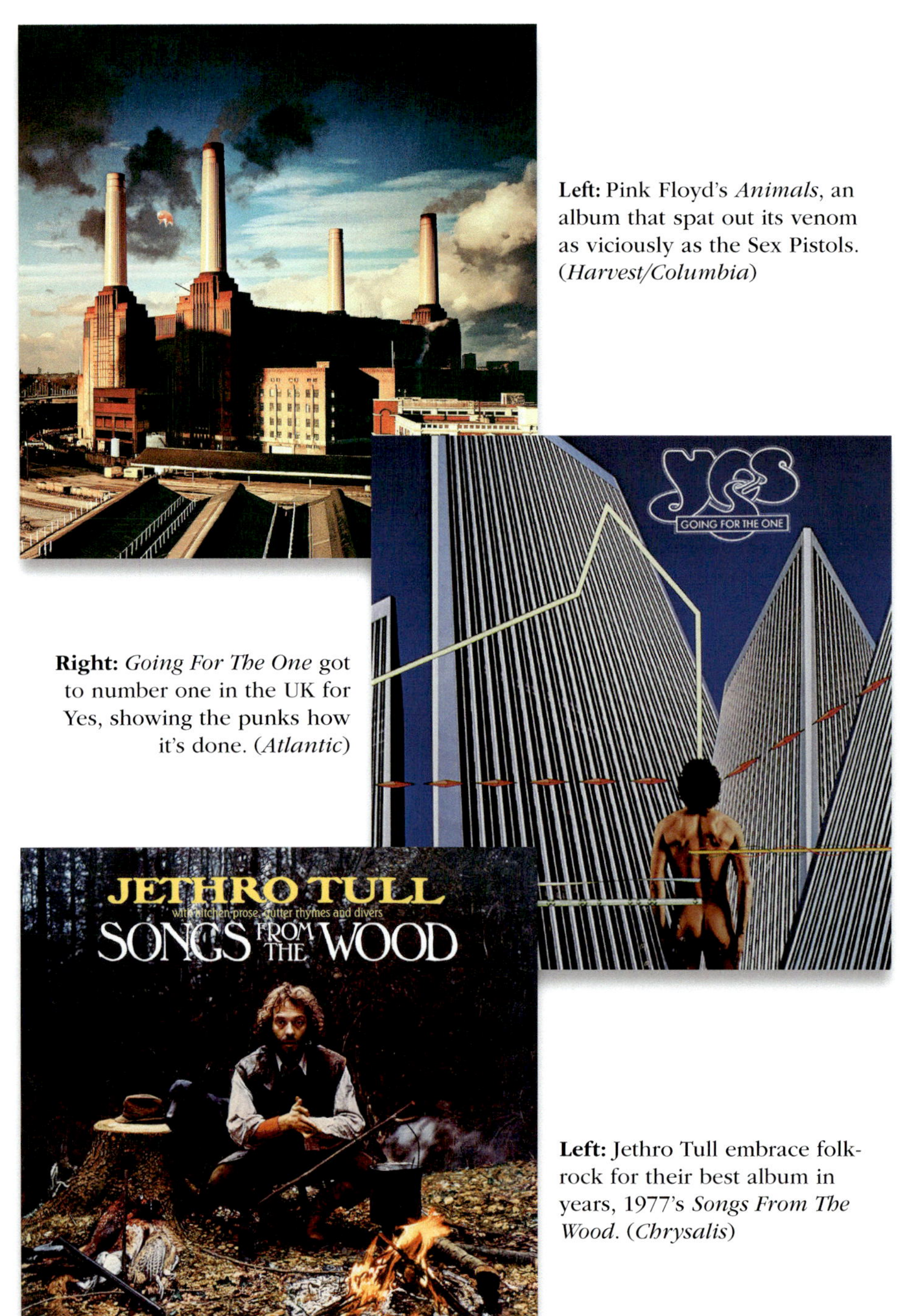

Left: Pink Floyd's *Animals*, an album that spat out its venom as viciously as the Sex Pistols. (*Harvest/Columbia*)

Right: *Going For The One* got to number one in the UK for Yes, showing the punks how it's done. (*Atlantic*)

Left: Jethro Tull embrace folk-rock for their best album in years, 1977's *Songs From The Wood*. (*Chrysalis*)

Right: A double album from Emerson, Lake & Palmer that included the hit single 'Fanfare For The Common Man'. (*Atlantic*)

Left: ELP's second release in 1977 was a hodgepodge of outtakes, solo tracks and new material. (*Atlantic*)

Right: A colourful cover for breakthrough album *The Grand Illusion* by American band Styx. (*A&M*)

Left: Welcome back my friends to the snow that never ends: ELP at Montreal Olympic Stadium. (*Getty*)

Right: US band Styx. From left to right: Tommy Shaw, John Panozza, James Young, Dennis De Young and Chuck Panozza. (*Michael Ochs Archives/Getty*)

Below: In your eyes: one of the pictures taken for the inner sleeve of Peter Gabriel's debut album. (*Hipgnosis*)

Right: Eric Woolfson and Alan Parsons were the creative forces behind The Alan Parsons Project. (*Michael Ochs Archives/ Getty*)

Left: Another dynamic duo, this time Lol Creme and Kevin Godley, formerly of 10cc. (*Getty*)

Right: Gentle Giant talents. From left to right: John Weathers, Ray Shulman, Derek Shulman, Gary Green and Kerry Minnear.

Left: Peter Gabriel's debut album, colloquially known as 'Car' from the Hipgnosis cover. (*Charisma*)

Right: The cover for *I Robot* by The Alan Parsons Project was shot at Charles de Gaulle airport near Paris. (*Arista*)

Left: There were *Consequences* for 10cc when Lol Creme and Kevin Godley made this groundbreaking (and immensely unpopular) album. (*Mercury*)

Right: What was *The Missing Piece* for Gentle Giant? According to their record label, it was a hit single. (*Chrysalis/Capitol*)

Left: Goblin found their chilling sound for the soundtrack of cult horror movie *Suspiria*. (*Cinevox*)

Right: *The Geese & The Ghost* is a 'lost' classic from Genesis founder Anthony Phillips. (*Hit & Run Music*)

Left: Italian soundtrack band Goblin. From left to right: Agostino Marangolo, Massimo Morante, Fabio Pignatelli and Claudio Simonetti.

Right: The original Ant music: Genesis founder and genius musician Anthony Phillips.

Left: Geddy Lee, Alex Lifeson and Neil Peart – together, they were Rush, Canada's finest prog band. (*Fin Costello/ Redferns*)

Right: Guitar wizard
Steve Hillage was
briefly fashionable
in the mid-1970s.
(*Getty*)

Left: Van der Graaf
in 1977. From left to
right: Graham Smith,
Nic Potter, Guy Evans
and Peter Hammill.
(*Robin Schwartz*)

Right: Lisa Herman, John
Greaves and, on the right, Peter
Blegvad in New York during
the making of *Kew. Rhone..*
(*Dana Johnson*)

Left: Rush recorded *A Farewell To Kings* in the very wet Welsh countryside. (*Anthem*)

Right: Steve Hillage went funky on *Motivation Radio*, foreseeing his later dance music experiments. (*Virgin*)

Left: Van der Graaf lost their 'Generator' for their stripped-down 'punky' album *The Quiet Zone/The Pleasure Dome*. (*Charisma/Mercury*)

Right: One of the most complex, baffling and fascinating prog albums of the 1970s: the enigmatic *Kew. Rhone..* (*Virgin/Europa*)

Left: Brian Eno teamed up with German electronic music group Cluster for this very listenable album of ambient melodies. (*Sky*)

Right: Eno's *Before And After Science* created an irresistible fusion of progressive rock and brittle, rhythmic pop. (*Island/Polydor*)

Left: Camel in 1977. That's Andy Latimer in the foreground, with Peter Bardens, Andy Ward and Richard Sinclair.

Right: The pioneering genius that is Brian Eno, who began his musical journey with Roxy Music before forging an idiosyncratic solo career.

Left: US proggers Happy The Man were heavily inspired by British bands, particularly Gentle Giant.

Above: Surprisingly, The Enid's blend of classical prog was catnip for punk fans.

Left: Space rockers Hawkwind may not have won any beauty contests, but they were frequent chart invaders in the mid-1970s.

Above: Supertramp in 1977 were leaving prog behind for the more lucrative shores of pop. (*Getty*)

Left: *Rain Dances* in 1977 was Camel's first album after sacking bass player Doug Ferguson, replaced by Richard Sinclair. (*Gama/Decca*)

Right: Happy The Man's debut album was a very accomplished slice of jazz-prog, with a nod to the Canterbury Scene. (*Arista*)

Left: Hawkwind's *Quark, Strangeness And Charm* crept into the top 30 UK albums chart. (*Charisma/Sire*)

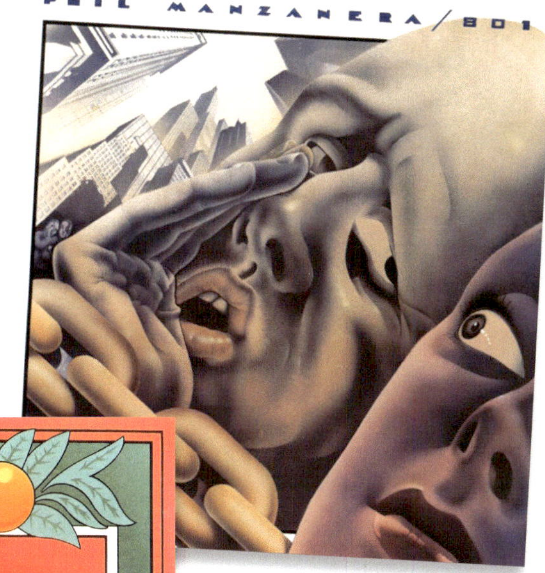

Right: 801's only studio album, *Listen Now*, was really the work of Phil Manzanera and Bill MacCormick. (*Expression/Polydor*)

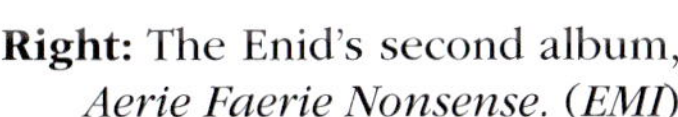

Left: *Garden Shed* by Kent band England is an overlooked gem that deserves to be heard. (*Arista*)

Right: The Enid's second album, *Aerie Faerie Nonsense.* (*EMI*)

Left: If industrial prog is your thing (if it is even a thing), then you may like *Interface* by French electronic band Heldon. Some people do, I believe. (*Cobra*)

Right: *Even In The Quietest Moments...* was not really a prog album, but included a bona fide prog track in the 11-minute 'Fool's Overture'. (*A&M*)

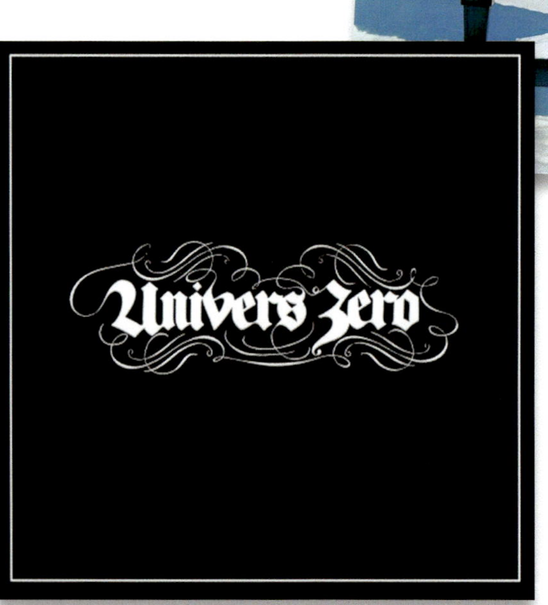

Left: Enter the dark, disturbing world of Zeuhl music with Belgian band Univers Zero's debut album. (*Eric Faes*)

Lyrically, the song was inspired by Woolfson's reading of the Asimov stories, some of which required their protagonists to hide their true feelings, to show a poker face to the rest of the world and to the Big Brother controlling things. Woolfson added in a video interview on the APP website: 'Superficially, it was fairly straightforward, but there were so many layers of meaning in that song that even I haven't got to the bottom of it yet!' It was originally recorded with an opening section of eight cellos. Woolfson said: 'It was a complete disaster! But I remembered there was a pipe organ in the studio from another session and we borrowed it!'

Another big name to join the ever-growing list of vocalists was Steve Harley, who at the time was just about to fold his band Cockney Rebel and embark on a solo career. He was asked to sing on 'The Voice', a song that suggests the idea of society being controlled by a human or robotic Big Brother. As the title suggests, the APP wanted a distinctive voice, and Harley was someone Parsons had worked with, co-producing the band's second album, *The Psychomodo*. Steve delivered the goods with a vocal stuffed full of paranoia and menace, while Parsons provided mysterious whoops and swoops through the Projectron.

'Nucleus' is another instrumental mostly improvised by Parsons on the Projectron, opening with indistinct 'rocket launch' chatter that fades into spacey chords washing in and out like the sea on a beach. Stuart Tosh provides a steady drum rhythm – there are water gongs, a cimbalom and the oohs and aahs of The English Chorale. It segues into a ridiculously catchy song, a gentle ballad based on a repetitive keyboard phrase supplied by the SynthiA sequencer, with pacey whoops on pedal steel guitar. Woolfson says 'Day After Day (The Show Must Go On)' suggests a starlit night on an alien beach somewhere, staring up into the sky and marvelling at the magnificence of the universe. The singer was Jack Harris, a regular collaborator with guitarist Bairnson and other members of Pilot, and the backing vocals include Woolfson and Parsons.

The only track on the album not written by the pair is 'Total Eclipse', a powerful, atonal mixture of doom-laden orchestra and wordless choir, composed by APP's musical director, Andrew Powell. He had worked with Parsons on several previous albums, including those by Cockney Rebel and Pilot, and orchestrated APP's debut. He would go on to work on all the APP releases, as well as Kate Bush's first album and her quirky number-one single 'Wuthering Heights'. 'Total Eclipse' suggests the moment human beings are eclipsed by their mechanical slaves – imagine a scene of future devastation from the *Terminator* movies and you'll see what I mean.

The fourth and final instrumental ends the album. 'Genesis Ch1 v32' is based on a repetitive four-chord sequence of Dm, C, Bb and A – the basic track is laid down by Woolfson and Duncan Mackay's keyboards, with Bairnson playing lead guitar over the top, supplemented by choir and orchestra. While there are no lyrics to give us a steer on the subject matter, there is a clue in the title: there are only 31 verses in Genesis Ch 1 in the Old Testament of the Bible, which ends with the Judeo-Christian deity sitting back and feeling very satisfied after having created the Earth and everything on it. So what could verse 32 be? Perhaps, suggests the album, it's when the meek-anicals inherit the Earth…

I Robot was released with a suitably sci-fi-looking cover of tube-like glass and concrete walkways and a robotic head with a rather large screw in the middle of it. In an interview on the APP website, Woolfson revealed that the inspiration came from Charles de Gaulle Airport in Paris:

> The system they had there, which was quite unique in its day, of a kind of people-moving belt in which you stood and were transported to various bits of the airport was very dehumanizing … when it came to the cover design for *I Robot*, I did recommend Hipgnosis – who had done the *Tales Of Mystery* cover and also worked with Pink Floyd on *Dark Side Of The Moon* – that idea; I gave them the clue that might be the approach for the cover of *I Robot*. In fact, the people on the cover are [Hipgnosis founder] Storm Thorgeson's assistants from Hipgnosis … you couldn't just photograph anybody, so they photographed themselves going up and down the escalators and tubes and they superimposed quite a lot of extra tubes, which don't actually exist in Charles de Gaulle Airport … I think after we had done that cover, they became very guarded about letting anybody else film in there.

The album received mixed reviews on release, encapsulated by the *New York Times*, who praised its 'really ingenious use of the possibilities of the modern recording studio' but dismissed the music as 'flatulent, self-important preening'. Of course, by July 1977, no publication worth its salt would praise a progressive rock album, so a better guide is its huge commercial success – going silver in the UK, gold in Germany and Spain, platinum in the US and Canada. Today, *I Robot* is seen as one of the band's best-loved albums and the moment when the formula for later successes was set in stone.

As I said before, there is modern relevance in its theme of Mankind creating the machines that would ultimately destroy us. According to the Centre for AI Safety, 'Mitigating the risk of extinction from AI should be a global priority alongside other societal-scale risks such as pandemics and nuclear war.' The Alan Parsons Project warned us nearly 50 years ago – but is Mankind ready to listen? Or shall we leave it to 'Some Other Time'?

Lol Creme/Kevin Godley – Consequences

Personnel:
Lol Creme: instruments and vocals
Kevin Godley: instruments and vocals
Peter Cook: dialogue
Sarah Vaughan: vocals on Lost Weekend
Judy Huxtable: dialogue as Lulu
Peter Wheeler: dialogue
Andy Peebles: dialogue
Recorded at Strawberry Studios, Stockport, Cheshire, and The Manor Studios,
Shipton-on-Cherwell, Oxon, in 1976 and early 1977
Produced by Godley & Creme
Engineered and mixed by Martin Lawrence
Label: Phonogram/Mercury Records
Release date: 17 October 1977
Chart places: did not chart
Tracks: 'Seascape', 'Wind', 'Fireworks', 'Burial Scene', 'Sleeping Earth', 'Honolulu
Lulu', 'The Flood', 'Five O'Clock In The Morning', 'Dialogue', 'When Things Go
Wrong', 'Dialogue', 'Lost Weekend', 'Dialogue', 'Rosie', 'Dialogue', 'Office Chase',
'Dialogue', 'Cool, Cool, Cool', 'Dialogue', 'Cool, Cool, Cool (Reprise)', 'Dialogue',
'Sailor', 'Dialogue', 'Mobilization', 'Dialogue', 'Please, Please, Please', 'Dialogue',
'Blint's Tune – Movements 1-17'
All tracks written by Lol Creme and Kevin Godley

The Story So Far…

Kevin Godley met Laurence 'Lol' Creme at art school and the pair joined various
bands in the north of England before forming Hotlegs in 1970 with fellow
Lancastrians Eric Stewart and Graham Gouldman, who owned their own studio
in Stockport. Following brief chart success with the single 'Neanderthal Man',
the band released several singles under various names and supported The
Moody Blues on a short tour before producing and playing on three Neil
Sedaka albums. Experience encouraged them to seek a new outlet for their
own work, persuading producer Jonathan King to release Godley and Creme
composition 'Donna' as a single. King renamed them 10cc, supposedly from a
dream he had in which he saw the name outside Hammersmith Odeon, but the
band claimed that it referred to the volume of semen produced in a particularly
virile male ejaculation. 'Donna' hit number two in the UK in October 1972,
followed by their first number-one, 'Rubber Bullets', in 1973. Their eponymous
debut album that year charted in the UK top 40, while their second album,
Sheet Music (1974), reached number nine. This lineup recorded two more
successful albums, *The Original Soundtrack* (1975) and *How Dare You!* (1976).
Notable singles include 'The Wall Street Shuffle', 'Life Is A Minestrone', 'I'm
Mandy, Fly Me', 'Art For Art's Sake' and the number-one smash 'I'm Not In Love'.
However, in 1976, creative differences forced Godley and Creme to quit.

The Album

Nature is revolting against Mankind's cruel domination. Hurricane winds sweep the planet, and a tornado flattens Manhattan. Wildfires consume everything in their path as stampeding animals flee in terror. Torrential floods turn cities into lakes as major rivers burst their banks. Feeble humans cower in fear as the elements wreak revenge...

It sounds like climate change in the 21st century, but it is also the main concept of a remarkably prescient, ambitious, musically loopy and commercially suicidal album released as a triple-LP box set in the middle of the punk explosion in 1977. *Consequences* is one-third mock-orchestral soundscape, created on guitars with the help of a device called the Gizmo – not to be confused with the nicely-behaved creature in the 1984 movie Gremlins – and two-thirds Monty Python-esque play written and performed by British comedian Peter Cook, interspersed with the kind of clever, literate art-rock songs Kevin Godley and Lol Creme used to write for 10cc.

If you have even heard of the album – and its poor record sales suggest few households possess a copy – you will either adore it as the ultimate expression of 1970s creative musical indulgence or scratch the bald spot on your head while muttering: 'WTF!!!' The Prince of Prog, Steven Wilson, is in the former camp. On his website, he says: 'Every moment of that record is crowned with brilliant ideas that, at the time, wouldn't have been easy to have realised … it's a masterpiece and deserves to be re-evaluated.'

However, Donald Guarisco, of website Allmusic, counters with: '*Consequences* is a disaster: its humour is laboured, its musical content is dull and the mind-numbing length of the album proved that neither Godley nor Creme knew when to quit.' Perhaps Godley himself summed it up best when he told the ProGGnosis website in 2007 that it was a mix of 'sheer brilliance and utter shit'. It sounds almost like a definition of prog to me.

It was also an album that didn't just ignore the changing musical landscape but acted as if it were living in an alternate universe. This is despite the fact that the Sex Pistols' 'God Save The Queen' was blaring out from the Dansette in the studio lounge. It is highly unlikely that Johnny Rotten secretly loved this one.

The story of *Consequences* goes back to 1969 when the four future members of 10cc were churning out pop songs for other artists at Strawberry Studios in Stockport, named after The Beatles' 'Strawberry Fields Forever'. Godley and Creme wanted to put some strings on a demo track but couldn't afford the cost of hiring an orchestra, and the primitive synthesisers available then were not up to the job. They wondered if it was possible to make an electric guitar sound like a violin or cello – not by bowing the strings like Jimmy Page of Led Zeppelin but by grinding something against them, in the same way that a rosined wheel vibrates strings in a hurdy-gurdy.

They began by wrapping rubber around the bit of an electric drill and holding it against the strings. The resulting vibrating hum didn't sound too bad, so they approached John McConnell, a physics lecturer at the nearby University of Manchester Institute for Science and Technology, who had assisted in the development of the engine for the Spitfire, for help. He made the first prototype, a battery-operated device with six nylon wheels that could be mounted on an electric guitar to stroke the strings. Dubbing it the Gizmo (and, occasionally, the Gizmotron because most technology sounds better with a 'tron' on the end), Godley and Creme used it on several 10cc album tracks from *Sheet Music* in 1974 to *How Dare You!* two years later. It also got its own instrumental, a B-side to hit single 'The Wall Street Shuffle' in 1974, mistitled as 'Gismo My Way'. A pretty, mid-tempo instrumental, it shows the device's ability to create slide guitar effects but doesn't really display its true noise-making potential.

A few other artists had a go with it, including Led Zep on their album *In Through The Out Door* and Paul McCartney on Wings' release *London Town*. But the Gizmo was notoriously unreliable. Despite constant development, it remained easily affected by temperature and humidity and was prone to creating strange, abrasive harmonics, like a musical chainsaw. Even Godley admitted that 'some days it sounded absolutely beautiful, and on other days it sounded like shit'.

Despite the Gizmo's shortcomings, its creators still had faith that it could revolutionise music and decided the best way to convince the world of their genius was to release an album created entirely by the device. So, they took three weeks off from the recording of *How Dare You!* to concentrate on grinding out some Gizmo sounds. The first three minutes of recording, which later became 'Wind', were played to their manager Harvey Lisberg, who supported their decision to quit 10cc. Godley told the website On the A Side:

> We were so excited by what we were doing and the noises we'd conjured up in that three weeks that when it came time to go back to the 'day job', as it were, and write songs for 10cc, it was like, 'Oh god this is really fucking boring, we don't want to do this anymore' … We threw it all away in order to do something that we felt was much more exciting musically and more challenging. It felt like what 10cc had felt like in the beginning, when we didn't know what we were, and that was always an integral part of Lol's attitude and my attitude toward making music. If we knew exactly what we were going to end up with at the end of the recording process, then it's almost pointless doing it.

The remaining duo, Eric Stewart and Graham Gouldman, thought they were crazy and delivered an ultimatum: It's the Gizmo or us! Later, Godley told Uncut magazine: 'Unfortunately, the band weren't democratic or smart enough at that time to allow us the freedom to go ahead and do this project, and we were in the unfortunate position of having to leave to do it.'

Bedded down in Strawberry Studios – and working nights because other artists had booked the day shifts – Godley and Creme slaved away to obtain musical sounds out of their unpredictable invention. Violins, saxophones, oboes – all the instruments bar a grand piano were created using the Gizmo and whatever bits and pieces they had lying around, such as tracing paper.

Three weeks turned into many months. According to the Radio DJ Paul Gambaccini's sleeve notes on the original LP release, by November 1976, there were ten minutes of music to play to record company executives that included: a burial scene, for which a microphone was placed under a board and Godley shovelled sand on top of it; an animal stampede, created by hitting a timpani with cat litter on top; and a fireworks display recorded by letting rockets off in a field in Stockport. The executives didn't understand any of it but assumed it was groundbreaking.

The first side of the album was completed in February 1977. It opens with 'Seascape' – a rich, warm chord fades in, there's a hint of a merry-go-round in a three-quarter-time accordion-like melody in the background, the music swelling gently and swooping like seagulls over a beach. After a short silence, the orchestral sound builds until it segues into 'Wind', with a steady beat and menacing riffs mixed with the sound of swirling atmospherics. Then, a vocal of sorts comes in, a rush of air within which you can make out the words, 'I am the wind, and I'll blow you away! Bye bye everyone!' The effect was achieved by forcing the vocals through a vacuum cleaner.

There are brief snatches of radio weather reports and then the music cuts abruptly to a man's voice announcing that there's someone at the door. He opens it and the wind tries to get in. There's a brief struggle before the wind wins, smashing its way through the house. It's the first instance of human beings and the elements colliding, a battle that would come to dominate the album later.

'Fireworks' is, as the title suggests, the sound of fireworks mixed in with various effects from the Gizmo, ending with a warning alarm. It goes straight into a powerful orchestral riff for 'Stampede', with Gizmo-created elephant trumpeting and buzzy bees. At one stage, Godley was on all fours lapping from a bowl in an attempt to mimic bison at a waterhole.

There's a brief interruption from a DJ at a disco, unaware that a raging fire is heading his way (and that's Radio 1 presenter Andy Peebles doing his best impersonation of an upbeat disc jockey). Here it comes now, with a breathy vocal warning, 'Fire! Fire! Where you gonna hide?', and the sound of crackling flames racing through a forest as it heads for human civilisation, created by bursting bits of polystyrene packaging through a noise gate on the mixing desk. Side one ends with the sound of a funeral in the pouring rain and the burial scene, followed by a beautiful piano solo backed by the voices of harmonious angels, created using an effect suggested by Phil Manzanera of Roxy Music – the Gizmo was fed into a tape machine with a piece of chewing gum stuck to the tape to make it wobble against the recording heads. That fades out on the melody of 'Honolulu Lulu', which would be played in full on side two.

With side one completed (it was all recorded in sequence), Godley and Creme played it to their managers. In the liner notes for the 2018 box set reissue, Godley said:

> We turned out the lights, pushed them into the control room, turned it up to 11, closed the door and left them to listen for 20 minutes [actually only 17]. They exited, glasses half hanging off, hair messed, their eyes spinning and their ears falling off. And we said, 'Well, what do you think?' They said, 'Oh man, extraordinary. It's the most strange, powerful thing we've ever heard.' We thought, this is fucking brilliant. We went back into our control room to carry on working, and they went into the live room to chat. What they didn't know was that there was a microphone in there and we heard things like, 'What the FUCK was that? What do they think they are doing?!!'

Undeterred, they persevered, painstakingly piecing together the material for side two, averaging a minute of music a day. Godley spent a lot of time snoring to obtain the sound of 'Sleeping Earth' over a repetitive guitar arpeggio. Then comes the first real song on the album. 'Honolulu Lulu' is a short but sweet Hawaiian-style pastiche that, musically, also visits Japan on its travels as a gentle breeze turns into a hurricane. 'Everybody's screaming, streets are teeming with kamikaze rickshaws', sings the geographically-confused Godley in a many-tracked falsetto.

The natural disasters reach a crescendo in 'The Flood', in which someone brushing their teeth starts a dripping tap that turns into a tsunami that levels cities across the world. The drips were created by dropping pieces of plasticine into a bucket of water, each drip recorded separately so they could be reassembled as a rhythmic backing track. More water was thrown at a wall for four hours to create the sound of a flood washing away fans at a rock concert.

With 35 minutes of music across two sides of vinyl, Godley and Creme had the makings of a slightly short but innovative album, the likes of which had never been heard before. But it still wasn't enough. Perhaps they didn't want their studio experiments to end and were looking for a reason to avoid facing up to the, er, consequences of quitting one of the biggest bands in the world. But someone – and no-one can quite remember who – came up with the idea of extending the album to examine the effects of the weather disaster on ordinary people. And what could be more ordinary and every day than a meeting in a lawyer's office to thrash out the details of a divorce while Armageddon raged outside?

They decided they wanted to make an 'ear movie' and needed someone to write a script. A meeting with Jack Rosenthal, author of early *Coronation Street* episodes and more than 150 TV and movie screenplays, went nowhere, so the record company suggested British comedian, actor and writer Peter Cook. In the 2018 liner notes, Godley said:

> I think the record company thought by then that we needed somebody grown up to work with these two madmen to make sure that a) they get something interesting, b) to add another name to the event and c) someone we could look up to, someone more sensible than us, perhaps. So, Peter Cook was suggested. We met and we said yes. But, my god, were they wrong – he was crazier than we were.

Famed for his TV and movie comedy partnership with Dudley Moore, by 1977, Cook was regarded as the father of modern satire. He was also an alcoholic, and when Godley and Creme moved into Richard Branson's Manor Studios for further recordings, Cook joined them with thousands of cans of Diet Pepsi and Coca-Cola but never drank any of them because he was on to wine. His working patterns were also completely at odds with the musicians'. He would be up at 6am, having breakfast, reading the morning papers and dictating his ideas. Then, he would start drinking and be totally bladdered by lunchtime. By the time Kev and Lol were up, observing rock star hours, Cook was asleep under the table, emerging in the evening to record until 4 am.

Slowly, a plot and some characters began to emerge. A musician called Mr Blint rents out his attic to a firm of lawyers who bicker over divorce proceedings between Walter Stapleton and his soon-to-be ex-wife, Lulu. Meanwhile, the weather continues to go ballistic outside their window – and only Mr Blint knows how to calm it down by composing and playing a piece of music with 17 movements.

The characters were a mixture of stereotypes and people Cook had worked with during his career – indeed, Walter's lawyer, Mr Haig (in the original script, his first name is Victor, but it is never used), could be Cook himself. Named after his favourite whisky, Mr Haig gets progressively more sozzled as the play goes on – just as Cook was doing each day in the studio. Then, there is Walter Stapleton, whose slow, pedantic Northern drawl is clearly a mickey-take of Yorkshire playwright Alan Bennett, who worked with Cook in the Beyond the Fringe comedy revue in the early 1960s.

Mr Blint was clearly based on E.L. Wisty, a fictional character created and played by Cook in comedy sketches throughout his career. Described as a 'bland, monotonal know-it-all', Wisty combined an unsmiling, plodding pedanticism with a desire for world domination. As Blint, Cook was also channelling the piano-playing talents of his long-term comedy partner, Dudley Moore. The final male character in the play is Lulu's lawyer, Malcolm Pepperman. Loud, paranoid and emphatic, he is portrayed as such a stereotypical Jewish character that modern listeners may find it offensive – Pepperman himself admits: 'I am a stereotype and always have been a stereotype. I'm not ashamed of it, and I'm not proud of it. The whole thing is not an issue to me.'

The two female characters are both played by Cook's then-wife, Judy Huxtable. Lulu, who speaks in a terrible cod French accent, is Pepperman's client and Walter's wife of convenience (and possibly a prostitute). Miss Farthing, who only has a few lines, is Mr Haig's secretary (and he calls her Judy, which may have been a mistake by Cook during the recording).

Central to the plot is the fact that there is a large hole (aaahhhh) in the floor of the attic, and it is from there that Mr Blint occasionally appears to address the bickering parties with gnomic warnings about the impending climate catastrophe. Every time the hole (aaahhhh) is mentioned, we hear a short burst of angelic harmonies, possibly in E flat minor.

There are also frequent mentions of the number 17, which appeared to have some significance for Cook – he was born on 17 November and once lived at 17 Church Row in Hampstead, London. The website Mr Blint's Attic lists all the 17s that appear in the play. They include:

> According to the sleeve notes, the action of the play takes place on 17 April
> Mr Blint's first words to the others are, 'I make it around 10:17'
> He says his bath takes 11 minutes to fill and six to empty – 11+6=17
> Lulu says she is 34 – that's twice 17
> The attic is 'exactly 17 points south west of the pyramids'
> Near the end, Blint says the time is 'six minutes past 11'. Six plus 11 equals … well, work it out yourself
> Pepperman gives his phone number or Ladbrokes account number as PEC2528. 2+5+2+8=17
> Mr Blint's tune has 17 movements
> He asks the others to lead him in with a count of 17

Also, the album was completed on 17 June 1977, released on 17 October and the original vinyl box set was given the catalogue number CONS17. Spooky, eh?

The play depicts the characters bickering about everyday things, including teeth and half-hairpins, while chaos reigns outside. Despite Mr Blint's hints, they at first seem completely unaware of what is going on, apart from Mr Pepperman's opening excuse for his lateness: 'I was delayed by headwinds on the M4. It's terrible out. Thank God for the Rolls, I say, Some of the cheaper cars were going backwards.' Later, Walter watches a woman with an umbrella being blown into a lamppost while talking to Lulu about hang-gliding. Then, Mr Pepperman tries to place a bet on the 'Nembutal Triumph Hurdle', only to be told the racecourse is flooded. There is also no dog racing because they can't find the dogs.

Haig's secretary asks to go home early because 'my niece is on fire'. 'Same excuse every time!' says Haig. There is the sound of chaos and screaming coming through the intercom, then Haig's goldfish jumps out of its bowl and through the window. As the storm builds to a crescendo, Haig's wife, Veronica, is blown into the office from her yacht in the Canaries, Big Ben bursts into flames, Pepperman's Rolls is swallowed by an earthquake, smoke obscures the sun, all the TV channels go dead and the building starts shaking.

The characters eventually realise they are possibly approaching the end of the world and beg Mr Blint to save them. They jump into his hole (aaahhhh) and seal the opening with tarpaulin and the wings from Stapleton's hang-glider. Then, with a count of 17, Mr Blint plays the music that will quell the elements.

There are a few amusing lines, particularly the muddled-up aphorisms from Mr Stapleton ('You can't teach ducks to dance' … 'Rome wasn't burnt in a day'), Mr Pepperman's bizarre rants and Mr Blint's strange obsessions with pyramids and precisely what chord people are, but your enjoyment depends on how much you appreciate Cook's Python-esque ramblings. The play certainly sags at points, and it can sometimes be difficult to know what on earth is going on. But it is helped immeasurably by the fact that the action is interspersed with some of the best songs Godley & Creme wrote outside of 10cc.

The undoubted gem is the opening number, 'Five O'Clock In The Morning', which sets the scene: someone wakes up, gets washed and dressed, eats some buttered toast, then drives to the factory for work. But, warns the song, 'something seems to be different and you can't quite put your finger on it at all'. It's almost all Creme's solo piano with vocal harmony backing and added birdsong. Creme sings the verses while Godley joins in on the middle eight, with just a single muted drumbeat beneath it all. Melodically sumptuous, the song reminds us that Godley and Creme were great singers, particularly Godley, ostensibly a baritone but with a wide vocal range.

The second song in the play, 'When Things Go Wrong', appears as Pepperman goes on a little rant about how Jewish he is and about how being Jewish is totally irrelevant. 'What's the point of inventing a problem when it isn't there?' he cries, as jazzy music swells beneath him and Godley's vocals softly sing 'I can't sleep, I can't sleep…'

Lyrically, it's Pepperman's angst set in song – almost a rap on one note in the verse as Creme sings, 'My doctor said I've got to stay in bed a week at least, a week or three but that would drive me crazeee' with a slightly raucous, stage song delivery. Other lyrics have a stereotypical Jewish bent – 'My yoga class said take the time to relax, relax, relax. But we're dining out with the Shultzes tonight and I hate the Shultzes'. Musically, the song alternates between just two chords, Eb and Ab, even during the simple chorus. There are two types of saxophone playing throughout, one generated by the Gizmo and the other played by Mel Collins, a frequent prog collaborator with the likes of Camel and King Crimson.

Walter and Lulu get a duet as they discuss their marriage and their futures apart, although their vocals are performed by Godley and jazz legend Sarah

Vaughan. 'The Lost Weekend' is a tender, moving ballad that could have been written by Irving Berlin or George Gershwin. It sounds old-fashioned and simple, yet it is deceptively complicated, with subtle key changes and surprising shifts in the melody.

Godley and Creme initially wanted Ella Fitzgerald, but she wasn't available, so the record company suggested Vaughan, who was younger than Ella and probably in better voice at the time. Her soulful delivery provides a welcome contrast to Godley's pristine but clinical vocal – and she did it in one perfect take. Creme plays electric and acoustic pianos, with the Gizmo providing warm string backing. As the title suggests, 'The Lost Weekend' is all about loss and regret – 'When the book finally is written,' sings Vaughan, 'just our luck, the last page will be missing'.

Loss and regret feature in Blint's song on side four of the original vinyl. During a discussion on each character's chord, Blint tells Lulu she is a C# minor, just like 'Rosie', who we assume was his wife or fiancée. He begins to play what sounds like an old 1940s ballad, speaking the lyrics over his out-of-tune piano: 'Rosie, I wish that you were here. I miss you so much, Rosie, my dear'.

Godley takes over lead vocals and the song lurches into some sort of East End of London pub knees-up as a V1 rocket lands in the 'next street' to the local Palais (a name frequently given to Victorian theatres that had been turned into dance halls). 'The next street? We live in the next street! Rosie!' For indeed, Rosie has been killed by a V1, the flying bomb developed by the Nazis and used to terrorise the British capital during the closing years of World War II. More than 10,000 of the missiles were launched at a rate of up to 100 a day, killing more than 6,000 people.

'Rosie' is a bit of a throwaway song and too much of a pastiche to be taken seriously, but it helps shed a little light on the character of Mr Blint, the pedantic loner obsessed with his piano. Another character who gets a song is, surprisingly, Roland the goldfish – the one that leapt out of its bowl, through the window and to, presumably, its death in the street below. Immediately after his demise, harmony vocals sing 'Your life is over – so is mine!' The piano-based opening is bluesy and jazzy before the song settles into a 6/8 stomp similar to the rhythm of 'Sail On Sailor' by The Beach Boys, and we hear the chorus of 'It's cool, cool, cool in the evening'. Then, we are back into another bluesy section in a minor key reminiscent of Peggy Lee's 'Fever' or 'Big Spender' from the musical *Sweet Charity*. The song ends with Blint's deadpan observation that 'it's not a good omen when goldfish commit suicide'.

'Cool, Cool, Cool' was originally the closing track on side four and is reprised for side five, where it is stopped abruptly by the crash of glass as Mr Haig's wife, Veronica, is blown into the office on a tsunami wave. This leads into 'Sailor', a bluesy and mysterious minor-key ballad that the folk at website Mr Blint's Attic believe is Veronica's song to her husband – 'Sailor, I love you, but you only love the sea'. The trouble is, Haig seems to love alcohol more than the sea, so it doesn't really stack up. Sung by Godley, with massed choir backing, it once again has an old-fashioned feel to it, almost something that could have been sung in a Hollywood musical.

'Sailor' is the last proper song on the album, but there are other musical sequences that are more tied into the action of the play. When Pepperman telephones Ladbrokes, the bookies answer with a barbershop quartet jingle: 'Ladbrokes, good morning. Gambling is our traaaade!' I have never used Ladbrokes, but I would be bitterly disappointed if they didn't answer their phones in the exact same manner.

During a monologue by Stapleton on the mysterious behaviour of his butcher, there are some spooky, random percussion effects punctuating his dialogue. When Pepperman starts getting into the nitty-gritty of who gets what in the divorce, he is soundtracked by a pretty vocal melody singing: 'Yours … Mine … Yours … You split yourself right down the middle'.

The Gizmo's slide guitar potential comes into play for 'Office Chase', a wild, unpredictable maelstrom of sound with added typewriters as the weather chaos bursts into the office of Miss Farthing, while Blint plays an early snatch of piano to quell the elements.

Later, as the characters become aware that their lives are in danger, they switch on a still-working TV showing scenes of the defence forces being mobilised over sinister, dramatic, martial marching music. When the TV dies and the lights go out, the characters beseech Mr Blint to help them, repeating 'Please! Please! Please!' over a steady, up-tempo rock backing.

Side five ends with everyone in Mr Blint's hole (aaahhhh) as he prepares to play the music he hopes will calm the weather and save the planet. He tells them: 'Lead me in with a count of 17…'

Convention would suggest that the musical finale should reprise at least some of the music that has gone before. Not so here. 'Blint's Tune' is 14 minutes of seemingly random piano and Gizmo-produced orchestra – blasts of sound, then repeated single keyboard notes, snatches of interesting melodies, occasional sweeping melodrama, weird sound effects and playful percussion. Every now and then, Creme plays a beautiful solo piano tune that is then upended and forgotten about, replaced by atmospheric random noises or a blast of strings.

Recorded at the very end of the process after 18 months in the studio, why didn't Godley and Creme simply stitch together fragments of the earlier tracks? Godley told Mr Blint's Attic: 'We didn't do that because we were knackered! I think we were on our last legs, if any, to do the last piece, and we did have some musical passages remaining that we hadn't included. So, it was simply a matter of attacking that and making them live on the record.'

While there are no reprises apart from the occasional orchestral motif, you can clearly hear certain sections that are similar in tone and approach to parts of the first LP, bits that would have fitted quite nicely into 'Wind' or

'Stampede'. The piece ends with the same birdcalls that opened side one of record two, suggesting that Blint has managed to save the world. If only it were that simple.

The album is also notable for its artwork, painstakingly produced by hand in the days before Adobe Illustrator. Both Godley and Creme were art school students, so they had a very visual approach to everything they did. The box set cover, which shows clouds forming a face with one glaring eye, was created by sticking cotton wool to a sheet of glass and shining a lightbulb beneath it. Another image in the lavish booklet shows the same face in the sky above a tank driving along a deserted autobahn. This wasn't a stock image – it was shot for the album by photographer Lew Long and was later used as the cover of an album by The Chemical Brothers. An image of a wave swallowing a yacht – presumably the one with Mr Haig's wife on it – was created by dripping wax onto a glass, then sticking a small model yacht into the mass before it cooled.

Retailing for £9 when the average album cost less than half of that, *Consequences* was a difficult sell at a time when popular music was changing so rapidly. With hindsight, it's clear to see why it flopped so miserably as a musical revolution went on outside the walls of Strawberry and Manor studios. Creme was sanguine about the failure of *Consequences* – Godley less so. He told the Mr Blint's Attic podcast:

For a long, long time, I drove myself away from it because we put so much effort, heart and soul into the thing, but we were on the wrong side of history and it failed commercially, which shouldn't really have an impact on how creative or how good it was, but it really pissed me off … Now, I've got very fond feelings towards it. The only bit I'm still not sure about is the playlet with Peter Cook. I think that may have been a misstep … I can't listen to that. I don't find it particularly funny. It was a great experience to work with Peter, but other than that, I'm not sure it actually worked.

While Creme told *Uncut* magazine in 1997:

Kevin was heartbroken; I don't think he's gotten over it yet. He was really, really upset about the way it was received, like a big turkey, really. I didn't take it the way Kevin did, to be honest, because I loved doing it so much and I learned so much, got so much out of it, a totally selfish thing; I didn't give a shit, I really didn't. And I never have; to me, it's the doing of something that's the vibe, it's not necessarily the result. It's always a bonus if what you do does well, but it's not that precious, you know. I've always thought like that. And I could see why it was laughed at; it does look like a pretentious pile of old stuff. We were self-indulgent pop stars, there's no question about it.

Today, *Consequences* has achieved cult status, so much so that there are websites and podcasts dedicated to exploring it at a granular level. I've already mentioned Mr Blint's Attic, created by Paul McNulty and Sean Macreavy – they also have 99 podcasts examining all things 10cc. Look them up if you want an hour-long examination of all 17 movements of 'Blint's Tune'.

It has also been praised in some quarters for its prophetic use of climate change as the main theme. Godley refuses to take any credit for that – it was just the idea that, given nature is so powerful, what would happen if it began to fight back against its human abusers?

These days, Godley is convinced that the human race is living on borrowed time – the planet will probably survive, he thinks, but our time is up. However, *Consequences* ends on a note of hope, so perhaps there's a Mr Blint somewhere who, with an out-of-tune piano, a guitar and a piece of rubber on the end of a power drill, will save us all.

Gentle Giant – The Missing Piece

Personnel:
Gary Green: electric and acoustic guitars
Kerry Minnear: Hammond organ, electric piano, piano, synthesiser, Minimoog, Clavinet, percussion, vocals
Derek Shulman: lead vocals
Ray Shulman: bass, 12-string guitar, percussion
John Weathers: drums and percussion, drum machine
Recorded at Relight Studios, Hilvarenbeek, Netherlands in May 1977
Produced by Gentle Giant
Engineered by Paul Northfield
Label: Chrysalis (UK), Capitol (US)
Release date: 26 August 1977
Chart places: Sweden: 50, US: 81, Canada: 81
Tracks: 'Two Weeks In Spain', 'I'm Turning Around', 'Betcha Thought We Couldn't Do It', 'Who Do You Think You Are?', 'Mountain Time', 'As Old As You're Young', 'Memories Of Old Days', 'Winning', 'For Nobody'
All tracks written by Kerry Minnear, Derek Shulman and Ray Shulman

The Story So Far...

Born the sons of a jazz trumpeter in Glasgow, Scotland, the three Shulman brothers put an r&b band together that eventually became Simon Dupree and the Big Sound (Derek was 'Simon') and had a psychedelic hit, 'Kites', in 1967. Follow-ups flopped, so, in 1969, the brothers recruited Dorset-born multi-instrumentalist Kerry Churchill Minnear, who had graduated from the Royal Academy of London, Londoner Gary Green and former Dupree drummer Martin Smith. The new lineup's name was a reference to a fictional 'gentle giant' who happens upon a band of musicians. Signed to Vertigo, their self-titled 1970 debut was challenging but criticised for poor recording quality. Their 1971 follow-up, *Acquiring The Taste*, showed a further experimental approach, after which Smith left and was replaced by Malcolm Mortimore. Their first concept album, *Three Friends*, came in 1972, after which Mortimore was injured in a motorcycle accident and replaced by Welshman John Weathers for the band's second album that year, *Octopus*. Phil Shulman left following arguments with his brothers, and the band released *In A Glass House* in 1973 and *The Power And The Glory* in 1974. Moving to Chrysalis Records, *Free Hand* (1975) reached the US top 50. *Interview* (1976) is seen as the start of a creative wane, although 1977's live album *Playing The Fool* showed they were at their peak as performers and musicians.

The Album

The vast majority of albums featured in this book were untouched by the punk revolution, partly because they were recorded before the gobbing brigade began to make their presence felt but mostly because progressive rock bands lived in a different, more sophisticated musical world and saw the three-chord snarls of yobbish teens as irrelevant.

So, it is ironic that one of the few prog groups to be openly influenced by punk was Gentle Giant – surely the proggiest of the lot. They were so outrageously talented that they played something like 30 different instruments between them, including a celeste and a donkey's jawbone. Their albums displayed their mastery of rock, folk, soul, jazz and the classics.

Their compositions were long and complex, with multi-part harmonies, unusual instrumentation and abrupt changes of tempo and style, frequently leaping from the 20th century to the 15th and back again, with time signatures that read like Fermat's Last Theorem and song structures like tangled knots or the interwoven strands of the Bayeux Tapestry (actually an embroidery, pedantry fans). Lyrically, they would draw on poetry, philosophy and psychology, being particularly inspired by the Renaissance writer Rabelais.

Their aim, made explicit in the sleeve notes of their second album, was to 'expand the frontiers of contemporary popular music at the risk of becoming very unpopular', and they were wildly successful at both pursuits. Not only did they expand popular music's frontiers, but they remained very unpopular, in the UK at least, until long after they broke up.

However, as with every cult musical endeavour, there was pressure from record companies to create a hit single or album, particularly by the mid-1970s when prog was increasingly being seen as past its peak. Gentle Giant were no exception – in fact, some of the members wanted commercial success almost as much as the label did. They tried writing a hit single in 1974, recording three tracks Derek Shulman described as 'atrocious'. The record label released the worst one, 'The Power And The Glory' (confusingly, it WASN'T on the album of the same name) before the band complained and it was withdrawn from the market.

Now, the pressure was on again, from both outside and inside the band. It was true that Gentle Giant were respected in the US and mainland Europe, where punk had yet to make an impact, but in their home nation, they were rapidly becoming seen as 'dinosaurs'. The live album *Playing The Fool*, released in January 1977, showed them being received with enthusiasm by European fans. However, in the 12-page booklet that accompanied the original double LP, Derek Shulman admitted: 'In Britain, it's not been low profile, it's been NO profile.' Perhaps that's why the band never played live in the UK again, apart from an appearance on the BBC TV show *Sight & Sound*.

They watched the musical barbarians storming the citadel and felt as if the world was crumbling around them. In the liner notes for the CD reissue of *The Missing Piece*, Ray Shulman recalls: 'It was like a kick in the teeth, but also a jolt to stop complacency – it was a general shake-up for everybody, really. With the pressure to become more commercially viable on the one hand and the fact that we had a very loyal audience on the other, we were in a dilemma.' In the same notes, Kerry Minnear says:

> At this stage, certainly, one or two members of the band were becoming frustrated by the straitjacket we'd made for ourselves ... Because of the nature of what we were, we felt obliged to play quite experimental music all the time. Ray was getting quite heavily into punk because it was just a total burst of energy and enthusiasm, and I think that appealed to him because it was so completely different to what we were. I confess I was a bit nonplussed by some of the things that were going on in the band ... Personally, I had much less enthusiasm for breaking free of these restrictions we'd placed on ourselves.

Despite Minnear's reservations, there certainly seemed to be a conscious effort to simplify things a bit. As the main songwriters, he and Ray would meet up a couple of weeks after the end of a tour to share musical ideas and see where the next album was going. This time, punk fan Ray was pushing the band in a more straightforward direction. Minnear told Prog magazine in 2024: 'Some of the songs were quite simple on this album, and they didn't need an awful lot – they were more or less presented as completed songs.'

There were two more influences helping to reshape Gentle Gant's music. One was the fact that some of the songs that ended up on *The Missing Piece* were road-tested before being recorded. 'Winning', 'For Nobody' and 'As Old As You're Young' were debuted on tour – in a live situation, playing songs the audience had never heard before, it seemed the shorter, simpler approach worked best.

The second influence was fellow prog giants Genesis, who were edging towards a more commercial sound after the departure of lead singer Peter Gabriel. Their 1976 album *Wind & Wuthering* – recorded at Relight Studios in the Netherlands because they could keep more of their earnings under tax rules – contained more obviously commercial material such as 'Afterglow' and the single 'Your Own Special Way'. The album sold 100,000 copies in its first week, reaching number seven in the UK charts. Gentle Giant followed them to the same studios, hoping to sprinkle the album with the same commercially successful fairy dust.

The Missing Piece was recorded fairly quickly in May 1977 and the result is deliberately schizophrenic. Side one contained what, to Gentle Giant, were the 'experimental' songs – exercises in concise, direct writing, usually in a straight 4/4 tempo, unadorned with baroque or medieval influences, all clocking in at less than four minutes. There was even an attempt to create a punk song! Side two, on the other hand, was the 'business as usual' approach, with longer, more complicated compositions, including the seven-minute 'Memories Of Old Days'.

The album kicks off with two tracks that were later released as singles. 'Two Weeks In Spain' is a bright, poppy opener taking the oh-so-gentle piss out of the typical British working-class summer holiday. Derek sings in a London accent as he praises the joys of spending a fortnight on the Costa Brava, drinking cheap Spanish wine and enjoying the carnival atmosphere. In the end, he concedes, 'Two weeks in Spain is not enough'. Catchy and jaunty, it could have repeated the chart success of, say, Yes's 'Wonderous Stories'. It didn't. Backed with a live version of 'Free Hand' from the *Playing The Fool* album, the single seemed to get lost in transit.

The power ballad 'I'm Turning Around' was written, says Minnear, as a deliberate attempt to create a chart hit – indeed, that's what gave the album its name; the 'missing piece' was the elusive hit single, the unadventurous all-green cover driving the message home by showing a missing bit of a jigsaw puzzle. Opening with a simple four-chord sequence on electric piano, admittedly in the un-punk-like key of Eb, Derek sings fairly corny lines about lost love before the song slips into C for a powerful everybody-join-in chorus. There's a cheesy organ instrumental over the verse chords, then it fades out on the chorus like every good power ballad should.

'I'm Turning Around' has been described as 'Genesis-like', and there are similarities to the two commercial tracks on *Wind & Wuthering*. Perhaps it could have repeated the success of, say, 'Your Own Special Way'? It was not to be – backed with 'Just The Same' from *Free Hand*, the single turned around and disappeared.

We then come to what is probably the most divisive track Gentle Giant ever recorded, and one that makes explicit the confusion and uncertainty the band felt at this time. 'Betcha Thought We Couldn't Do It' is their attempt at a punk rock song, a three-chord wonder with lyrics spat out by Derek in a laughable attempt at a nasal snarl. Unfortunately, it is let down by a polite, middle-class guitar sound and words that are much too clever and ironic. 'I betcha thought we couldn't do it,' Derek sings to disbelieving GG fans, 'and if you did we wouldn't try … We built our house stone by stone … Now we can't stick in our old ways. Now it's out we'll see how you feel'. Never has punk sounded this insecure.

In the bouncy 'Who Do You Think You Are?', GG created something that sounds simple but actually isn't – there's plenty of the band's trademark 'stop-start' approach and a scattering of unexpected chords, particularly during a short but sprightly instrumental section. The chorus is in A major, but the verses are in D minor and E minor – hey, it's not Shostakovich, but it's beyond anything the punks could come up with in 1977. Side one ends with another finger-snapper in 'Mountain Time' – a fun, funky number with a pulsing bassline about meeting a girl for a date, apparently on a mountain. I hope they both wrapped up warm.

For side two, we get tracks that sound more like the Gentle Giant of old – generally longer with plenty of acoustic guitars and baroque keyboards (and you know what they say – if it's not baroque, don't fix it). 'As Old As You're Young' does indeed open with some medieval-sounding flourishes on keyboards and bass before Minnear takes lead vocals, sounding like a minstrel setting the scene in Sherwood Forest. There are stop-starts galore, clever key changes and intricate counterpointed instrumentals and vocals. Lyrically, the song is about getting old – a nod perhaps to how out-of-touch the band were feeling at this time – but it concludes by suggesting that 'coming of age never comes'.

All the songs on the prog side of the LP seem to reference time passing and regret for days gone by. Perhaps Gentle Giant were feeling their age. The title of 'Memories Of Old Days' is pretty explicit – 'with sadness today, hopes of joy yesterday', sings Derek. The song is inspired by George Orwell's fourth novel, *Coming Up For Air*, in which an insurance salesman returns to his birthplace in an attempt to recapture his childhood innocence. Published in 1939, on the cusp of World War II, it looked at how idyllic England was being destroyed by capitalism ('the city lights flickered where lake waters gleamed') while a new, deadly threat lay just over the horizon.

Musically, 'Memories Of Old Days' opens with exquisite and intricate interplay between Gary Green on acoustic guitar and Ray on a 12-string, reminiscent of early Genesis, while Minnear plays synth and Hammond organ, particularly effectively in a heart-wrenching key change towards the end. The guitars seem to chime like church bells, and Derek's voice is full of loss and yearning. There's the occasional sound of children playing in the background, providing a connection to 1972's *Three Friends* concept album, where this would have fitted perfectly.

There's even a sense of loss in the up-tempo rocker 'Winning' – the protagonist has everything, but 'no one knows him … What did he miss, needing nothing? Rising winner but falling man, gaining the day'. Guitarist Green and Minnear on Minimoog, piano and organ are locked together in intricate, weaving melody lines, but it is drummer John 'Pugwash' Weathers who is the star of the show, driving everything along with versatile percussion in which he seems to be hitting everything within reach.

Finally, 'For Nobody' is an even busier track than 'Winning' – again, Weathers drives things along with muscular drumming, along with busy bass work from Ray and an excellent guitar solo from Green. The lyrics are about running away, probably from a failed relationship – 'Tried to forget everything that we did … I'll be responsible for nobody'. But, once again, the song is laced with regret for the past and what might have been.

When *The Missing Piece* was released, the UK charts were being invaded by the barbarians – The Stranglers at number six, Elvis Costello and the Attractions at number 14 and The Jam at number 36. However, it would be wrong to think that punk was dominating music – the number-one album on 27 August 1977 was, um, *20 All Time Greats* by 1950s and 1960s US singer Connie Francis. The singles chart was topped by The Floaters (Float … float onnnn…). Both Yes and Emerson, Lake and Palmer had albums in the top 30, so a release that straddled both pop and prog should have done well.

Nevertheless, as Derek Shulman pointed out, Gentle Giant had NO profile in the UK, and perhaps their pop was a little too clever, while their prog was also a little too clever. Whatever the reason, it failed to make much impact except in Sweden and has generally been regarded as a low point in the band's catalogue.

However, in 2024, it was given a spruce-up by the ubiquitous Steven Wilson, who boosted the bass (the original recording was quite tinny), lost some unnecessary vocal effects and created a 5.1 surround sound version. Suddenly, everyone realised that *The Missing Piece* is probably Gentle Giant's last great album – both *Giant For A Day!* (1978) and *Civilian* (1980) went down the pop-rock route before the band called it quits, finally defeated by the 'no profile' problem.

Here was a genuine attempt by a prog rock band to explore the new musical landscape and inject some of the urgency and immediacy of punk into their own creations. It may not have been a resounding success, but we can certainly say it was a heroic failure. In the *Prog* article, Green admitted:

We were just a bit flummoxed as to what was going on. We just weren't built like that; that's not who we were. So, any attempt we had to cross over was going to fall foul. The shoes we had just weren't the right fit, and we were stumbling over the cobbles … But I think we'd made a good album, absolutely. We never didn't think that.

Goblin – Suspiria

Personnel:
Agostino Marangolo: drums, percussion, vocals
Massimo Morante: electric guitars, acoustic guitars, bouzouki, vocals
Fabio Pignatelli: Fender Precision Bass (fretless), Rickenbacker bass (fretted), tabla, acoustic guitar, vocals
Claudio Simonetti: Mellotron (presets: 3-violins, church organ and 8-choir), Elka organ, Logan violin, Celesta, Fender Rhodes electric piano, grand piano, Moog synthesisers (Minimoog and System 55)
With:
Antonio Marangolo: saxophone (on 'Black Forest')
Maurizio Guarini (uncredited): additional keyboards
Recorded in 1976 at Orthophonic Recording Studio, Rome
Produced by Goblin
Engineered by Pino Mastroianni
Label: Cinevox
Release date: 15 June 1977
Chart placings: no chart data available
Tracks: 'Suspiria', 'Witch', 'Opening To The Sighs', 'Sighs', 'Markos', 'Black Forest', 'Blind Concert', 'Death Valzer'
All tracks written by Goblin

The Story So Far...

The band was formed by Brazilian-born Italian Claudio Simonetti, Masimo Morante, Fabio Pignatelli and drummer Walter Martino. Between 1972 and 1973, they recorded demos under the name of Oliver, inspired by British progressive rock groups Genesis, King Crimson and Yes. Taking the recordings to London in the search for a recording contract, they met Yes producer Eddy Offord, who urged them to move to England. When they arrived (with new drummer Carlo Bordini and vocalist Clive Haynes), they found Offord away on tour, so they returned to Italy penniless. They signed with Cinevox Records, formed mostly to release soundtrack albums, and changed their name to Cherry Five. Also signed to Cinevox was Italian film composer Giorgio Baslini, who was scoring a horror movie, *Profondo Rosso* (translated as 'Deep Red'), for director Dario Argento. Argento was unhappy with Baslini's music, which he described as 'awful'. After failing to get Pink Floyd, he turned to Cherry Five, who impressed him by coming up with two compositions in one night. They composed the majority of the score, and the resulting soundtrack– released under the name of Goblin to avoid clashing with the imminent release of the first Cherry Five album – sold more than a million copies and spent 52 weeks in the Italian charts. New drummer Agostino Marangolo joined during the recording process. By the time of the release of their second album, *Roller*, in 1976, they were officially Goblin.

The Album

'You can run from Suspiria! You can hide from Suspiria! But you cannot escape Suspiria!' So warned the hysterical (and hysterically funny) trailer for Dario Argento's 1977 horror movie classic. To the accompaniment of more screaming than Fay Wray in *King Kong*, the trailer added: 'The only thing more terrifying than the last 12 minutes of *Suspiria* … are the first 92!'

From a distance of nearly 50 years, it all looks laughably overwrought, hammy and too desperate to scare. The acting is terrible, the dialogue (in the English version) is inaudible, while the music and sound effects are ear-shatteringly loud. But it is seen as one of the most influential films in the genre, containing all the cliches that have become key ingredients of modern horror movies – the death trap setting, the victims slowly picked off one by one, the expert who provides vital background and 'the final girl' who survives. Even now, it is revered as a cult classic for its visual and stylistic quirks.

Why is a book on music rabbiting on about a movie? Because all good horror films rely on an effective score that can unsettle the viewer and heighten the terror, otherwise they are just shots of people running around dodging visual effects. In the case of *Suspiria*, it was the Italian progressive rock group Goblin who provided an experimental soundtrack that is as disturbing as the film. Not only is it regarded as the band's finest album, but it also inspired other filmmakers, particularly John Carpenter, and the electronic music scene. Clever little Goblins.

The de facto leader of the group and chief composer was Claudio Simonetti. Music was in his genes – his father was celebrated Italian musician and entertainer Enrico Simonetti, who was living in Brazil, where he had his own TV show, when his son was born. In fact, father and son saw their careers run almost in parallel – Enrico's most famous composition was the theme song for a 1975 Italian TV science fiction thriller called *Gamma*, recorded by his son's band and released as a single after they completed work on the music for *Profondo Rosso*. It was Enrico who helped his son get a contract with Cinevox.

His background meant young Claudio had a foot in both the popular and serious music worlds, playing guitar in beat groups but also studying piano at an Italian conservatory. He was a big fan of horror movies, so working with 'Master of the Thrill' Dario Argento was a dream – or perhaps a nightmare – come true. Simonetti told revok.com in a 2010 interview: 'We were only in our 20s. He had a lot of faith in us, giving us such a great job. We were young and inexperienced, but our music was close to what Dario wanted.'

In return, Dario helped create Goblin. Without him, they may have remained Cherry Five, churning out accomplished but derivative British-style prog. Listen to the band's only Cherry Five album, released in 1975, and you will hear what I mean. At times, it's more Yes than Yes. But scoring horror movies encouraged Goblin to absorb jazz, heavy metal and musique concrete into their DNA, which came together most impressively on their score for *Suspiria*. Even on the rare occasion that the band recorded and released a non-soundtrack album, such as *Roller* in 1976, it still sounded like the score to a horror movie.

Profondo Rosso had been composed and recorded in a matter of days after the film had been cut; Goblin were given three months to come up with the music for *Suspiria*, which allowed them the opportunity to use the screenplay as inspiration. But that turned out to be a mistake. Simonetti said in the revok.com interview:

> The only time we tried to write music from a screenplay was with *Suspiria*. Dario gave us his script and we started writing some music, which he also played on the studio set to create an ambience. Then, when we saw the completed film, it was so different from what we'd imagined that we had to start all over from scratch.

The film they saw was inspired by Suspiria De Profundis, a collection of essays by 19th century writer and journalist Thomas de Quincey about a dream he had after staying at a supposedly haunted house in Milan. Argento and his partner, Daria Nicolodi, fashioned a screenplay about a student who enrols in a prestigious dance academy, only to find it was founded by a witch and is home to a coven practising black magic.

There are scenes of extreme violence as one girl is disembowelled with a knife, a second girl's throat is slit and a third is nailed to a coffin, while a dog inexplicably turns on its owner and tears him to pieces. In one scene, actress Stefania Casini had to force her way through a room full of wire. It was shot only once because she suffered cuts and scratches all over her body.

Suspiria was shot in the gothic settings of Freiburg im Breisgau in Germany and the Black Forest, and photographer Luciano Tovoli created deep, accentuating colours by hanging tinted fabric in front of arc lights. Argento had wanted to use teen actresses but was forbidden by strict German laws – instead, all the door handles were placed higher than normal to suggest the cast were younger than they actually were, and much of the acting by the mostly female characters is childlike and hysterical.

Suspiria is sometimes mistakenly described as 'giallo' – an Italian term to describe particularly bloody murder mystery novels and films, particularly those involving serial killers. *Profondo Rosso* was a typical giallo film – a series of gruesome murders is carried out by a mysterious figure wearing black leather gloves. But Argento had other ideas about *Suspiria*. In a 2015 interview with vice.com, Simonetti recalls:

> When he called us to do the film, he said, 'This is not about a serial killer or not the typical Italian giallo, but a film that talks about witches. I need music that always lets the audience feel that witches are there, even if there is

nothing on the screen.' We recorded *Profondo Rosso* in just ten days, but not for *Suspiria*. For *Suspiria*, we stayed in the studio for almost three months. We also experimented with different ethnical instruments like a Greek bouzouki and Indian tabla, and we used a lot of different synthesisers like the Mellotron and the big System 55 Moog.

The band employed a number of canny tricks to heighten the suspense in the score. First, there is the simple, repetitive music-box melody in D minor as the main theme. Clearly influenced by director William Friedkin's use of Mike Oldfield's 'Tubular Bells' in 1973's *The Exorcist*, it shows that a child-like lullaby can sometimes sound more terrifying than any amount of orchestral bombast. It is played on a celesta over the opening credits with random strums of a bouzouki and the bouncy boom of a tabla. On the original LP, it is part of the six-minute opening track 'Suspiria', which builds to a crescendo with keyboards and sound effects.

Second, the constant presence of evil is suggested by whispered voices. 'Witch!' they hiss, even when there's no witchy person in sight. There's also a lot of heavy breathing and strange animalistic cries, growls and yells as if demons are gathering to watch someone being whipped to death. Along with choral effects created by the Mellotron, these are the only vocals on the album – there are no songs here, only strange, disturbing instrumentals.

Third, the band use plenty of percussion and sound effects to suggest the existence of violent acts. Sheets of metal are crashed together, acoustic guitars are strummed abrasively so they are more rhythmic noise than melody, and drums and cymbals are thrashed apparently at random, while keyboards play strange whooping noises. Where real instruments are used, they are frequently treated to sound brutal and aggressive, such as Pignatelli's fuzzed-up bass on 'Markos', or to provide menacing washes of synthesised backing.

Two tracks on side two take a more conventional tack – indeed, on later issues, they would be merged into one 12-minute piece. 'Black Forest' opens with finger-picked acoustic and electric guitars, a short keyboard melody and a thrumming bass so deep it could dislodge your fillings. Antonio Marangola (Agostino's brother) provides jazzy saxophone phrases before drums come in and drive the track through a lurching riff, then electric guitars take things in a more funky direction, with Morante, Marangola and Simonetti trading licks on guitar, sax and keyboards.

'Blind Concert' starts with tinkling percussion as the musical-box main theme fades in before funky bass and guitars take over to suggest some sort of concert – it is used in a scene where the blind pianist, sacked by the ballet school, drowns his sorrows in a club. But commercial club music this ain't – it's jumpy and angular with wild guitar licks and atonal piano flourishes. Finally, the original soundtrack album ends – after a paltry 34 minutes – with a sprightly piano waltz. Later releases would include alternate and extended tracks, but they don't add much to what is already there.

All this was achieved without modern-day samplers, although Goblin did push the boundaries of what could be achieved with synthesisers in movie scores. Simonetti told *Factmag* in 2014:

You would never use a synth to do soundtracks [then]. Normally, it would be made with an orchestra or with a band. No one was using a synthesiser for that. I think we were maybe one of the first using [the synthesiser], then in the 1980s, the synthesiser and drum machine became more famous and it became more usual.

Simonetti hired a System 55 Moog, the final and biggest model the company made, as played by his hero Keith Emerson. It was so complicated to wire up and play that he also brought in Italian composer Felice Fugazza, who had just released an album of Moog music and could translate the band's ideas into sound. Keyboardist Maurizio Guarini is also sometimes listed as playing on the album – he had joined Goblin in 1975 but left after just three days of recording *Suspiria*. Simonetti says Guarini's contributions were limited to the early demos.

It is fair to say that the *Suspiria* soundtrack has aged better than the film – it is still a chilling and disturbing listen, while the movie now looks a bit shoddy and amateurish (and the 2018 remake is just baffling). Allmusic says 'it represents their sound carried to its most powerful and intense', while film critic Mark Kermode praises its 'witchy shrieks and synthy strains'. Simonetti is in no doubt about its importance, telling vice.com: 'I think that *Suspiria* is the real Goblin sound, more than *Profondo Rosso* because *Profondo Rosso* is similar to a lot of different prog stuff of the 1970s. With *Suspiria*, we invented the Goblin sound. *Suspiria* is our masterwork.'

Anthony Phillips – The Geese & The Ghost

Personnel:

Anthony Phillips: acoustic 12-string, 6-string, classical, electric 6- and 12-string guitars, bass guitar, dulcimer, bouzouki, synthesiser, Mellotron, harmonium, piano, organ, celeste, pin piano, drums, glockenspiel, timbales, bells and chimes, gong, lead vocals on 'Collections' and 'Master Of Time (Demo)'

Mike Rutherford: acoustic 12-string, 6-string and classical guitars, bass guitar, organ, drums, timbales, glockenspiel, cymbals, bells

Phil Collins: lead vocals on 'Which Way The Wind Blows', 'God If I Saw Her Now' and 'Silver Song'

Rob Phillips: oboe on 'The Geese & The Ghost' and 'Sleepfall: The Geese Fly West'

Lazo Momulovich: oboe, cor anglais on 'Henry: Portraits From Tudor Times' and 'The Geese & The Ghost'

John Hackett: flute on 'God If I Saw Her Now', 'Collections' and 'Sleepfall: The Geese Fly West'

Wil Sleath: flute, baroque flute, recorder, piccolo on 'Henry: Portraits From Tudor Times'

Jack Lancaster: flute, lyricon on 'Sleepfall: The Geese Fly West'

Charlie Martin: cello on 'Chinese Mushroom Cloud' and 'The Geese & The Ghost'

Kirk Trevor: cello on 'Chinese Mushroom Cloud' and 'The Geese & The Ghost'

Nick Hayley (with 'friend'): violin on 'The Geese & The Ghost'

Martin Westlake: timpani on 'Henry: Portraits From Tudor Times', 'Chinese Mushroom Cloud' and 'The Geese & The Ghost'

Tom Newman: heckelphone, bulk eraser on 'Master Of Time (Demo)'

Vivienne McAuliffe: vocals on 'God If I Saw Her Now'

Send Barns Orchestra

Jeremy Gilbert: conductor

Barge Rabble: voices of several friends

Ralph Bernascone: soloist

Recorded at Send Barns in Woking, Surrey, and Argonaut Galleries in London between October 1974 and November 1976

Engineered and produced by Anthony Phillips, Mike Rutherford and Simon Heyworth

Label: Hit & Run Music (UK), Passport Records (US)

Release date: March 1977

Chart places: US: 191

Tracks: 'Wind-Tales', 'Which Way The Wind Blows', 'Henry: Portraits From Tudor Times – (i) Fanfare (ii) Lute's Chorus (iii) Misty Battlements (Iv) Lute's Chorus (Reprise) (V) Henry Goes To War (Vi) Death Of A Knight (Vii) Triumphant Return', 'God If I Saw Her Now', 'Chinese Mushroom Cloud', 'The Geese & The Ghost – Parts I & II', 'Collections', 'Sleepfall: The Geese Fly West'

All tracks written by Anthony Phillips, except 3, 5 & 6 by Phillips/Mike Rutherford

The Story So Far…

Like Peter Gabriel, Anthony Phillips (born Chiswick, England) was one of the founders of Genesis at Charterhouse School. Between 1967 and 1970, he was the band's lead guitarist and one of the main songwriters. However, he quit Genesis after the second album, *Trespass*, suffering from glandular fever and stage fright. It was inevitable that he would produce his own album, but he probably didn't suspect it would take him seven long years.

The Album

The music business is full of people who quit or were pushed out before 'the band made it big'. The most famous is probably Pete Best of The Beatles, cast aside in favour of Ringo Starr before the Fab Four recorded their debut single. But there were many others, including Doug Sandom (a drummer forced to resign from The Who in 1964), David Marks (who quit The Beach Boys in 1963 after clashing with Brian Wilson's dad) and Tony Chapman (another drummer, who stepped aside for Charlie Watts in The Rolling Stones). Then, there was Anthony Phillips.

Who? Well, I forgive you if you don't recognise his name. But Ant, as he is known to his friends, could have been Steve Hackett if he hadn't found the whole process of live performance so stomach-churning. Even sadder was the fact that he was – sorry, still is – a multi-talented musician and composer whose name dominates the songwriting credits on *Trespass*, the second Genesis album.

But why am I featuring an artist and an album that you probably haven't heard of? Well, first of all, it's a great recording, full of sublime 12-string and classical guitars, delicate keyboards and medieval-style woodwind, a combination of folk, classical music and progressive rock. Secondly, it's almost a 'lost' Genesis album as it includes the instrumental talents of Mike Rutherford and the voice of the ubiquitous Phil Collins. There's also Steve Hackett's brother, John, on flute.

It shifted very few copies in 1977 as punk swept across the UK – Phillips recalls meeting someone who confessed to selling his copy because he was too embarrassed to be seen with it. However, it has gradually become a cult album over the last five decades, and Phillips himself is revered as a 'pure' musician who turned his back on commercialism to follow his own idiosyncratic muse. In 2015, it was re-released as a three-disc definitive edition with outtakes, an aborted single and a 5.1 surround sound mix. Not bad for an album hardly anyone has heard of.

The story of *The Geese & The Ghost* stretches back to 1969, when Phillips was still a member of Genesis, writing material with Charterhouse School pal Mike Rutherford for *Trespass*. The band's debut, *From Genesis To Revelation* – a collection of pleasant little pop songs originally written with other singers in mind, such as Dusty Springfield – had sold a grand total of 649 copies, and Dusty inexplicably failed to get in touch. But, in a triumph of optimism over experience, they agreed to have another crack at full-time musical careers, hunkering down at a cottage in Surrey to write and rehearse for up to 11 hours a day.

The plan was to make an album of heavier, more complex songs, and they largely succeeded – *Trespass* contained just six tracks, all more than six minutes in length, with the longest, the heavy, brutal 'The Knife', clocking in at nearly nine. The 18-year-old Phillips provided material for all the songs – he is the only member of the *Trespass* lineup to have a credit on every track – but a lot of the stuff he and Rutherford were composing was of the gentle, wistful variety, the two of them working together with their 12-string guitars, the top strings tuned down to D from E. In an interview for *The Pavilion* magazine in 1992, conducted by Jonathan Dann and Alan Hewitt, Phillips said:

> The problem is that there were lots and lots of bits in the same tuning that got shunted off into different areas. There was an abundance of material which Mike and I recorded during the summer of 1969, the period when the group were switching from the *From Genesis To Revelation* period to 'The Knife' and 'Looking For Someone', and doing the heavy electric guitar stuff. Some of the stuff that we recorded, and which ironically ended up on the CD re-issue, were things like 'Lucy: An Illusion', 'Stranger' and 'Silver Song' … most of it never ended up going through Genesis.

Phillips was also no mean pianist but was sensitive about offering up any piano compositions in front of the band's keyboard player, Tony Banks. So, 'Collections', a stately, hymn-like ballad with some heart-wrenching melodies, didn't go through the group. Other compositions – including 'D Instrumental' with that tuned-down string – were later grouped together and ended up as the title track for *The Geese & The Ghost*.

Then came the split – Phillips was suffering from stage fright, and it got increasingly worse as time went on. Brought down by a bout of glandular fever and the belief (despite the album credits) that a lot of his material was being overlooked, he eventually took his doctor's advice and quit the band, playing his last gig in July 1970. Genesis nearly split up at this point – they later said it was the one departure that seriously threatened the band's survival – but, as we know, they found a new guitarist in Steve Hackett and a new drummer in Phil Collins and the rest, as they say, is history.

For Phillips, the departure should have freed him up to work on a solo album and it is true that a lot of material came flooding out at that point, mostly songs he had been working on during the last five or six months of his time in the band: 'God If I Saw Her Now', 'Which Way The Wind Blows' and what eventually became the seven-part suite 'Henry: Portraits Of Tudor Times'. But then, he started listening to the classical composer Sibelius and realised he was 'terribly limited' as a musician. Any thoughts of a solo career were put on ice as he took piano and guitar lessons and studied orchestration and harmony at the Guildhall School of Music and Drama in London. He also became a qualified music teacher.

Phillips and Rutherford drifted apart over the next few years before reuniting in about 1972, when they took another look at the material they had. But there wasn't much they could do because things became very busy for Rutherford as Genesis really took off following the release of *Foxtrot* and the recordings of 1973's *Selling England By The Pound* and 1974's torturous double album *The Lamb Lies Down On Broadway*.

When they eventually got going at Phillips' home, Send Barns, using equipment bought thanks to an advance of £3,000 from record label Charisma, they were plagued with technical problems. In the 1992 interview, Phillips explained:

> We kept getting static clicks from these TEAC machines, which were notorious for being a bit odd. 'Which Way The Wind Blows' was the first piece we kicked off with and that was on electric guitar, but it was played to sound like a classical guitar and was very quiet and gentle with a round sort of gentle strumming sound and we had all these static clicks and all these sorts of boffins came down and it was a nightmare ... just when we wanted to get going and we had all this technical stuff! We decided that the budget was so small that we had to do most of it at home – quite what would happen later on, we weren't sure, but we bought these two four-track TEACs and a desk for two or three thousand pounds, and that set us up basically. So, we thought we could do it very simply and make it sound convincing on a small level of tracks. What we didn't realise was that some tracks wouldn't sound full enough and would need still more.

During this time, Phillips and Rutherford attempted to record a single with Phil Collins. The result was 'Silver Song', written in 1969 about departed early Genesis drummer John Silver – 'Dear friend, when you have gone/ There'll always be this song/To remind you of where you once belonged', said the poignant lyrics, over strummed and picked acoustic guitars. It was recorded at Island Studios in London in November 1973, along with a projected B-side called 'Only Your Love', but was never released, possibly because Charisma felt it wasn't the right time for any current Genesis member to have a solo career. So, Collins would have to wait until 1981 to do his own thing.

After a further break, during which Rutherford toured with Genesis to promote *The Lamb Lies Down On Broadway*, he and Phillips moved to the Argonaut, a recording studio on a barge moored in London's Little Venice, owned by British record producer Tom Newman. But even that proved a challenge, with more equipment malfunctions and breakdowns and the vessel being rammed by other water dwellers. But at least they were able to complete the overdubs of woodwinds, flutes and percussion, with the help of engineer

Simon Heyworth, and, in July 1975, Collins was back to lay down his vocals on 'Which Way The Wind Blows' and 'God If I Saw Her Now'.

Other musicians who added their talents to the recordings included Ant's brother Rob, a talented oboe player, and students from the Guildhall School of Music and Drama. A second vocalist, Vivien McAuliffe, who sang with various bands in London, was recruited to add her voice to 'God If I Saw Her Now'. The sessions ended with the recording of massed vocals on the 'Triumphant Return' part of 'Henry: Portraits From Tudor Times', a group of friends dubbed the Barge Rabble.

By October 1975, the album was ready for release, but it took another 18 months to hit record shops. Why? Phillips believes it was partly because Rutherford was too busy with a rejuvenated Genesis to get involved with pushing the record label and partly because executives saw the project as too similar to Mike Oldfield's *Ommadawn*. It was a deeply frustrating time for Phillips, who returned to teaching and studying while recording material on his home equipment that would surface on later albums.

Then came the surprise news that Passport Records, an independent label founded in 1973 by Martin Scott, Jeff Tenenbaum and Ed Grossi, were going to release the album in the US. Phillips was booked onto a promo tour of the States, and there was talk about selling 17,000 copies in New York in just ten days. In the UK, the album was put out by Hit & Run Music, run by Genesis manager Tony Smith, but there wasn't much promotion, and by 1977, punk was sweeping the boards.

For those record buyers who weren't too embarrassed to be seen with *The Geese & The Ghost*, there were some musical treasures to be found in the grooves. The cover, by artist Peter Cross, set the scene – a Tudor-looking lute player sits beneath an oak tree, gazing across England's green and pleasant land as a ghostly fairy rises from a silver pond. This clearly wasn't The Damned.

The album opens with a brief one-minute introduction of synthy washes that is actually a portion of the orchestral finale from the last track, played backwards. The first proper song is the beautiful 'Which Way The Wind Blows', sung (and harmonised) by Collins with admirable simplicity and restraint against a background of chiming 12-string guitars. Its bittersweet sense of yearning makes this one of Phillips' best-loved compositions.

'Henry: Portraits From Tudor Times' is a seven-part instrumental inspired by the life of Henry VII, the first Tudor King of England, who snaffled the throne in 1485 after defeating Richard III (himself a usurper and murderer of the princes in the Tower of London). Almost entirely played on acoustic instruments, with added timpani, piccolo and cor anglais, it opens with a lusty fanfare, moves through the courtly melodies of the 'Lute's Chorus', solemn spookiness of the 'Misty Battlement's, furious strumming on 'Henry Goes To War', the melancholy 'Death Of A Knight' and, finally, the return of the fanfare as Henry comes home in triumph (he fought further battles to secure his throne and to stop France claiming Brittany).

Side one ends with another gentle, wistful ballad, 'God If I Saw Her Now', in which Collins and McAuliffe duet most effectively and John Hackett plays a lovely flute solo. Side two opens with another short snippet, this time from the title track, but played at half speed. 'The Geese & The Ghost', split into two parts, clocks in at a mighty 16 minutes and is probably the most musically dense instrumental on the album, with both electric and acoustic guitars, Mellotron, a string quartet and Phillips himself on drums. It is a stunning recording, showing his ability to match anything his old mates in Genesis could dream up.

The penultimate track is 'Collections', which we've already mentioned – a gentle piano ballad sung by Phillips himself in a thin, plaintive voice that nevertheless effectively conveys the bittersweet sentiments of disillusion and loss. Finally, the album ends on 'Sleepless: The Geese Fly West', a soaring instrumental based on a repetitive four-chord cycle that grows in intensity before melting into the mist. Why the apparent fixation on geese? Listen to 'Title Inspiration' on the separate CD of bonus tracks included with the 2008 remaster – a short snippet of sounds produced by Phillips on an ARP Pro-soloist synthesiser that mimics the distinct call of geese as they fly west.

It's estimated that some 100,000 copies of the album were sold in the US and UK in 1977, enough to squeeze it into the American charts but not enough to give it any sort of showing in Britain. Not even a sticker reminding buyers of the Genesis connection made much difference. Critics were respectful rather than ecstatic, with *Sounds* calling it 'civilised music … Elegant. Wistful. Graceful. Tasteful. Quiet, subdued and fragile.'

Record labels recognised Phillips' talent and tried to push him into more commercial areas without much success (despite co-writing an album track for UK Eurovision winners Bucks Fizz). With around 40 albums to his name by 2024, including collections of TV and film music, he remains a cult figure – in other words, someone people have barely heard of. But to those in the know, Phillips is the lost genius of Genesis, a true original who combines intense musicality with a fine ear for a moving melody.

Today, *The Geese & The Ghost* is recognised as one of his finest works – maybe his finest. I will leave the last word to actress Rosanna Arquette, a surprise Ant fan. She said: 'It's like Genesis but taken to another level. When all the guitars sound like hundreds together at the end and there is this feeling of hope, innocence and fantasy and when you make music for the sake of music, rather than a single or hit record, it's a whole experience – not just a chapter, but the book read cover to cover.'

Rush – A Farewell To Kings

Personnel:

Geddy Lee: vocals, bass and 12-string guitar, Minimoog, bass pedal synthesisers

Alex Lifeson: electric and acoustic six- and 12-string guitars, classical guitar, bass pedal synthesisers

Neil Peart: drums, orchestra bells, wind chimes, bell tree, vibraslap, triangle, tubular bells, temple blocks

With:

Terry Brown: spoken vocals on 'Cygnus X-1 Book I: The Voyage'

Recorded at Rockfield Studios, Wales, between June and July 1977

Produced by Rush and Terry Brown

Engineered by Terry Brown and Pat Moran

Label: Anthem

Release date: 29 August 1977

Chart placings: Canada: 11, UK: 22, US: 33

Tracks: 'A Farewell To Kings', 'Xanadu', 'Closer To The Heart', 'Cinderella Man', 'Madrigal', 'Cygnus X-1 Book 1: The Voyage i) Prologue, ii) 1, iii) 2, iv) 3'

All tracks written by Geddy Lee, Alex Lifeson & Neil Peart, except 'Closer To The Heart' (Lee, Lifeson, Peart, Peter Talbot) and 'Cinderella Man' (Lee, Lifeson)

The Story So Far...

The band was formed in Toronto, Canada, in 1968 by guitarist Alex Lifeson (born Aleksandar Zivojinovic, also known as Lerxst, in British Columbia), drummer John Rutsey and bassist/vocalist Jeff Jones. Jones was swiftly replaced by Geddy Lee, from Ontario. Various lineups were tried with additional keyboards and a second guitarist, and, at one point, Lee was sacked and replaced by bassist/vocalist Joe Perna. However, Lee was invited back after a disastrous gig with Perna. An initial demo tape had no takers, so the band formed their own label, Moon Records, with manager Ray Danniels. Their first single, 'Not Fade Away' (a Buddy Holly cover), released in September 1973, reached number 88 in the Canadian charts. Their self-titled debut album was released in March 1974 and hit number 86 in Canada.

A copy of the album was sent to Mercury Records, who signed the band. Rutsey quit due to dissatisfaction with the band's new complex music, distaste for life as a touring musician and health problems caused by Type 1 diabetes. His replacement was Neil Peart, also from Ontario, who swiftly established himself as the band's primary lyricist. The second album, *Fly By Night* (1975), reached number nine, but third album *Caress Of Steel* (1975) fared badly (even though it's great. There's no pleasing some people). The band's fourth make-or-break album, *2112* (1976), was a career-saver – making number five in Canada and number 61 in the US – followed by a live release, *All The World's A Stage*.

The Album

Picture, if you will, the Wye Valley in Monmouthshire, Wales – very green and, frequently, very wet. See the sheep and cows grazing in the fields, hear the sound of Welsh birds discussing the results of the Eisteddfod. Feel the rain on your face, on your hands and squelching in your socks. Did I mention that it's very wet? Now, imagine being inspired by these moist surroundings to write a song about … a black hole located 2.22 kiloparsecs from the Sun.

Difficult, eh? They don't really seem to go together unless it rains in black holes. But it was here, on a farm converted into a recording studio, that Canadian proggers Rush recorded their fifth and one of their best albums, *A Farewell To Kings*.

Rush came quite late to prog, and it took them a bit of time to make some truly great records. When *2112* gave them the artistic and commercial success they and the record company needed, the glory days of progressive rock were on the wane. But that didn't deter the trio, who pretty much ignored modern music trends until succumbing to synthesisers on *Signals* in 1982. They even had a hit single in 1980 with 'The Spirit Of Radio' – the first Rush song I ever heard.

But in 1977, the band were receiving very little radio airplay outside of Canada, and the music papers at the time had entered their 'sneer at anything clever' stage. For example, an interview in the *New Musical Express* compared their vague political beliefs – Neil Peart was an admirer of Ayn Rand, the Russian-born philosopher and author whose principle of 'rational self-interest' has become an article of worship for the Right – to the horrifically ironic slogan placed by the Nazis on the gates of Auschwitz, 'Arbeit macht frei' – or Work Makes You Free. As you can imagine, that didn't go down well with Lee, whose Jewish parents were both incarcerated in Nazi concentration camps during the Second World War.

One exception was music journalist Geoff Barton, who gave the band a positive write-up in the UK's *Sounds* publication, which then led to a short British tour, during which Rush debuted a few new songs. They decided to capitalise on the momentum they had built up by immediately going into a studio in the UK to record their next album, but finding the right place proved to be a challenge. It had to have accommodation, space to contain all the instruments they were planning to bring and be cheap enough for the band to spend time there rehearsing and writing, as well as recording.

That meant looking outside London for a start – perhaps even further afield. It was Rush's longtime producer and engineer, Terry Brown, who found Rockfield in Monmouthshire, Wales, and convinced the band to book the studios. They probably didn't need much persuading because it had already been used by Dave Edmunds to record his hit single 'I Hear You Knocking' and by Queen for parts of *Sheer Heart Attack* and *A Night At The Opera*. Black Sabbath were already there when Rush moved in, and Ozzy

Osbourne popped his head into their studio to borrow some hash! In his autobiography, *My Effin' Life*, Geddy Lee said:

> It was the first time we had worked in a residential recording environment, and we found that living on the premises was exactly (as they say in England) what it said on the tin: a rustic, chilled-out yet efficient place with a snooker table, television set and a dining room overlooking the fields (after loading in, a few of the guys went for a stroll, only to be chased across the mud moments later by rampaging cows.) It was a welcome change from eating takeout food while crowding around the console at Toronto Sound … Pretty ideal.

By this time, Rush's arsenal of instruments had grown from the basic drums, bass and guitar of their early years. Lee also had a Minimoog, while both he and Lifeson used bass pedals. Peart, meanwhile, had added all kinds of percussion, including tubular bells, wind chimes, temple blocks and vibraslap. The studio was equipped with a purpose-built echo room that provided further opportunities to experiment with sound, while there was always the great outdoors, with its cast of birds, sheep and cows, to add atmosphere to the music – although the band found themselves recording mostly at night when the wildlife was asleep.

The songs on *A Farewell To Kings* are divided between a few that were road-tested during the tour to promote the live album *All The World's A Stage* and those that were put together in the studio. The band tended to have a clear divide between writing duties: Peart, with his voracious reading and broad interests, crafted the lyrics, while Lee and Lifeson were responsible for the music. There are exceptions, of course, but the vast majority of Rush songs were created in this way. Movies also provided a big inspiration, partly because watching films was how they passed their time on long tour journeys across Canada and the US, and at least two are specifically referenced on this album.

In his autobiography, Lee explained how the music-writing process worked: Lee would sit with a cassette recorder while Lifeson picked out spontaneous riffs, chords and licks, almost immediately forgetting what he had played. When Lee heard something special, he would say, 'Whoa! Let's build a song around that!' and they would go back through the tape to find the gem. It seems rare that Lifeson would come up with a fully realised song built around one or two themes – Lee would do it occasionally – which may explain why so many of their compositions seem to squeeze in half a dozen different musical ideas, almost tumbling over each other.

The earliest track to make a live appearance was the 11-minute 'Xanadu', inspired by both the Samuel Taylor Coleridge poem 'Kubla Khan' and the classic 1941 Orson Welles film *Citizen Kane*. In a 2010 interview in British newspaper *The Guardian*, Neil Peart explained:

In the summer of 1976, in a cottage in Southern Ontario, I was working on the lyrics for a song called 'Xanadu'. (I didn't have any opium, but I might have smoked a little hash.) The song idea was originally inspired by the movie *Citizen Kane* and its main character, Charles Foster Kane, and I had planned to build something on that theme. At the beginning of the movie, the opening lines from 'Kubla Khan' were quoted: 'In Xanadu did Kubla Khan, a stately pleasure dome decree.' As research, I looked up the poem, and I was so powerfully impressed by it that the poem took over the song. In the end, there was entirely too much 'honeydew' in it – too much Coleridge, that is to say – and though musically the song was one of our earliest big 'epics', I never cared much for the lyrics.

Luckily for Peart, the band were trying to concentrate more on music than lyrics, feeling that '2112' had been very word-heavy. Lee told Stereo 104FM Toronto: 'With *A Farewell To Kings*, we had a lapse of about a year and a half when we could learn our instruments better, as we learned a lot of things about music, especially the new instruments that we were playing. We wanted to put the point on music because we had learned a lot about it.'

That's why 'Xanadu' has one of the longest intros ever recorded, taking up nearly half the song's total running time. Listen carefully and you can hear birds tweeting (in Welsh) while the echo room is used to add effects to the guitar and percussion. Peart brings out his tubular bells before the song bursts into life with the guitarist's circular seven-note riff. The music is allowed to fade away almost to nothing before a new, more rhythmic riff bursts in, followed by slashing guitar chords with understated keyboards from Lee. We go back to the tubular bells, and after five minutes of the intro, we finally get the first vocal line in the song: 'To seek the sacred river Alph, to walk the caves of ice…'

Lyrically, the song is a very close adaptation of Coleridge's 'Kubla Khan: Or A Vision In A Dream', written in 1797 after the poet read a book about Shangdu, a sprawling palace founded in the 13th century by the Emperor Shizu of Yuan (also known as Kublai Khan) as his summer capital in what is now Inner Mongolia. Coleridge then took copious amounts of opium before falling asleep and dreaming about the palace in such detail that he was able to jot down most of the lines. Initially denounced by his contemporaries, it is now regarded as one of his three best poems.

Peart's lyrics use the last two lines to create what passes as a chorus in the Rush song – 'For I have dined on honeydew and drunk the milk of paradise'. As Peart says, there is probably a little too much honeydew and paradise milk – think of the calories for a start. Less directly, the Orson Welles film also played its part. Lee said he visualised the 'News On The March' sequence in the early moments of the movie while mixing the intro. 'Xanadu' is without doubt one of the band's signature songs, rated at number six in a top ten list of Rush tracks by *Rolling Stone* magazine. In his Stereo 104FM Toronto interview, Lee said:

'Xanadu' was a good example because that was one song we had been playing for two months on the road before we recorded it, and it was the first time we had an opportunity to do that in many years because of our touring schedule. We got it broken in on stage and it felt right, and when we finally got to Britain, it was getting a remarkably amazing response, and even our hardcore fans were coming up saying it was one of the best things we'd done. We had a lot of confidence; we felt very up when we went into the studio to do it.

On the day Xanadu was recorded, the band played it once to get the levels and balances correct, then ran through the entire song a second time – and that's the one you hear on the album. In an interview with *Prog* magazine in 2017, Lifeson said: '[Recording engineer] Pat Moran was shocked that we ran an 11-minute song down in one take. It did feel like we were moving in another direction and into this whole other level of performance. 'Xanadu' was also one of the greatest live songs we've ever done; it was a tour de force, a moment for the lights, a moment for the double-neck guitars. It was a big moment! Though not so much for my poor back.'

'Cinderella Man' was also debuted live in early May 1977. One of the few Rush songs with lyrics by Lee, it was inspired by the 1936 Frank Capra film *Mr Deeds Goes To Town*, starring Gary Cooper as an honest greeting card poet and tuba player who inherits $20 million and falls prey to a scheming reporter, who dubs him the 'Cinderella Man'. Lee's lyrics pretty much follow the story of the film, telling of a 'modest man from Mandrake' who 'travelled rich to the city'. Musically, it's a combination of Lifeson-composed riffs and a sing-along chorus set to strummed acoustic guitar. There's a middle instrumental section that, unusually for Rush, is almost funky.

The Welsh birds make another appearance in the title track, which opens the album (let's hope they never sue for royalties). Lifeson plays a short classical guitar passage recorded in the courtyard of the studio complex – he walked quietly around a stereo microphone so the sound moved from speaker to speaker, trailed by Lee playing a Minimoog. As they did so, the birds chirped their approval from the studio rooftops.

The title was adapted from Ernest Hemingway's novel *A Farewell To Arms*, published in 1929, about an American lieutenant in the Italian army having an affair with an English woman during World War I. It's a story of disillusion and loss – the soldier bids farewell to his armaments when he deserts and farewell to the loving arms of his mistress when (spoiler alert!) she dies. The 'kings' in Peart's lyrics are all the tyrants, warmongers and hypocrites – 'Withered hearts and cruel, tormented eyes/Scheming demons dressed in kingly guise' – who have caused misery for Mankind throughout history. 'Can't we learn to feel what's right and what's wrong?' asks Peart – a question that is still very relevant today as the Far Right marches across Europe and America.

Ayn Rand's influence is all over the song – she was 12 when she and her family were forced to flee Saint Petersburg when Bolshevik soldiers seized her father's shop during the October Revolution. She denounced the savagery of Communism and warned: 'We are fast approaching the stage of the ultimate inversion: the stage where the government is free to do anything it pleases, while the citizens may act only by permission, which is the stage of the darkest periods of human history, the stage of rule by brute force.' 'A Farewell To Kings' makes a plea for reason to replace tyranny – its use of monarchist metaphors and stately acoustic guitar reminding us that oppression isn't new and has plagued societies back through the ages to the beginnings of history.

The track ends by making a reference to another song on the album, the band's first hit single in the UK, reaching number 36 in the charts. 'Closer To The Heart' is a stately rocker that opens with a beautiful acoustic guitar arpeggio before Lifeson strums through the chords of the first verse. It has a similar theme to the title track in that it calls for the 'men who hold high places' to create a more harmonious society. It was written with Peter Talbot, a friend of drummer Peart and the first original Rush song to give a writing credit to a non-member. Taylor was a hippie who lived on Vashon Island in the Pacific Northwest – he and Peart became close friends, and he gave the drummer some poems that were moulded into shape for 'Closer To The Heart'. Lifeson calls it 'the ultimate Rush song', which is debatable, but it is surely one of their most-loved compositions, even finding its way into an episode of Canadian TV sitcom *Trailer Park Boys*.

'Madrigal' is a pretty love song, almost Genesis-like in its gentle, wistful musical approach and medieval imagery, working almost as the calm before the storm of album closer 'Cygnus X-1 Book 1: The Voyage'. This is the 'black hole' track I alluded to earlier, and one that is continued on the next album, *Hemispheres*. It is the hardest-sounding tune on the album and a complex piece with dense, stop-start music that demands intense instrumental discipline. In the *Prog* interview, Lee said:

That was something we jammed out; I think that grew from all three of us sitting in a room together, trying to work it out. I had an idea for the opening and Neil started playing the drum part, and then, just as any band does, and perhaps that's the organic nature of a band like Rush, you figure out the part and you put it together. Neil had this story in his mind and we loved it – it was really expressive for us. That whole idea of using sci-fi stuff really worked for Rush because there are no boundaries, there are no limitations – you can use all your goofy, weird sounds because that's what's happening out in space.

Clocking in at ten and a half minutes, nearly half the track's length is once again given over to the intro. After a spooky opening with slow bells and echoing percussion, a whispering alien voice tells us that 'in the constellation of Cygnus there lurks a mysterious, invisible force, the black hole of Cygnus X-1'. The alien is right: it is a five-million-year-old astronomical object that is 21 times the mass of our sun, detected by a rocket flight in 1965 from its strong X-ray emissions. A black hole is so dense that its strong gravitational field sucks everything into it, including light (which is why it looks black).

In the Rush song, Peart is piloting his ship, the Rocinante – Spanish for a broken-down old horse – directly into the heart of Cygnus X-1, following the path of x-rays, 'headlong into mystery'. The music charts the journey through the quiet bleakness of space, well, quiet except for rhythmic tubular bells. Then, in comes Lee's funky slap bass, staccato percussion and dramatic guitar riffs and chords.

Lee's vocals begin low-key and mysterious before he very impressively leaps up an octave. His high-pitched vocal style has been compared to Jon Anderson of Yes, except that he is able to project more powerfully because he is a tenor singing as a soprano. He would lower his range on later albums after discovering that the songs on 1978's *Hemispheres* were almost too high for him to sing comfortably. But on *A Farewell To Kings* – and on this track in particular – those high vocals still have the power to cut through the busy instrumentation.

With a cover by longtime Rush art director Hugh Syme, showing a puppet king slumped in front of a derelict building shot in Buffalo, New York, *A Farewell To Kings* was a chart hit in the UK, US and, of course, in Canada. Critics hailed it as 'a lavishly orchestrated extravaganza that has a rock opera feel to it' (*Billboard*), while Allmusic said the band 'had improved their songwriting and strengthened their focus and musical approach', calling 'Xanadu' 'an outstanding achievement'.

For me, *A Farewell To Kings* begins a fantastic four-album run that transformed Rush from stodgy Yes clones into prog giants. *A Farewell To Kings, Hemispheres, Permanent Waves* and *Moving Pictures* – what a great catalogue of superb progressive rock music, a standard the band did not reach again until *Vapor Trails* in 2002.

Obviously, the album made no concessions to punk, but it is wrong to think the band ignored the new musical revolution – in fact, it benefited the band, says Geddy Lee. Rush had been considered a pale imitation of Yes and Led Zeppelin – but compared to the crude simplicity of punk, they were up there with Yehudi Menuhin. Well, within spitting distance…

Steve Hillage – Motivation Radio

Personnel:
Steve Hillage: guitar, synthesiser, vocals
Reggie McBride: bass
Malcolm Cecil: synthesiser
Miquette Giraudy: synthesiser
Joe Blocker: drums
Recorded at Record Plant, TONTO and Westlake Audio, Los Angeles, California, in July 1977
Produced and engineered by Malcolm Cecil
Assistant engineers: Dion Forrer (at TONTO), Ron Alvarez, John Newsham
Label: Virgin
Release date: September 1977
Chart placing: UK: 28
Tracks: 'Hello Dawn', 'Motivation', 'Light In The Sky', 'Radio', 'Wait One Moment', 'Saucer Surfing', 'Searching For The Spark', 'Octave Doctors', 'Not Fade Away (Glid Forever)'.
All tracks written by Steve Hillage and Miquette Giraudy, except 'Not Fade Away (Glid Forever)' by Norman Petty and Charles Hardin

The Story So Far...

After taking piano lessons as a child, Walthamstow lad Stephen Simpson Hillage switched to guitar when the skiffle boom hit the UK in the early 1960s. Inspired by seeing Jimi Hendrix live five times, Hillage formed Uriel in 1967 with musical schoolmates Dave Stewart on keyboards, drummer Clive Brooks and bassist Mont Campbell. Despite leaving the band in mid-1968 to go to the University of Kent in Canterbury, he returned a year later to record the psychedelic album *Arzachel* (not released until 1974). At university, he met members of the 'Canterbury Scene' that included Soft Machine and Caravan, and through them, signed to Deram, a subsidiary of Decca Records, and formed the band Khan with bassist Nick Greenwood, organist Dick Heningham and drummer Eric Peachey. Their sole album, *Space Shanty* (1972), saw Stewart replace Heningham on keyboards. Khan broke up in October 1972 and Hillage joined Kevin Ayers' group Decadence, playing on his 1973 album *Bananamour*. During a tour in France, Hillage met and joined anarchic space rock band Gong and played on their celebrated 'Radio Gnome trilogy' – *Flying Teapot* (1973), *Angel's Egg* (1973) and *You* (1974). During this time, Gong leader Daevid Allen introduced him to French keyboard player Miquette Giraudy (born on 9 February 1953 in Nice), who became a lifelong musical and romantic partner. Hillage recorded his first solo album, *Fish Rising* (1975), with Stewart and some members of Gong. Allen quit Gong in 1975 and Hillage followed soon after, although he contributed some guitar parts to *Shamal* (1976). Record label Virgin said US musician Todd Rundgren was interested in producing an album, so Hillage and Giraudy went to Woodstock, New York, to record *L* with Rundgren's prog band Utopia. Released in 1976, *L* reached number ten in the US charts.

The Album

Back in 1978, I read a review of Steve Hillage's *Live Herald* album in one of the music papers, which, by that time, were sneering at anything that wasn't just three chords and 'the truth'. The reviewer predictably mocked Hillage's hippie music and his preoccupation with fish and suggested the guitarist spent too much of his time talking to cabbages. But one comment really stood out – in a tone of surprise and disbelief, the critic admitted that you could actually DANCE to some of the songs.

He was no doubt referring to tracks that originally appeared on Hillage's 1977 release *Motivation Radio,* a progressive rock classic with more funk and fewer fish. It may not have been his most commercially successful album of the 1970s, but it was certainly his most influential, pointing the way to an intriguing future in which the hippie-haired string-bender became a sleekly shorn purveyor of hypnotic beats with his electronic dance music band System 7. So, how did the hippie become funky?

A quick trawl through Hillage's albums with Gong reveals that he always had a bit of funk in him. Tracks such as 'The Isle Of Everywhere' on *You*, mostly written in conjunction with bassist Mike Howlett, have an irresistibly bouncy feel that makes your limbs twitch rhythmically in response. Even on *L*, his second album (or third if, like Hillage, you count *Space Shanty* as his debut), there are hints that Hillage would be quite prepared to 'get down' if given the opportunity. Listen to 'Electric Gypsies' and tell me it doesn't make you want to at least nod your head along with the beat.

You see, Hillage had a guilty pleasure – he loved funk music and was a big fan of George Clinton's Funkadelic and the Chicago hitmakers Earth, Wind & Fire. That would have been fine if he had kept his embarrassing music tastes to himself, but he made the mistake of admitting his funky inclinations to fans, who reacted with narrow-minded horror. Steve Hillage loves funk? Prog traitor!

It may not have mattered if he had remained an obscure cult figure, but in 1977, he was actually becoming popular. His Todd Rundgren-produced album *L* was a critical and commercial success, and the live tour that followed saw him supporting the Electric Light Orchestra across the US. He told the website Terrascope in 2012:

We had all these fans coming to us and saying (affects American accent), 'Aw Steve, I really love your work, and I really love Van der Graaf Generator and King Crimson and all your British rock, tell me what are you listening to at the moment.' I'd say, 'Well, I'm really into Bootsy's Rubber Band and P. Funk, and they'd say, 'What, you like disco?' It's like I'd killed their pet cat. I got this feeling of musical apartheid over there, and I thought sod all that, and this sort of propelled me further down that road. That's what led to *Motivation Radio*, really, although we already had some ideas in that direction, but this gave me the stimulus.

Hillage had struck up a friendship with Tony Andrews, a far-sighted PA designer who believed bands could sound just as good live as they did on stage. He had a company called Turbosound, and Hillage would go to his house in Surrey, where he had a rehearsal studio equipped with the latest cutting-edge amplification equipment. Hillage told *Prog* magazine in a 2016 interview: 'He was into funk and we used to have these parties where he would set up this system and have a party with funk records – it was like a pre-rave rave! So, I was getting into funk quite a lot.'

The *L* tour concluded with a triumphant gig at London's Rainbow Theatre, then Hillage and Giraudy shut themselves away in a cottage in Crofton, West Yorkshire, to write the next album. It wasn't just funk that was influencing their songwriting – Hillage was well aware of the punk revolution taking place in the UK and realised he could no longer write long-winded, multi-sectioned epics about fish, no matter how much he loved his scaly friends (as a boy, he got into trouble for liberating some eels from a fishmongers and helping them to escape into the drainage system). He needed to write shorter, snappier songs with funky beats. He had also ditched pot and got heavily into meditation, so the lyrics he and Giraudy crafted had a decidedly more spiritual bent.

A quick aside here: As stated in other parts of this book, the punk fraternity were not really as anti-prog as they made out. Hillage recalls bumping into Johnny Rotten of The Sex Pistols, expecting a barrage of abuse. Instead, Rotten gave a thumbs up and said: 'Flying Teapot!'

The Crofton retreat proved to be extremely productive, so much so that they had enough material for two albums, plus a few that would turn up two years later on *Open*. They divided the songs into 'red' and 'green' – the upbeat tracks would be issued as *The Red Album*, the more mystical and spacey ones as *The Green Album*. But first, they had two prior appointments to keep. One was for Hillage to play Mike Oldfield's guitar parts in two live performances of the latter's instrumental epic 'Tubular Bells' in Glasgow with the Scottish National Orchestra (reprising the role he played when the work had its live premiere back in 1973). The other was a Gong reunion at London's Hippodrome on 28 May, released in 1979 as *Gong Est Mort: Vive Gong*. Then, Hillage and Giraudy flew to California to start work on *The Red Album*.

During the US tour with the *L* band, Hillage had been introduced to Malcolm Cecil, a British musician and producer who was now one-half of TONTO's Expanding Head Band with US audio pioneer Robert Margouleff. Back in 1968, they had created a ground-breaking synthesiser they called The Original New Timbral Orchestra, aka TONTO – a massive one-ton beast the size of a caravan that linked up multiple keyboards and made them play more than one note at a time. The sound of TONTO became ubiquitous in the early 1970s, particularly on classic albums by Stevie Wonder, the Isley Brothers and Gil-Scott Heron. For a short while, until advancing technology overtook them, Cecil and Margouleff were the go-to people for pop and funk stars, and they released two influential albums of their own showcasing their polyphonic monster.

Hillage was so enamoured by the sound of TONTO that he wanted Cecil to produce his next album and give it a more modern, funky sound. He told *Electronics & Music Maker* in 1983: 'I'd become interested after hearing his album *Zero Time* with Robert Margouleff, which has some fantastic synthesised voices, and when we went down to see him in Santa Monica, he was in the middle of an alpha rhythm biofeedback experiment with the synth.'

It was Cecil who chose the other musicians on the album, all from a non-prog background. On bass was Detroit-born Reggie McBride, who learned his trade by listening to Motown records and had played with Stevie Wonder, Funkadelic and Billy Preston. On the drum stool was Joe Blocker, a session musician with Arthur Lee's Love and jazz-funk group Karma among his credits. Cecil and Giraudy completed the studio lineup on synthesisers.

The rhythm tracks were recorded at the Record Plant in Los Angeles in early July before the band moved to Cecil's home in Santa Monica. By this stage, the number seven had become an important talisman for Hillage and Giraudy. All the glissando guitar parts were recorded on 7 July – 07/07/77 – and the album was given the catalogue number V2777. This numerical superstition continued with the later System 7 and its albums *777*, *Power Of Seven*, *Seventh Wave* and *Café Seven* [That's enough sevens. Ed]. Another important decision was made just before the recording started – instead of *The Red Album*, the title would be *Motivation Radio*, linking the titles of two of the tracks.

The result is an album that bristles with great melodies, funky rhythms and Hillage's trademark guitar sound. Opener 'Hello Dawn' sets the scene, marrying a cheerful Bo Diddley beat with a sunny, optimistic lyric as Hillage greets the new day. Multi-tracked acoustic and electric guitars, popping bass and busy but rhythmic drums drive the track along, and there's also room for a brilliant, echo-drenched lead guitar break. At just 2:48, it is the shortest song Hillage had so far recorded that wasn't about fish.

The funk really kicks in for 'Motivation' – McBride, in particular, drives the song with complex but precise bass patterns, locked in with Blocker's drums, as Hillage offers more positive vibes in his uplifting lyrics. It is a sound that would be repeated on 'Unidentified (Flying Being)' from the next album, *Green*.

'Light In The Sky' has a heavier feel, based on a stately guitar riff with a stop-start pattern that allows Giraudy to state the song title in a childish, sing-song voice. Lyrically, it starts off as something to do with aliens – 'We're picking up the pieces of the puzzle of the saucer machines', sings Hillage, perhaps inspired by media coverage of alleged sightings of flying saucers in Wales earlier in 1977. Played live, Hillage would tack onto the end the five notes of Steven Spielberg's alien language from *Close Encounters Of The Third Kind*, released in the US at the end of the year. The song was also used as the theme music for the 2005-2008 TV comedy show *The Friday Night Project* (renamed *The Sunday Night Project* from season eight).

Side one closer 'Radio' is more like the material on *L* and *Fish Rising* – less funky, more ethereal in places – and it would have also fitted perfectly on Hillage's spacier album *Green* the following year. Solo acoustic guitar opens proceedings with some bluesy twiddling before a wash of synth strings and gentle electric guitar arpeggios join in. The acoustic guitar sets up some sort of rhythmic plucking that is picked up by gentle bass and drums. Acoustic guitar is replaced by electric, but things don't really pick up until more than three minutes in when Hillage's vocal enters. It ends with a sequence of descending chords under repeated vocal lines that gently fade out.

Side two opens with 'Wait One Moment', a slowish ballad with strummed major seventh chords that leads to a pretty ascending and descending electric guitar line. 'Saucer Surfing' is another track that could have appeared on the earlier albums, having a short, very repetitive guitar riff similar to 'The Salmon Song' and a typically hippy chorus suggesting we are all 'reality gypsies'.

'Searching For The Spark' is the track that really points to a possible musical future. Fading in on twinkling, swirling synth, it launches into a fast and furious dance beat, punctuated by offbeat sections in a strange time signature that would have any dancers tying their limbs in knots. It's accompanied by a fiendishly complicated guitar riff, but one that's buried in the mix. Hillage sings vocal lines that sound almost made up on the spot, and there's a key change for a soaring guitar solo. But it's the beat that matters here, as it would later in his career with System 7. Blocker pounds away relentlessly, probably wishing someone would invent the drum machine.

'Octave Doctors' is a slower instrumental, still with a steady beat, that descends through seemingly unrelated chords, named after the alien beings who apparently beamed a vision of the Planet Gong into the head of Gong founder Daevid Allen. Finally, the album ends on a cover of the Buddy Holly song 'Not Fade Away', which utilises the Bo Diddley shuffle pinched by Hillage for 'Hello Dawn'. He introduced the song into the live set during the *L* tour, and it became the only single to be released from *Motivation Radio*, backed with 'Saucer Surfing'.

Released with a cover showing Hillage and his Stratocaster guitar superimposed over the Parkes Observatory radio telescope dish in Australia, *Motivation Radio* failed to match the commercial success of its predecessor, with Hillage putting that down to the funk influence alienating his hardcore fans. But it was well-received by critics – *Billboard* praised the 'further extension of [Hillage's] unique rock vision consisting of electronic galactic-seeming mind excursions filled with heavy synthesiser and a philosophy built around ancient Eastern culture' – and has since been recognised as a key stepping stone in Hillage's career towards the later dance-oriented System 7.

He would go on to mix funk and space rock with *Green* (1978) and *Open* (1979) before succumbing almost completely to synthesisers on a pair of 1983 releases, *For To Next* and *And Not Or*. From 1989 onwards, Hillage and Giraudy concentrated on electronic dance music with System 7 and 'chill-out' sister project Mirror System, working with the likes of Alex Patterson of The Orb.

It seemed Hillage had turned his back on his prog roots – until 2006, when he dusted off his guitar and played 'Hello Dawn', among others, at the Gong reunion weekend in Amsterdam. That led to more live performances as he realised there was a big demand among us ageing prog fans for his musically adventurous 1970s material and he embraced it all once again.

Along with *L* and *Green*, *Motivation Radio* is a must-have album for every prog fan and an example of how bands and artists tried to straddle the past and the future during a time of momentous musical upheaval.

Van der Graaf – The Quiet Zone/The Pleasure Dome

Personnel:
Peter Hammill: vocals, electric and acoustic guitars, piano
Graham Smith: violin, viola
Nic Potter: bass guitar
Guy Evans: drums, percussion
With:
David Jackson: saxophone (7, 9)
Recorded at Foel, Morgan and Rockfield Studios between 13 May and 12 June 1977
Produced by Peter Hammill
Engineered by Dave Anderson, Ian Gomm and Pat Moran
Label: Charisma Records
Release date: 2 September 1977
Chart placings: did not chart
Tracks: The Quiet Zone – 'Lizard Play', 'The Habit Of The Broken Heart', 'The Siren Song', 'Last Frame'. The Pleasure Dome – 'The Wave', 'Cat's Eye/Yellow Fever (Running)', 'The Sphinx In The Face', 'Chemical World', 'The Sphinx Returns'
All tracks written by Peter Hammill, except 'Cat's Eye/Yellow Fever (Running)' by Hammill, Graham Smith

The Story So Far...

Formed in 1967 by Manchester University students Peter Hammill and drummer Chris Judge Smith, the band name was a misspelling of the particle accelerator developed by physicist Robert J. Van de Graaff in 1929. Hammill and Smith recruited organist Nick Pearce in a bid to ape the style of The Crazy World of Arthur Brown and recorded a demo of songs that would later appear on a Hammill solo album. Mercury Records offered them a contract, but Pearce quit to continue his college studies. The band moved to London, where Birmingham drummer Guy Evans, organist Hugh Banton and bassist Keith Ellis joined. Then, it got a bit complicated. New manager Tony Stratton Smith decided the Mercury deal was with the original trio, not the new lineup, so he could release their debut single 'People You Were Going To' on Polydor Records. Mercury disagreed and forced Polydor to withdraw the single, but refused to let new members sign up, so only Hammill was on the contract. He started recording a solo album with the new members as backing musicians, then Mercury agreed to release it as VdGG (as we shall call them for the sake of brevity) quiet freed the band from their contract. So, *The Aerosol Grey Machine*, released in September 1969, was VdGG's debut album but also the first and last album for Mercury. Manager Smith formed Charisma Records, and the band were his first signing. The second album, *The Least We Can Do Is Wave To Each Other*, released in February 1970, solidified the band's sound and reached the top 50 in the UK. The album saw Wiltshireborn Nic Potter replace Ellis on bass. The band also gained David Jackson on sax and flute. Subsequent albums *H To He, Who Am The Only One* (1970) and *Pawn Hearts* (1971) were critically praised but commercially dead in the water, although the band built up a devoted cult following and were particularly popular in Italy. The strain of touring led to the first VdGG breakup. Reuniting in 1975, that year's *Godbluff* and 1976's *Still Life* and *World Record* continued VdGG's tradition of being critically acclaimed but commercially ignored by everyone except diehard worshippers and Italians. Banton and Jackson quit (although Jackson made guest appearances), and Londoner Graham Smith joined on violin. Phew! Now, on to the album.

The Album

I'm going to outrage every VdGG fan here with a controversial admission: I don't like Peter Hammill's voice. I think he declaims rather than sings as if he is hollering Shakespeare on stage at The Globe Theatre and trying to reach anyone in the loos at the back. Musically, VdGG are brilliant – complex, challenging and dark. Hammill called the music 'the blues in wonky time signatures' but totally unlike any blues you have ever heard – the blues funnelled through classical music, krautrock and King Crimson. But those vocals … that's why my favourite VdGG album is 2012's *ALT* because it is totally instrumental.

However, I fully accept that I am a minority among prog rock appreciators who view this group as bold and influential. I mean, even The Sex Pistols' Johnny Rotten liked Peter Hammill – on Tommy Vance's Capital Radio show in 1977, he chose two solo songs by the VdGG founder and said: 'Oh yeah, Hammill's great, a true original. I've liked him for years. If you listen to his solo albums, I'm damn sure Bowie has copied a lot out of that geezer. The credit he deserves has just not been given to him.'

In his view, Hammill was punk, and there is a certain belligerent, punkish attitude to his vocals. Of course, Hammill didn't sing about anarchy in the UK or being pretty vacant. In fact, his lyrics are as dense and impenetrable as some of the music, even when, in 1977, he was trying to be a bit more straightforward and conversational. 'I was a prime believer in the faith of 'I' – yellow fever in the cat's eye', he sings on one of the tracks on *The Quiet Zone/The Pleasure Dome*. Yep, clear as mud.

To be fair, *TQZ/TPD* (as we will call it to save my poor aching fingers) is one of the more accessible VdGG albums – *Melody Maker* at the time said it was 'an album that finally approached the band's long-promised potential', and there are certainly hints that Hammill was aiming at a slightly more commercial, even new wave, approach. It didn't help sales, of course – the only VdGG album to have any serious chart success in the UK was the (so far) final one, 2016's *Do Not Disturb*. However, *TQZ/TPD* is certainly seen as a reaction to the more energetic and aggressive music hitting the UK charts. It was also the last album until 2005, as the commercial realities of being a cult band finally hit home.

In fact, VdGG virtually broke up after *World Record* in 1976, when Hugh Banton and David Jackson both quit, the latter to spend more time with his baby son, leaving just Hammill and Guy Evans holding the torch. In the liner notes for the 2005 reissue of *TQZ/TPD*, Banton explained:

The whole thing had just got too tiring and intense. Financially speaking, things weren't secure, and I had just got married and felt that I didn't want to be on the road any more. For me, being in a band and being married didn't go together. I went back to work in electronics and that's what I continued to do. I never stopped playing, but music ceased to be a full-time activity.

However, Hammill was determined to keep soldiering on – in fact, he saw it as an opportunity to refocus the band and to try a different instrumental approach. Hope you like our new direction. In 1976, he recorded his sixth solo album, *Over*, with old and new friends. Bassist Nic Potter had been persuaded to return – he had left the group during the recording of *H To He, Who Am The Only One* in 1970 but had stayed in touch, even leaping out of the audience during a 1971 gig to play with the band after Hugh Banton's bass pedals broke down. The other, newer, arrival was violinist Graham Smith, formerly of Scottish folk-rock band Steam Driven Thing, who were also on the Charisma label until their breakup in late 1975. When Banton and Jackson left, it seemed a no-brainer to absorb Potter and Smith into the new-look VdGG.

The other change around this time was in Hammill's writing, which became more personal, even angry. He had just come out of a long-term relationship with a woman called Alice – she apparently left him for a roadie – and felt the need to put his feelings into songs. He told the *New Musical Express* in 1977: 'I did it at a time when it was absolutely necessary to write songs to survive in a human sense. The more the channel of songwriting is dug, the more the other means of expression dry up.'

Those breakup songs, with titles such as 'Crying Wolf' and 'Betrayed', were probably too personal for VdGG, so they were recorded for *Over*. The bitter, almost hysterical, lyrics – 'I don't give a damn any more – I've only wound up betrayed/It's been absolutely worthless – all of the efforts I've made to be gentle and kind/Are repaid with contempt … I don't believe in anything/Anywhere in the world!' – demanded a harder, more direct musical approach. So, Hammill started playing more electric guitar, with heavy, repetitive riffing, resulting in sharper, snappier and shorter songs. In fact, the cover showed him sitting on a windowsill next to his guitar. He may not have been spitting phlegm, but he was certainly gobbing out his bitterness.

The leaner approach spilt over into the next VdGG album. In the liner notes for the 2000 compilation *The Box*, Potter revealed: 'We did a lot of jamming and it worked very well. The four-piece was a very powerful unit, close to the edge even, and I was developing some different bass sounds.' Graham Smith told *Mju:zik* magazine in 1998: 'It was really Peter on vocals, guitar and piano, either one or the other, then drummer, bass and me on violin. So, it was quite linear, quite sparse, and yet we got quite a big sound with that.' Here's Hammill talking to *Sounds* in March 1977:

> It would have been a fruitless exercise to get another sax player and another keyboard player. Comparisons would have been odious, and it would just have turned into something like a production line. What we're doing now is dangerous and difficult and may well turn off a lot of people who've been into us in the past, but that's simply how it's got to be at the moment. The time for safety and analysis and holding back and being careful is over. We're diving straight into the deep end.

Jackson stayed for a while to rehearse with the new lineup, but he felt it didn't work musically without Banton, so his saxophone graces just two tracks, 'The Sphinx In The Face' and 'The Sphinx Returns'. The stripped-down four-piece made its live debut at the Roundhouse in London in February 1977, revealing a revitalised Van der Graaf (the 'Generator' had been dropped to make the name as lean as the band) – indeed, a live album recorded nearly a year later was titled *Vital* to reflect the band's new energy. Suddenly, the prog 'dinosaurs' sounded as angry and aggressive as the young punk upstarts. In the liner notes, Hammill says:

> It was 1977 and music had moved on. Although we were oldsters, it seemed perfectly reasonable to have a band that was so highly charged. I felt an empathy with punk as rock music had become very pompous. It had gotten to the point where it had become impossible for people to form a band with their mates, the lifeblood of the music industry, without having Wakeman-esque towers of keyboards instead of an amp and a guitar and a lot of passion … Suddenly, rock had become accessible once more.

The Roundhouse set consisted of four songs from *Over*, plus two new compositions rehearsed in January that year. A fairly gentle piano-based ballad, 'The Siren Song' shows Hammill hadn't finished with the soul-baring from his solo album. Indeed, the lyrics suggest that 'Alice' still wasn't far from his mind. 'Laughter in the backbone', he sings, 'laughter impossibly wise. That same laughter that comes every time I flash on the look in your eyes'. In Greek mythology, sirens were alluring female creatures offering dangerous temptation to innocent sailors through their irresistible songs. Hammill sings about being 'lashed to the mast' as the siren's laugh 'chills my marrow' – his, shall we say, idiosyncratic vocals working to his benefit here as he sounds fragile and broken. The song is punctuated by a faster instrumental section led by piano with a Smith violin solo.

'The Siren Song' displays a looser VdGG – without the organ, there is more space around the notes and more contrast between loud and soft. At slightly over six minutes, the track still sounds concise and more simply structured than most of the band's previous compositions. The same applies to 'Last Frame', the second song to be unveiled during the February/March 1977 tour. Hammill is on electric guitar this time, but with a chorus effect to give it a shimmering sound, while Smith's violin intro smacks of David Cross in King Crimson.

For those of us who complain that Hammill talks rather than sings, here is exhibit number one, m'lud. The first two lines are spoken, the rest sung, but I can't really tell the difference. Taken at a faster, rockier pace than 'The Siren Song', there is an extended instrumental section in the middle that allows Smith to let rip on the old fiddle, ending with a fade-out on a descending fuzzy bassline.

Lyrically, this may confuse younger readers – it equates his memory to a photograph and displays some understanding of the processes one had to go through in a darkroom to get a finished product. Chemicals! Strange lights! Negatives! None of that point, shoot and upload it to Google Drive. I used to work in a newspaper office with a darkroom and I still vividly remember the acrid acid smell. In 'Last Frame' (see what he did there?), Hammill is leading up to a rather laboured punchline – 'I only have a negative of you'. Sounds like 'Alice' has got into his head again.

In May, Van der Graaf, as they were now known, went into Foel Studio to begin work on *TQZ/TPD*. Like Rockfield, Foel is in Wales and claims to be the second oldest residential recording studio in the world (Rockfield being the first). Unlike Rush, who incorporated some Welsh wildlife into their recordings, this is the sound of an urban band – lean, edgy and exciting. Hammill plays a lot of acoustic guitar but manages to make it sound hard and jagged, almost on the verge of breakdown. Opener 'Lizard Play' is a prime example – Hammill plays a jumpy, unpredictable acoustic guitar riff, Smith joins in with some Jean-Luc Ponty-style jazz violin, followed by funky bass and quite tinny drums.

By VdGG standards, it is an open sound with empty spaces surrounding the instruments, as if they are waiting to be filled by overdubs. Of course, there are tricky-dicky time signatures galore – parts are in 5/4, others in, well, pick a number – but, at four and a half minutes, it is a tight piece of music that skips along nicely. Hammill once again sings about a woman – she's an iguana, she's a chameleon, she's into snakes, she's a lizard! It's not the most flattering metaphor, particularly when she starts shedding her skin. Oh, Alice, what did you do? The song ends with a common VdGG device, a repetitive chord sequence that descends from B to A, up to D, then down to C, while Hammill repeats 'Will you dance with me?'.

Acoustic guitar also kicks off 'The Habit Of The Broken Heart', a slower, bluesier number reminiscent of Traffic at their most laid back. Talk about sparse – at times, there's just acoustic guitar, drums and bass here as Hammill once again picks at the scabs of his emotional wounds by postulating the idea of an order of Sisters giving him a lecture about succumbing to self-pity. I have to grudgingly admit that there are times when Hammill is actually singing here, and he manages to pack plenty of anger into his performance.

Thus ends side one of the original vinyl release, the so-called Quiet Zone – although all four songs have their loud moments. The second side was supposed to be more spiritual and contemplative – the Pleasure Dome – and opens with 'The Wave', a short(ish) ballad led by piano and violin. It's about, well, a wave that hits the beach and wipes away words written in the sand. Is it also about living in the moment – 'let's not trade sand and sea for brick and cement', sings Hammill. He also says, 'I think we're all pretty out to lunch', and few of us would disagree with that.

The only single released from the album was 'Cat's Eye/Yellow Fever (Running)', which was issued in France backed with non-album track 'Ship Of Fools'. In some ways, you can see why it was chosen – it has the angry, manic approach of a punk song, with Smith sawing away on violin like 'Larks Tongues In Aspic' on speed. There are also elements of early Electric Light Orchestra in the dramatic strings, while Hammill plays some dirty, overdriven guitar. On stage, the four-piece would be augmented by a cellist, Charles Dickie.

However, one wonders what the record buyers made of the lyrics. At a time when bands were spitting out death threats and venom, here's a song about being a cat in the grip of a mad compulsion to run. I think. Perhaps it's a metaphor for fearlessness, for laughing in the face of death and adversity. 'I'll let you know how it goes in the ninth life', sings Hammill.

David Jackson's only contribution to the album is on 'The Sphinx In The Face', an uptempo, poppy number with some inexpertly played electric guitar (for a long time, Hammill was self-conscious about his guitar skills, and rightly so) and funky, fuzzy bass. Hammill overdubs piano and organ, Smith is quietly supportive on violin and Jackson … well, he's almost inaudible. The lyrics are something about being young and wanting answers, but the face of the Sphinx is inscrutable, a common trait of sphinxes. The music fades out at the end to leave the voices chanting, 'You're so here, so gone, so near, so wrong'.

The final song on the album (because 'The Sphinx Returns' is a reprise of track seven) is 'Chemical World', probably the least straightforward track, as it twists and turns through various forms. There's a folkie opening on acoustic guitar and violin, an eastern-sounding section with guttural vocals, a louder workout with electric guitar and screeching violin and a gentle, contemplative ending. The lyrics may have something to do with drugs – 'Chemical World' is a bit of a giveaway, as are lines that warn 'from the moment that it's embraced … all the diamonds turn to paste'.

We should mention 'Ship Of Fools', the B-side of the single that appears on CD versions of the album. Van der Graaf do heavy metal! Hammill has both guitar and voice turned up to 11 as he sings bizarre lyrics about 'the captain's in a coma, the lieutenant's on a drunk; the owner's in his cabin with his special friend the monk'. Oooerr! Captain Pugwash it isn't. (Or is it? After all, there was Seaman Stains, wasn't there?)

Both the band and the record label separately came up with album covers, so they were both used – the band's, showing a trapeze artist high above a fiery Earth, on the front and the label's – a shot of the four-piece larking about – on the back. Along with the title, it encouraged a schizophrenic feeling about the album, although that is, of course, lost on CD and streaming listeners. Suffice to say, it rammed home the idea that this was a new VdGG, one that could no longer be pigeonholed as readily as before.

There was no schizophrenia in the reviews, which were all positive about the band's new direction. 'The combination of verbal dash and musical down-the-line power shown on the album indicates the spark is still there', said *Melody Maker*. 'Brilliant and unpredictable production challenges the ears and imagination', said *The Sunday Times*. 'This is music worth getting to know … VdG are still moving towards a wider musical appreciation and acceptance', intoned *Sounds*.

Of course, none of that praise translated into sales. However, nearly 50 years later, *TQZ/TPD* is recognised as a unique entry in the band's catalogue, an album that showed Peter Hammill refusing to stand still and absorbing the influences of the new musical barbarians. As *Sounds* said, this is music that's worth getting to know.

John Greaves, Peter Blegvad & Lisa Herman – Kew. Rhone.

Personnel:
Peter Blegvad: guitar, vocals, tenor sax on 5
Carla Bley: tenor sax on 1 and 7, vocals
Andrew Cyrille: drums, percussion
John Greaves: piano, organ, bass, vocals, percussion on 7
Lisa Herman: vocals
Dana Johnson: vocals on 2
Boris Kinberg: claves on 5
April Lang: vocals on 5 and 8
Michael Levine: violin, viola, vocals on 9
Mike Mantler: trumpet, trombone
Vito Rendace: alto sax, tenor sax, flute
Recorded at Grog Kill Studio, Woodstock, US, in October 1976
Engineered by Mike Mantler
Artistic contributions: Peter Blegvad
Label: Virgin (UK), Europa (US)
Release date: March 1977 on Virgin (UK), Europa (US). Reissues on Voiceprint and Le Chant du Monde
Chart places: did not chart
Tracks: 'Good Evening', 'Twenty-Two Proverbs', 'Seven Scenes From The Painting 'Exhuming The First American Mastodon' By C. W. Peale', 'Kew. Rhone.', 'Pipeline', 'Catalogue Of Fifteen Objects And Their Titles', 'One Footnote ('To Kew. Rhone.)', 'Three Tenses Onanism', 'Nine Mineral Emblems', 'Apricot', 'Gegenstand'
All tracks composed by John Greaves and Peter Blegvad

The Story So Far...

Welshman John Greaves played bass in his father's orchestra, then joined newly-formed avant-rock group Henry Cow in 1969. Musician, writer and cartoonist Peter Blegvad, a New Yorker, moved to the UK in 1965, then formed avant-pop trio Slapp Happy with musical collaborator Anthony Moore and German singer Dagmar Krause. Greaves first worked with Blegvad when Henry Cow and Slapp Happy merged briefly in 1974, recording two albums. Blegvad left because the music was too complicated and serious for him and reunited with Greaves to record *Kew. Rhone.*

The Album

Knowhere? We're Honk? Henre Kow? There are meanings hidden in *Kew. Rhone.* – the album as well as the title – but you'll get no help from Peter Blegvad. In his view, it's inexplicable. In a 2015 interview with website *The Quietus*, he said:

It invites interpretation even as it resists it. When considering the meanings of *Kew. Rhone.*, we can only guess, we can't know – which will put some people off. People who want definitive answers are unlikely to get whatever there is to be got from the *Kew. Rhone.* experience. Personally, I feel more at home with doubt than I do with certainty – what Keats called Negative Capability.

So far, so … baffling. Thirty years after recording *Kew. Rhone.* (the full stops are important, apparently. They represent the distance between the words … or something), Blegvad wrote a book about it. The only copy I could find cost £167.95, plus £9.96 delivery. I have viewed a few choice extracts and, trust me, you would be none the wiser. Save your money.

The fact is, I don't think there is any unifying meaning to *Kew. Rhone.* Not lyrically, anyway. Blegvad included some diagrams in the album artwork that refer to the tracks, but they are about as illuminating as a torch shining black light. Perhaps the music will help, but even that is dense, complicated and seemingly unstructured, full of melodic leaps and contortions, more avant-garde jazz than anything resembling the traditional definition of rock. So, we still avant-garde a clue.

And yet … perhaps the search for meaning is somehow the whole point. There is something about *Kew. Rhone.* that draws you in and makes you go back to it time and time again in an attempt to unlock its mysteries. Perhaps meaning is there, but it is tantalisingly out of reach, and all it will take is one more listen. Perhaps you cannot discover meaning by listening to both music and lyrics; listen to the music first, then turn it off and read the lyrics in conjunction with the diagrams. That's Blegvad's advice anyway.

Most of the albums in this book are well-known to progressive music fans. A few may not be because it took many years, even decades, for their genius to be recognised. In the case of *Kew. Rhone.*, critics knew it was special from the off. They just didn't know why. They certainly couldn't convince the record buyers, who ignored it and still do. I mean, how do you sell an album with song titles such as 'Seven Scenes From The Painting 'Exhuming the First American Mastodon' by C. W. Peale' and 'Catalogue Of Fifteen Objects And Their Titles'? It made 'Close To The Edge' sound like 'Da Doo Run Run'.

The album, which Allmusic judges 'an unfortunately neglected masterpiece of 1970s progressive rock', grew out of a musical movement called Rock in Opposition – weird experimental groups, mostly from Europe, who were opposed to producing commercial music and opposed to record labels who refused to sign them because of it. Many of them were avowedly left-wing, such as Stormy Six in Italy, Samla Mammas Manna in Sweden and the UK's Henry Cow.

The Cow – whose name was chosen, said drummer Chris Cutler, because it was 'silly' – played music that was complex, challenging, uncompromising and frequently in time signatures more likely to be seen written on a physicist's blackboard. 'Nirvana For Mice', for example, has a section in 21/8, whatever the hell that is. John Greaves met them because he was at Cambridge University with band founders Fred Frith and Tim Hodgkinson, and he fitted in perfectly, contributing several mind and ear-boggling compositions to the repertoire over the following four and a half years. They included 'Teenbeat' on the 1973 debut album *Legend* (pronounced with a hard 'g') and 'Half Asleep, Half Awake' on follow-up *Unrest* (1974).

Greaves first met Blegvad when Henry Cow toured with German experimental rockers Faust in 1973 – both bands had been signed by Richard Branson's Virgin Records. Blegvad's band Slapp Happy – formed just to take the piss out of popular music – had recorded their debut album *So Far* (1972) at Faust's studio in Germany, with members of Henry Cow as the rhythm section, and he joined them on the tour. When Polydor Records rejected Slapp Happy's second album, Henry Cow persuaded Branson to sign them up, too, so everyone was happy.

The two groups joined forces in 1974 when they collaborated on what was originally going to be Slapp Happy's first album for Virgin. *Desperate Straights* was eventually released the following year as a joint effort, and it included 'Bad Alchemy', the first recorded song written by Greaves and Blegvad together. In an interview with me, Greaves said about the song: 'It was a kind of fortuitous, serendipitous kind of thing – he'd got these words and I'd got this bit of a tune and they just seemed to fit together. And that was the beginning of a lifelong collaboration. We just seemed to hit it off.'

Dig out your copy of *Desperate Straights* and listen to 'Bad Alchemy' (what do you mean you don't have a copy? Buy it, quick!) and you will hear the seeds of *Kew. Rhone.* Pounding, discordant piano chords in a marching tempo, like an army with banners; a female voice ranging up and down through offbeat, discordant notes; a juddering, stop-start rhythm; and dense lyrics jam-packed full of bizarre imagery, such as 'I dream Hermaphrodite and I sit up all night/Our eyes on the horizon of a wobbling bowl'. Yes, a wobbling bowl.

By the time of their second collaboration, 1975's *In Praise Of Learning*, Blegvad and fellow Slappers Dagmar Krause and Anthony Moore had pretty much been absorbed into Henry Cow. But it was a short-lived lineup as Blegvad and Moore quit soon after, the former returning to the US to work as a cartoonist. Greaves stayed with the Cow a while longer before quitting in 1976 in circumstances that he says were 'quite traumatic – I just realised it wasn't going anywhere for me and I just had to make the leap and get out of there.'

Greaves was homeless for a while, although please don't feel too sorry for him because he was living in Richard Branson's luxurious country house in Surrey. While there, he started writing some of the melodies that eventually became *Kew. Rhone.* using the Virgin boss's upright piano before persuading the record label to give him a deal for a collaboration with his old pal. Virgin gave Greaves a minuscule budget that just about got him to Blegvad's apartment in John Street, New York, where they worked on the material through the summer of 1976. He told me:

> It was a long, slow process because Peter was very long and slow! He comes up with one word a day, really, that's it – but what a word, a great word! It's something like that. A lot of the time, he worked damn hard trying to fit his stuff to my rather tortuous melodies, and it sometimes drove him quite mad. But he really settled into it, and I remember for some reason coming up with that very English expression 'nowt as queer as folk', and he said, 'You're damn right, these notes are queer as fuck!'. That sort of summed up his approach to my work. And by the end of the summer, we got the makings of an album.

The experimental music community was a small one in those days – perhaps it still is – and there was a mutual respect between the practitioners that stretched across the Atlantic. When Blegvad and Greaves were ready to record in October 1976, they were immediately offered the use of Grog Kill Studios in Woodstock, owned by adventurous jazz pianist Carla Bley and her second husband, trumpeter Mike Mantler.

Greaves cites Bley as an influence on his music, and that is hardly surprising, as she was an inspiration to modern jazz musicians everywhere from the 1960s until her death in 2023. Her three-LP set *Escalator Over The Hill*, released in 1971, featured contributions from such jazz giants as bassists Charlie Haden and Jack Bruce, saxophonist Gato Barbieri, guitarist John McLaughlin, trumpeter Don Cherry and Frank Zappa keyboardist Don Preston. Recording *Kew. Rhone.* at Grog Kill meant not only the chance to use the talents of Bley and Mantler but also access to other talented US jazzers such as drummer Andrew Cyrille and Michael Levine, known as 'the Jimi Hendrix of the violin'.

It was one of the many decisions that helped shape the sound of the album. If it had been made in the UK, Greaves said he would probably have used Henry Cow's Chris Cutler or King Crimson's Bill Bruford on drums, which may have made it a more straightforward progressive rock album. Instead, the musicians he was able to call on provided a free jazz approach that took the music into strange, uncharted areas.

One name that somehow found its way onto the cover of the album was that of Lisa Herman. Who? She was a family friend of Blegvad's parents, who were living in New York at the time, and she was doing backup vocals on disco songs. Greaves explains: 'We'd got the very beginnings of this album, and we were looking for someone to sing it – it was clear neither Peter nor I were going to do it. So, we interviewed a couple of people. We had one wonderful woman who had just come from the musical *Oh! Calcutta!* but we couldn't get her in the end. Lisa got the gig because she had actually heard of us.'

The album opens with a short introduction, a kind of overture played by saxes and trumpet, a stately, 34-second tune that is repeated later in the title track. It is the most conventionally accessible piece of music on the album and really just an opportunity to showcase Bley and Mantler. After that, it all gets a bit weird.

Track two is called 'Twenty Two Proverbs', and it does indeed consist of 22 proverbs. Some are in common usage – 'A cat may look at a king', 'Would ye both eat your cake and have your cake?', 'Dead as a doornail' – while others seem to make little sense at all – 'Milk the mosquito to serve your king', 'To cut into another man's ear is like cutting into another man's hat', 'Herring in the land, the doctor at a stand'. Greaves told me:

> With this song, I had written pretty much the whole thing and Peter was struggling to fit some words to these rather tortuous melodies and rhythms. He went away for a weekend to Cornell University in Ithica, New York, and when he came back, he said, 'I've got it!'. He had been to the library and found this book of proverbs and he just stuck them in and made them fit. And by God, they do! So whether you understand them or not, they are all real.

So, the one about the herring is probably the Danish equivalent of 'an apple a day keeps the doctor away', fish being more plentiful than fruit in Denmark. Meanwhile, the third track is inspired by a painting Blegvad had seen in an art gallery (it's now in the Smithsonian American Art Museum in Washington) that is used as the front cover of the album. 'Exhuming The First American Mastodon', by artist and naturalist Charles Wilson Peale, does what it says on the tin, showing Peale and his team digging up the bones of the extinct mammoth from a marl pit in Newburgh, New York State, in 1801. Apart from being a fine landscape and marking an important moment in the history of palaeontology, the artwork also served to counter claims by European naturalists that there were no large, powerful creatures in the US because of the country's cold, damp climate and its 'social degeneracy'.

Blegvad focused on seven parts of the painting that are highlighted on the album cover and wrote lyrics both fanciful and prosaic about what he saw. On the far right of the artwork, a 'youth with no name cuts out of the frame with an axe', while elsewhere, a 'neophyte fast … ogles aghast a bone of gold' and 'Three green umbrellas are shown in all/These denote degrees by which a fall (a fall from grace) may be measured'. Opening with sombre piano chords and accompanied by gentle cello, Herman's singing guides you through the painting so you can follow her words across the album cover.

Title track 'Kew. Rhone.' almost didn't make it as a song, let alone onto the album. Greaves found the lyrics in Blegvad's wastepaper basket – it was an intellectual exercise that he had literally thrown away. Unsurprising, perhaps, as it consisted of random words that could be found within the eight letters that make up the title, arranged into strange, pithy little phrases such as 'We who knew no woe' and 'We won renown' before ending with one of the longest grammatically-correct palindromes, 'Peel's foe, not a set animal, laminates a tone of sleep'.

Greaves had a fast, nimble instrumental that he used to perform with Henry Cow and always wanted to develop into something more substantial. For 'Kew. Rhone.', his piano is augmented by trumpet and trombone from Mantler as it offers up more mysterious, darker melodies for the various iterations of the palindrome, sung with both male and female voices. Greaves admits it is one of the most pretentious things on the album, but 'it kind of works'. He liked it so much that he included it on a later solo album and often performs it live.

'Pipeline' is a track that references some more artwork on the album sleeve, this time drawn by Blegvad himself. Three people stand over a hole in the ground, within which there is a short piece of what appears to be a pipe. But its real nature is obscured – it could be the shaft of an axe, a piece of bone (from a mastodon, perhaps), the top (or bottom) rung of a ladder or part of an umbrella. Perhaps it's even 'the projection or the shadow of an entity of four dimensions', the lyrics suggest. Whatever it is, it illustrates the ambiguity of the situation. Greaves explains:

> It's a phenomenological study, really [that's the study of subjective experiences. KF]. As Peter says, the two gentlemen and a lady are contemplating a length of dug-up pipeline – Lisa is singing that line; you look at the picture and there they are looking at the pipe and they're wondering what it is. Peter speculates that it could be a third-dimensional representation of a fourth-dimensional object, which is the big question mark. All this is going on to a kind of cha-cha rhythm in 7/4, of course. Peter cooked up the idea that the whole album could be a phenomenological study somehow, but thankfully, we didn't.

Greaves already had the music for 'Catalogue Of Fifteen Objects And Their Titles' – a series of discordant piano chords followed by a faster section almost in three-quarter time, punctuated by random blasts of saxophone, followed by a funereal march that slowly speeds up into a frantic ending – so Blegvad went away to cook up some words. What he came up with is a list of bizarre objects, ranging from a 'cylinder of dust', a 'pillar of yeast in linoleum jacket' to 'a yolk of leather in a tobacco egg', followed by their titles or names. So, the cylinder of dust is a 'silo' – yes, I can see the logic in that – while the pillar of yeast is a 'dry cell'. Mmm, a bit more challenging, that one. The yolk of leather? That's 'October seventh'. Go figure. 'Peter is a painter,' said Greaves, 'so he looks at things in a very visual manner. He looked kind of sheepishly at Lisa and said, 'I've got it, but do you really think you can sing this?' And she said, 'Of course I can, give it to me."

'One Footnote (To Kew.Rhone.)' is, as the title suggests, a sort of reprise to the title track that suggests more anagrams hidden in the words, such as horn, honk and heron. 'You can no doubt eke out a couple more', say the lyrics – 'eke' being another word hidden in the title. 'That was an afterthought', says Greaves. 'I think I fitted that to a piece I'd already written with a lyric originally by Chris Cutler called 'No More Political Innocence, No More Parades'. Peter would never have written a lyric like that!'

'Three Tenses Onanism' was based on a poem that previously existed – Greaves puts some quite beautiful, evocative piano accompaniment to his own voice singing the first few lines about masturbation before it erupts into strange, tuneless noises, ending on – appropriately enough – an organ. 'Nine Mineral Emblems' is a metaphysical love song that uses the properties of minerals as emblems for passion. 'As carbon will become diamond when pressured', sing female vocalists over piano, bass, crashing drums and wild trumpet, 'so we come through love to realise our maximum'.

'Apricot' was a Blegvad poem set to music and sung mostly by Greaves – it is about discovering, very early, the pleasure of singing, and APRICOT is an abbreviation for Attain Perfect Realisation In The Cot. Finally, 'Gegenstand' came about almost as a result of a challenge. Blegvad went to study poetry once a week at New York University, and his tutor looked at one of his creations and said: 'It's good, Peter, but you can't imagine anyone singing it, can you?' So, he set out to prove the tutor wrong. Herman sang it to a backing of odd noises and percussion, and later, Robert Wyatt covered it for a Greaves solo album. So, there.

Packed full of strange prog and jazz influences, channelling Soft Machine, Matching Mole, Frank Zappa, Carla Bley and Magma, *Kew.Rhone.* is a challenging but rewarding listen that, thanks to riddles and wordplay in the lyrics, never ceases to offer up new insights. It was certainly brave to release it in the middle of the punk explosion and was probably the last of this type of stubbornly uncommercial music from Virgin Records – a few months later, the same label put out *Never Mind The Bollocks, Here's The Sex Pistols*. So, what is it that has given *Kew.Rhone.* a reputation as a 'lost classic' that persists to this day? Greaves told me:

I guess, in all modesty, it kind of stands alone. I don't even know whether it IS a progressive record – I guess you would have a better definition of prog than I would. It came about as a culmination of all the kinds of influences I've been through, from going back to my father's dance band to Henry Cow, Kurt Weill, Zappa and all sorts of things [Mmm, that sounds like prog, John!], and we just had this opportunity to wing it with Blegvad. It's very much a close symbiotic collaboration with Peter because those lyrics are pretty extraordinary. I thought the whole concept – because that is what it would have been called at the time, a concept album, where all the lyrics are tied up to the artwork and so on [Mmm, that also sounds like prog, John!] – I think that sort of sets it apart.

Camel – Rain Dances

Personnel:

Andrew Latimer: electric guitar, acoustic guitar, 12-string guitar, panpipes, flute, backing vocals, fretless bass on 'Tell Me', electric piano, Minimoog, synthesiser and fuzz guitar on 'Elke', piano on 'Elke' and 'Rain Dances', rhythm guitar and bass on 'Skylines', glockenspiel on 'Rain Dances', lead vocals on 'Highways Of The Sun' and 'Unevensong'

Peter Bardens: organ, piano, electric piano, Minimoog, synthesiser, Hohner Clavinet

Andy Ward: drums, percussion, ocarina, glockenspiel, talking drum

Richard Sinclair: bass, lead vocals on 'Metrognome', 'Tell Me' and 'Unevensong'

Mel Collins: alto saxophone, tenor saxophone, soprano saxophone, clarinet, bass flute, brass arrangements

With:

Martin Drover: trumpet on 'One Of These Days I'll Get An Early Night', flugelhorn on 'Skylines'

Malcolm Griffiths: trombone on 'One Of These Days I'll Get An Early Night' and 'Skylines'

Brian Eno: Minimoog, electric piano, piano on 'Elke'

Fiona Hibbert: harp on 'Elke'

Recorded at Basing St. Studios, London, between February and August 1977

Produced by Rhett Davies

Engineered by Dave Hutchins

Sleeve design by Paul Henry

Label: Gama/Decca

Release date: September 1977

Chart placings: Norway: 17, Spain: 18, UK: 20, Finland: 29, Sweden: 30

Tracks: 'First Light' (Peter Bardens, Andrew Latimer), 'Metrognome' (Bardens, Latimer), 'Tell Me' (Bardens, Latimer), 'Highways Of The Sun' (Bardens, Latimer), 'Unevensong' (Bardens, Latimer, Andy Ward), 'One Of These Days I'll Get An Early Night' (Bardens, Mel Collins, Latimer, Richard Sinclair, Ward), 'Elke' (Latimer), 'Skylines' (Bardens, Latimer, Ward), 'Rain Dances' (Bardens, Latimer).

The Story So Far...

The band was formed as The Brew in 1971 in Guildford, Surrey, by guitarist Andrew Latimer, drummer Andy Ward and bassist Doug Ferguson. The trio backed singer/songwriter Phillip Goodhand-Tait on his album *I Think I'll Write A Song* before advertising for a keyboard player, finding Londoner Peter Bardens through *Melody Maker*. Renamed Camel, they toured through 1972, signing with MCA Records and releasing their unsuccessful eponymous debut the following year. Moving to Decca Records' Deram label, their second album, *Mirage* (1974), was a respectable hit in the US. 1975 instrumental album *Music Inspired By The Snow Goose* was a breakthrough hit, while *Moonmadness* (1976) was the last recorded by the original lineup.

The Album

It's fair to say that Camel never quite reached the top rank of British progressive rock bands. The likes of Yes, Genesis, Jethro Tull and Emerson, Lake & Palmer sold more records, made more money and got more column inches in the music press. Perhaps it was because Camel concentrated on instrumental music rather than songs and were fronted by someone who came across as quiet and unassuming, perhaps even shy.

But there was genuine surprise and delight when, in 2013, Camel guitarist, songwriter and leader Andy Latimer announced a return to live touring, a decade after the band's 14th studio album, *A Nod And A Wink*. It was a surprise because, in 1992, he was given just 20 months to live after being diagnosed with the blood disorder polycythaemia vera. Chemotherapy and a bone marrow transplant saved his life, but required years of recovery. He also developed arthritis in his hands, which is not a welcome condition for a guitarist (tell me about it).

Yet, Latimer managed to overcome his many health challenges and embark on a tour that, five years later, culminated in a sell-out gig at the Royal Albert Hall in London.

It was a delight because, well, they did some great stuff. That run of early albums by the original lineup is essential listening for anyone who loves melodic, guitar-based progressive rock. *The Snow Goose* and *Moonmadness*, in particular, are classics of the genre. And there's no denying that Latimer has an instantly recognisable guitar style – fluid and melodic, with hints of David Gilmour. Some Camel fans can be a bit sniffy about the rest of the discography, but personally, I believe they recorded two or three more albums that deserve to be on every discerning music lover's playlist.

One of those is *Rain Dances*, released in September 1977 at the height of the punk revolution. In Camel terms, it was a hit, beaten only by *Moonmadness* the previous year. In musical terms, it showcases a slightly looser, jazzier approach and contains some of their most enduring songs and instrumentals. It also illustrated Camel's ability to survive personnel upheavals – good job, too, because there were plenty of those to come.

In the case of *Rain Dances*, we can blame Soft Machine. Camel were supporting the Canterbury Scene band in 1974, and every night, Peter Bardens and Andy Latimer would sit at the side of the stage, mouths open, watching guitar virtuoso Allan Holdsworth conjure up intricate jazz melodies. That's when they decided they wanted to write jazzier music, starting with 'Lunar Sea' on *Moonmadness*. Hope you like our new direction.

Except that Doug Ferguson didn't. Ironically, it was his idea to add Mel Collins of King Crimson fame on sax and flute – a decision that jazzed up the music even more. Collins played on the *Moonmadness* tour, and Latimer and Bardens couldn't wait to get together with him in the studio to make a jazz noise. Even drummer Ward was keen. Then, it all began to unravel. Latimer told *Record Collector* in 2013:

What happened was that Andy was getting very good and wanted to move into a much more technically demanding area. Doug was very solid in his playing; he didn't really want to get into this jazzy thing – he wanted to stay really simple and solid. So, there was this rift coming between them. Andy said, 'It's either me or him', so we went with Andy and Doug left. That was our biggest mistake because, as soon as Doug went, the whole unit changed.

It was Latimer's role to give Ferguson the bad news. In the 2003 Camel documentary *Curriculum Vitae*, the latter revealed: 'It all happened very quickly. We'd all got together after one of our rare breaks to start rehearsing for the *Rain Dances* album, and within ten minutes, Andy Latimer had informed me of their intentions. I think they must have had a few informal meetings before then. It was a complete surprise, but there wasn't anything I could do about it. As far as I was concerned, the eggs had been scrambled, and as everyone knows, you can't unscramble them.'

To continue the analogy, it was Latimer who ended up with egg on his face as, in retrospect, he realised Ferguson was part of the unique chemistry that bound the quartet together, as well as someone who happily took on some of the managerial duties. As a former soldier, he had a regimented way of doing things that every band needs. As proof of this, consider the fact that, after *Rain Dances* and its follow-up, *Breathless*, no two further Camel albums had the same lineup. But at the time, Latimer and Bardens saw this as an opportunity to approach someone they had long admired, the former Caravan bassist and singer Richard Sinclair.

Caravan were part of the Canterbury Scene along with Soft Machine, both bands that grew out of the unique jazz-rock atmosphere of the Kent cathedral town (where, historians will tell you, Thomas Becket [a Becket is a later, inaccurate spelling] got his comeuppance at the hands of four followers of King Henry II in 1170. 'Who will rid me of this turbulent priest?' cried Henry. Although what he probably said was: 'What miserable drones and traitors have I nourished and brought up in my household, who let their lord be treated with such shameful contempt by a low-born cleric?'. Not quite as pithy, I know.)

Musically, Camel and Caravan had many differences, particularly in the vocal department. Caravan had two distinctive singers in Sinclair and Pye Hastings; Camel had Latimer and Bardens, neither of whom would win any warbling contests. So, here was a chance to augment the Camel sound with Sinclair's warm, English baritone. Sinclair was also a superior bassist and well able to cope with the band's new direction, as his three years in experimental jazz-rock outfit Hatfield and the North proved.

When Camel's Canterbury-born manager Laurie Small came a-calling, Hatfield had broken up and Sinclair had started a kitchen-fitting and carpentry business in Canterbury. Despite having never heard any Camel, he said yes, put down his lathe and picked up his bass to become a working musician once again. By the time he arrived, Latimer, Bardens and Ward had already kicked things off in the studio, recording the instrumental 'Skylines' and the backing track for the ballad 'Tell Me', with Latimer fulfilling bass duties.

However, Sinclair says all was not well in the Camel camp. He told JoeSmithMusicStuff in 2021: 'Latimer and Pete were falling out all the time in the studio when we were recording … because Pete had more expansive ideas whereas Latimer was really tight on it – 'this is how it needs to be done.' He'd spend weeks and months sometimes playing the same solo till he perfected it … there were so many glasses of brandy and god knows what else while we were outside the studio waiting for Latimer to finally get the right solo.'

For Sinclair, learning the parts to the already-written songs was 'simple' as everything was pretty much set in stone – there was little opportunity for him to express himself and contribute to the writing as there had been with Hatfield. The only exception is on 'One Of These Days I'll Get An Early Night', which started life as a Sinclair bass riff before the rest of the band improvised over it. Jazzy and laidback, it is the least Camel-like track on the album, apart from 'Highways Of The Sun'.

Like all prog bands in 1977, Camel were under pressure from their record company to have a 'hit'. The result is the worst track on the album, 'Highways Of The Sun', a keyboard-heavy plodder that uses an unremarkable three-chord sequence for the verse and then, er, uses it again for the chorus, which, to be fair, is what practically every modern pop song does. At least there's a slight difference in the pre-chorus. Released as a single, it failed to leave planet Earth, let alone reach the sun.

Thankfully, the rest of the album is much, much better. Opener 'First Light' is a superb instrumental, fading in on Latimer's guitar arpeggios and Bardens' swirly synth before Sinclair makes himself known with slightly funky bass and Mel later adds expressive, soaring sax. 'Metrognome' is a lovely tune – over a ticking clock, Sinclair's very English, almost whimsical vocal works well with the simple, childlike lyrics. Then, the song jumps into a bouncy instrumental in 5/4 before Sinclair's fast, repetitive bassline takes it into a third section, in which Latimer lets rip on electric guitar.

'Tell Me' is one of the two songs on which Latimer plays bass, this time a nice, fruity fretless on a gentle minor key ballad that was issued as the B-side of 'Highways Of The Sun'. Again, Sinclair raises the material with his warm vocal, while Collins and Bardens complement each other on flute and keyboards. It is a mystery, however, why Sinclair didn't rerecord the bass on this and on 'Skylines'.

Side two opens with 'Unevensong', a play on words – Evensong is a religious service that usually takes place in a church in the evening. Camel's song is a more secular affair, a love song with a driving beat that consists of four sections: the opening verses in a minor key, punctuated by a staccato descending guitar phrase; a slower but funkier major key instrumental led by

Collins on sax that ends on the staccato guitar phrase; a gentler version of section two with Sinclair vocals; and a final reprise of the closing instrumental melody from section two. It was the only song from *Rain Dances* to be played at the Royal Albert Hall in 2018.

The album ends with three instrumentals. 'Elke' is a beautiful, sombre tune showcasing Collins' flute, with added keyboards from Brian Eno. Latimer told music journalist Mal Reding in 1981:

> That was through the producer, Rhett Davies. He was producing us at the time, when we were doing *Rain Dances*, and he was also producing Eno. I liked a lot of Eno stuff, especially all the ambient stuff that he was doing then, so I thought: 'Wow! This would be a fantastic chance to rearrange this number and get Eno through Rhett'. I asked Rhett if he would be interested in coming in, and he said, 'I don't know. I'll ask him', and Eno replied: 'Yes, I would love to come in'. So, he came in and he worked as hard as I did on a piece, and it was such a fabulous experience because he is a very hard-working person and very inventive, too.

It is followed by the aforementioned 'Skylines', with Latimer on bass (although Sinclair played the bassline live and did it better!). It's an instant Camel classic – the fast, funky bass drives it along, with guitar and keyboards playing unison melody lines while the tune gently shifts from key to key. The melody lines are fast and difficult to play but still immensely enjoyable. There is supposed to be flugelhorn and trombone on the track, but they are used to support the keyboard washes and are set well back in the mix. Finally, the title track is a gentler and slower reprise of the ending of 'First Light'.

Released with a somewhat dark and subdued cover, *Rain Dances* did well enough in the UK and European charts to justify the slight change in musical style – it seemed people liked the new jazzy direction. To be fair, I have seen reviews that range from calling it Camel's most consistent effort to one of the worst in their catalogue (they're wrong; that's *The Single Factor* in 1982). It probably doesn't match up to the previous four, but it was the right album at the right time – another *Snow Goose* may well have sunk without a trace in 1977.

Sadly, *Rain Dances* and its follow-up, *Breathless*, heralded more changes for the band. The partnership of Latimer and Bardens had gone adrift to the point where they were recording in the studio at separate times, and the latter quit the band in 1978. Sinclair was also asked to leave – Latimer believed he wasn't as loyal and reliable as Ferguson had been and had his own agenda. Sinclair's view is that Latimer dominated the band to such an extent that it was difficult for anyone else to make a contribution to the music. But he also told JoeSmithMusicStuff: 'I had a lovely experience. It was the most professional [band] because it was really dedicated to the perfection of entertainment.'

Eventually, Latimer became Camel, with a revolving door of musicians around him. The 2013 comeback saw one more album, a somewhat needless remake of *The Snow Goose*. A planned tour in 2023 was suddenly cancelled after he suffered a sharp pain in his lower back that spread to his leg and foot. The last bulletin was that he was recovering at home after urgent surgery.

Does it mean the end of the line for Camel? As I write this, it seems unlikely that the 75-year-old guitarist will ever tour again. But who knows – he has beaten the odds before and may do so again. Get well soon, Andy.

Brian Eno – Cluster & Eno/Before And After Science

Personnel on Cluster & Eno:

Hans-Joachim Roedelius: composer

Dieter Moebius: composer, synthesiser

Brian Eno: composer, primary artist, synthesiser

With:

Holger Czukay: bass on 'Ho Renomo'

Okko Bekker: guitar on 'One'

Asmus Tietchens: synthesiser on 'One'

Recorded at Conny's Studio, Cologne, Germany, in June 1977

Engineered and produced by Conny Plank

Assistant engineer: J. Kramer

Cover artwork: Cluster

Record label: Sky

Release date: August 1977

Chart placings: did not chart

Tracks: 'Ho Renomo', 'Schone Hande', 'Steinsame', 'Wehrmut', 'Mit Simaen', 'Selange', 'Die Bunge', 'One', 'Fur Luise'

Personnel on Before And After Science:

Brian Eno: voices (on all tracks, except 4 and 9), piano (tracks 1, 2, 5-7), synthesiser (1, 3), guitar (1, 7), synthesised percussion (1), rhythm guitar (2, 5), brass (2), chorus (3, 4), 'jazz' piano (3), keyboards (4, 9, 10), vibes (4), metallics (5), Yamaha CS-80 (6-8), Moog synth (6, 9), EMS Synthi AKS (7, 10), Minimoog and bell (7), melody guitar (9)

Paul Rudolph: bass (1, 2, 5-7), rhythm guitar (1), harmonic bass (7)

Percy Jones: fretless bass (1, 4), analogue delay bass (3)

Phil Collins: drums (1, 4)

Rhett Davies: agong-gong and stick (1)

Jaki Liebezeit: drums (2)

Dave Mattacks: drums (3, 6)

Shirley Williams (Robert Wyatt): brush timbales (3), time (9)

Kurt Schwitters: voice sample (from 'Ursonate') (3)

Fred Frith: modified guitar (4), cascade guitars (9)

Phil Manzanera: rhythm guitar (5), guitar (6)

Robert Fripp: guitar solo (5)

Andy Fraser: drums (5)

Achim Roedelius: grand piano and electric piano (8)

Möbi Moebius: bass Fender piano (8)

Bill MacCormick: bass (9)

Brian Turrington: bass (10)

Recorded sporadically at Basing Street Studios, London, and Conny's Studio, Cologne, between 1975 and 1977

Producer and cover design: Brian Eno

Producer and engineer: Rhett Davies

Engineers: Conny Plank and Dave Hutchins
Cover artwork: Cream
Label: Polydor (UK), Island (US)
Release date: December 1977
Chart placings: New Zealand: 18, Sweden: 25
Tracks: 'No One Receiving', 'Backwater', 'Kurt's Rejoinder', 'Energy Fools The Magician', 'King's Lead Hat', 'Here He Comes', 'Julie With…', 'By This River', 'Through Hollow Lands (For Harold Budd)', 'Spider And I'

The Story So Far…

Born Brian Peter George Eno in the village of Melton, Suffolk, he went to art school before forming the Black Aces in 1964 with youth club friends, playing drums. In the late 1960s, he was the frontman in various avant-garde performance groups, including Merchant Taylor's Simultaneous Cabinet, The Maxwell Demon and The War Damage. Moving to London, he was invited to join saxophonist Andy Mackay, singer Bryan Ferry, bassist Graham Simpson, guitarist Roger Bunn and drummer Dexter Lloyd in a group that, in 1970, became Roxy Music. Eno saw himself as a 'non-musician' but could operate a synthesiser and reel-to-reel tape machine. Signed to Island Records, Roxy Music's eponymous debut album was recorded in 1972 with a changed lineup that replaced Lloyd with Paul Thompson and Bunn with the band's roadie, Phil Manzanera. Their debut reached number ten in the UK, and the 'Virginia Plain' single was a number-four hit. Eno quit the band after the second album, *For Your Pleasure* (1973), following disagreements with Ferry, then collaborated with King Crimson founder and guitarist Robert Fripp on electronic ambient albums *No Pussyfooting* (1973) and *Evening Star* (1975). In between, he released the critically acclaimed solo album *Here Come The Warm Jets* (1974), a collection of avant-garde pop songs featuring Fripp, John Wetton and members of Roxy Music. His second solo album, *Taking Tiger Mountain (By Strategy)*, inspired by a Chinese revolutionary opera, was released later the same year and featured Robert Wyatt on percussion, Phil Collins on drums and the Portsmouth Sinfonia. Third album *Another Green World* (1975), recorded after several weeks' recuperation following a car accident, was heavily instrumental and is regarded by critics as a 'masterpiece'. That year also saw the release of minimalist electronic experiment *Discreet Music*, which brought him to the attention of David Bowie. Eno worked with Bowie on *Low* (1977), *Heroes* (1977) and *Lodger* (1979). He was also in experimental rock supergroup 801 with Manzanera, Bill MacCormick from Matching Mole, Francie Monkman from Curved Air and soon-to-be Judas Priest drummer Simon Phillips, appearing on sole release *801 Live* (1976).

The Album

Eno had a strange premonition that he was going to have an accident. He had just finished working on a song for a Phil Manzanera album and thought: 'I wonder if that's the last thing I'll ever record?' With those dark thoughts swirling about in his head, he left Island Records' Basing Street studio and absent-mindedly walked in front of a taxi.

It ran over his legs and threw him against a parked car, cracking his skull. As he was rushed to hospital, he held on to his head in case his brain fell out. He told *NME* in 1977: 'The whole thing was horrible. I was conscious all the way through, and I was thinking, 'You stupid c**t, you brought this on yourself."

However, the gods of music (there are 37) work in a mysterious way because it was while convalescing at home that he heard something that inspired his pioneering journey into the world of ambient electronic sound. A friend had brought him an LP of 18th-century harp music and put it on his record player. The volume was very low and only one channel was working, so what Eno heard was HALF a recording that seemed to blend in with the sound of rain outside his window.

He hit upon the idea of 'environmental music', created deliberately to be played in the background or as a complement to other natural and artificial sounds. In later years, he would create ambient – defined as 'relating to the immediate surroundings of something' – music for, among other things, airports and outer space. It is true that he had already dabbled in that world with Robert Fripp, but his first solo step, and the album that epitomised his new 'less is more' minimalist approach, was *Discreet Music* in 1975, which included a 30-minute piece created using synthesiser and tape delay.

But is it prog, and should Brian Peter George St John le Baptiste de la Salle Eno, to give him his full confirmation name, be in this book? Well, if progressive rock is all about pushing the boundaries of music, then Eno is as prog as they come. The words most often used in connection with him are 'pioneering', 'influential' and 'innovative' – all descriptions we would apply to the very best of the prog bands within this tome. Just look at the artists and bands who have worked with him: Roxy, Fripp, Robert Wyatt, John Wetton, Phil Collins, Percy Jones, John Cale, David Bowie, Fred Frith, John Paul Jones, Cluster, Can – the big prog beasts respect Eno, and who are we to argue with them?

In 1977, he released two albums that showed both sides of his creativity – the electronic, avant-garde experimentation and the quirky, innovative pop-rock that made up the bulk of his early work and to which he would very occasionally return in his later years. The first to appear was *Cluster & Eno*, a collaboration with German synthesiser duo Dieter Moebius and Hans Joachim Roedelius.

It is no surprise that Eno was an early fan of what has been rather unkindly dubbed 'Krautrock'. Much of it is synthesiser-heavy but also has a shambolic, homemade feel that no doubt appealed to the self-confessed 'non-musician'. Bands such as Can and Neu! seemed to deliberately shun American and British ideas about song structures and melodies, opting instead to generate rhythmically hypnotic improvisations that came and went without any apparent musical development.

Cluster's Moebius and Roedelius met at the Zodiak Free Arts Lab, an experimental live music venue in what was then West Berlin and formed the band – initially with a capital 'K' – along with Conrad Schnitzler in 1969. Their self-titled debut album in 1971 also featured Konrad 'Conny' Plank, an influential record producer and musician who was a pivotal character in the development of many of the great Krautrock bands, including Kraftwerk, Ash Ra Tempel and Kraan.

Cluster were fans of Roxy Music's first album and saw them in concert in Hamburg. Later, it was in the same city that they met Brian Eno when he attended one of Cluster's shows. In a 2015 interview at the Red Bull Music Academy, Moebius said: 'He spoke to us during the interval and asked if he could join us for the second half. We were thinking, 'Oh no, does this guy have to come on stage with us?' Of course, we said okay and he played with us and we invited him to come and visit Cluster in Germany two years later.'

When he arrived, an instant friendship was struck up – Moebius and Roedelius took Eno into their home in the forest, showed him how to find edible roots for lunch and took him shopping. Roedelius even used Eno as a babysitter for his first child.

In between his domestic duties, Eno and Cluster first recorded with Neu! guitarist Michael Rother in a so-called 'supergroup' called Harmonia, but the tapes stayed in the vaults until 1997. After a break to work with David Bowie, Eno returned to join the Cluster duo in fashioning an album of mostly gentle, repetitive drones and soundscapes. Eno softened Cluster by introducing more organic sounds, such as a grand piano, while Cluster gave him important lessons in the use of tape loops and repetition.

Instead of one long, interminable track, the album is split into nine easily digestible pieces lasting from one and a half to six minutes, and there is a considerable amount of variety in their tone and mood. 'Fur Luise' features a haunting piano, with echoes that merge into background drones and surges of sound, while 'One' evokes a busy Indian street with tablas and sitar. 'Steinsame' is built around slabs of disturbing processed sound, and 'Selange' offers the only proper beat on the album, with rhythmic, pounding piano chords and rudimentary drums.

Released in June 1977 on the German Sky label, *Cluster & Eno* failed to achieve any noticeable commercial success – there is, after all, only a small market for truly challenging progressive music. But it is now regarded as one of the many important albums Eno has made or contributed to. Contemporary reviews are hard to find, so we must rely on more recent judgements – Allmusic says, 'The best of this album's instrumental pieces are too emotionally rich to waste as mere background music', while Amazon's editorial review adds, 'Meshing Cluster's affinity for loops and repetition and Eno's penchant for processing sounds, the trio prove that ambient music does not merely consist of drawn-out drones and insipid keyboard tapestries.'

Cluster's influence on Eno can be distinctly heard in his production work on David Bowie's 'Berlin Trilogy' of albums, particularly *Low*, so the German pair could be forgiven for feeling Eno was achieving commercial musical success on the back of their talents. But they don't – in fact, they take pleasure in Eno's success and appear to have nothing but the greatest respect for him. As evidence of that, they joined forces for a second album, 1978's *After The Heat*.

One track was inspired by the forest environment of Cluster's home but never made it onto the album. Eno, Moebius and Roedelius composed the beautiful 'By This River' as they gazed upon a waterway flowing past the house. Recorded at Conny Plank's studio with the Cluster duo on pianos and Eno on a Yamaha CS-80, it is a pretty ballad over which Eno sings sad, slow lyrics: 'Here we are/Stuck by this river/You and I/Underneath a sky that's ever falling down, down, down'. Short, sweet and sparse, the playing sounds hesitant, almost clumsy, yet is a magical interlude on Eno's second 1977 album, *Before And After Science*.

Cluster & Eno was recorded in a matter of weeks – *BAAS* took two years, during which time Eno recorded more than a hundred tracks, discarding some, splicing others together and, eventually, whittling them down into a smaller set of ideas that he thought sounded promising. In a 1977 interview in *New Musical Express*, he revealed:

I abandoned the album three times before I finished it. It really caused a lot of sweat – and heartache, I suppose. At one point, I thought that I could never achieve anything more musically. Not that I'd achieved everything, just that there was nowhere else for me to go, you know? It affected everything I did in the end. I found myself saying, 'You're just a dilettante. You're not doing anything with the kind of intensity that it deserves.' It was a crisis of confidence that went very deep.

Helping him through the process – and sometimes leading him astray – were a series of cards produced with his friend, the artist Peter Schmidt. Called Oblique Strategies, each of the 100 cards suggests 'a course of action or thinking to assist in creative situations' – they are still available from Eno's website at £50 a pack. I guess they may be helpful when suffering from some sort of creative block – pick a card at random and follow its advice, which may be 'Do nothing for as long as possible'. However, Eno told *NME* that they didn't always help him tame and shape the monster that *BAAS* had become:

Some of the tracks went through so many changes. I'd start with a bit of instrumental, three minutes long. Then, I'd copy it and edit it together so that it was eight minutes long. Then, I'd put on a bit of song at the end and stick a whole load of instruments on. Then, I'd listen to it and decide that that was all wrong and I'd strip all the instruments off again and remix it and decide that what it needed was a bit of song at the beginning ... I was going mad.

In the end, having bust three deadlines, I just had to get it out. It had grown so enormous – I just had to burst the balloon.

The balloon went 'pop' – as, indeed, does most of side one of the album, featuring four uptempo songs that, on first listen, may appear alarmingly commercial. But delve deeper and you'll find he is channelling Krautrock in the relentless repetition, avant-funk in the guitar work and the harsh, jagged rhythms of Talking Heads, topped by vocals that are almost robotic in their absence of warmth and tone.

Yes, it all sounds a bit of a mess, but Eno manages to create bouncy little melodic gems with dense, futuristic lyrics that sound as if they've been badly translated from an obscure foreign language. Opener 'No One Receiving' is a case in point – a driving, funky number that foreshadows Bowie's 'Let's Dance', based on two repetitive chords and a drum pattern that Phil Collins would later use on 'In The Air Tonight'. An instrumental section shuns traditional lead guitar for rhythmic metallic noises and what sounds like the distant cawing of seagulls.

'Backwater' uses pounding piano chords and synthesised brass to create a dumb but catchy, lightweight pop song. 'Kurt's Rejoinder' is driven by Percy Jones's busy, funky bass and Eno's repetitive nonsense vocals – 'Burger Bender bouncing like a ball, ball, ball so Burger Bender bargain blender shine'. The track is named after avant-garde writer Kurt Schwitters, who is sampled reciting his surrealist 1932 poem 'Ursonate'.

'King's Lead Hat' is an anagram of Talking Heads, the new wave band led by David Byrne that Eno met at a concert while they were supporting The Ramones. Eno loved their debut and produced their next three albums, including their masterpiece, *Remain In Light*. 'King's Lead Hat' is a tribute to the Heads' rhythmic, minimalist approach, fading in on a three-chord sequence that is repeated practically throughout the song.

The remaining track on side one, 'Energy Fools The Magician', once again showcases the bass talents of Percy Jones, who improvises over atmospheric, minor-key synth chords, with occasional drum interjections from Phil Collins. Side two opener 'Here He Comes' is pop-soul, sounding at times like a dead ringer for The Drifters' 'Save The Last Dance For Me', with a slight country and western feel in Phil Manzanera's guitar and the laidback drumming of Fairport Convention's Dave Mattacks.

The rest of the album shows us Eno's more contemplative side. Eno told the *NME*: 'They're sort of post-atomic tracks. They're all about the sea, in fact. They're to do with either drifting away or getting lost or being part of the flow of things.' 'Julie With…' is a slow, minor-key ballad that fades in with a synth drone before he sings lyrics about drifting on the open sea with the eponymous Julie, who is trailing her fingers in the water. 'I wonder if we'll be seen here or if time has left us all alone', he asks. Eno appears to play every instrument here, including a hesitant, rudimentary guitar solo, except for Paul Rudolph on bass.

We have already talked about 'By This River' – it's followed by 'Through Hollow Lands (For Harold Budd)'. The dedication refers to an American minimalist composer who was discovered by Eno in 1976 and signed to the latter's record label. In fact, Budd claims he owes 'everything' to Eno, telling *The Los Angeles Times*: 'I was plucked from the tree, and suddenly I had flowered.' Eno's tribute borrows from Budd's long, slow piano playing style to create a beautiful, melancholy soundscape. Bill MacCormick from Matching Mole and 801 is on bass while Fred Frith plays 'cascade guitars', whatever they are.

Finally, 'Spider And I' is another slow one, heavy on synth keyboards and little else except occasional bass, with touching lyrics in which 'Spider and I sit watching the sky on a world without sound'. Perhaps it is a reflection of the way Eno was trying to catch the sounds he wanted in his own web.

Released with a cover showing a close-up of Eno's face in stark black and white, the original LP pressing included four prints of watercolours by Peter Schmidt – the back cover carried the subtitle 'Fourteen Pictures', which referenced the ten songs and prints. As for the title, Eno explained: 'I use the word 'science' to indicate techniques and rational knowledge. And what the title implies is that the condition 'before science' is similar to the condition 'after' it – that there's a kind of circle thing and that science is the isolated one.' Yell bingo if you understood that.

Before And After Science was critically acclaimed on release and is still regarded as one of Eno's most important works. *Downbeat* magazine called it 'another typically awesome, stunning and numbing Brian Eno album', *Rolling Stone* said 'the execution here is close to flawless' and *The Village Voice* voted it the 12th best album of the year. Nearly 50 years later, it still gets five stars from Allmusic and is credited with foreseeing the new wave revolution. In fact, the only negative comments really came from Eno himself, who told *NME*: 'I still don't know how pleased I am with what I've done. Robert Wyatt said to me once that you commit yourself to what you're left with – you know that this is the only thing left that you can do.'

As it turned out, Eno was wrong. *Before And After Science* is a hugely influential musical triumph – and he had plenty of other things left to do.

Happy The Man – Happy The Man

Personnel:

Stanley Whitaker: electric guitar, acoustic guitar, vocals

Frank Wyatt: keyboards, backing vocals, saxophone, flute, piano

Kit Watkins: Minimoog, acoustic piano, Rhodes piano, ARP string ensemble, Hammond B3 organ, Hohner clavinet, flute, marimba

Rick Kennell: electric bass

Mike Beck: drums, percussion

Recorded at A&M studios in Hollywood between November and December 1976

Produced by Mike Scott

Engineered by Wayne Garber

Label: Arista Records

Release date: August 1977

Chart places: did not chart

Tracks: 'Starborne' (Kit Watkins), 'Stumpy Meets The Firecracker In Stencil Forest' (Stanley Whitaker), 'Upon The Rainbow (Befrost)' (Watkins, Frank Wyatt), 'Mr Mirror's Reflection On Dreams' (Watkins), 'Carousel' (Wyatt), 'Knee Bitten Nymphs In Limbo' (Whitaker), 'On Time As A Helix Of Precious Laughs' (Wyatt), 'Hidden Moods' (Watkins), 'New York Dreams Suite' (Wyatt)

The Story So Far...

Guitarist Stanley Whitaker, from Missouri, formed first band Shady Grove with keyboardist David Bach in Germany, where his father, who became a full colonel in the US Army, was stationed. He met bassist Rick Kennell (born in Indiana), who had just been drafted, at a Shady Grove gig in 1972. Back in the US, they recruited former Kennell bandmates Mike Beck on drums and singer/flautist Cliff Fortney. Whitaker then met saxophonist/pianist Frank Wyatt at James Madison University. The band name came not from the 1972 Genesis single but from a quote from *Faust* by Johann Wolfgang von Goethe: 'Happy the man who early learns the wide chasm that lies between his wishes and his powers.' JMU piano teacher's son Kit Watkins, from Virginia, replaced Bach, while Fortney quit. Moving to Washington, DC, the band signed to Arista Records.

The Album

'Wow! I don't really understand this music. It's way above my head, but my head of A&R, Rick Chertoff, says you guys are incredible, and we should sign you. So, welcome to Arista', said record label boss Clive Davis. So began the stop-start story of the most British of American progressive rock bands, Happy the Man.

They never achieved any noticeable commercial success and released just six albums over 30 years, two of them deep dives into the band's demo archive. Yet, their eponymous debut has become something of a cult record, their complex, dynamic and meticulously arranged music chiming with fans of Canterbury Scene bands such as Hatfield and the North and National Health, with a splash of Frank Zappa and The Enid.

In fact, I assumed they were British when I first came across them. Not only did they have the same name as a Genesis single (see above), but they had silly, Monty Python-esque song titles, just like Hatfield were wont to do. Instead, they were American boys but heavily influenced by British bands, from The Beatles through Led Zeppelin to the big proggers. If any band helped shape HTM's music, it was Gentle Giant. In a 2024 interview, Whitaker told me:

> We all had a great love for the typical British prog groups that were huge – we were big Genesis fans, King Crimson and all those, but Gentle Giant was my personal favourite out of all of them. They were always a cut above, and part of that was after I'd first seen them and they were opening for Colosseum in Frankfurt, their very first ever show in Germany. We were 15 years old and so knocked out that we went backstage after they played and didn't even go back out for the Colosseum set. We found them to be the most humble, beautiful human beings in music that we had ever met!

As well as the prog influences, the band also drew from classical music, from Debussy, Ravel and Stravinsky. HTM began by covering their favourite prog classics, but soon, the composing talents of Whitaker, Wyatt and Watkins came to the fore. Wyatt was a jazz man, equally at home on sax as he was on piano. Watkins, meanwhile, was something of a gifted prodigy who could faultlessly recreate Keith Emerson's keyboard parts in 'Hoedown'.

They quit university and lived together in a house, just like bands used to do in the 1960s, each doing odd jobs such as working in a paint store, in a chicken plant and as an orderly in a hospital. At the same time, they concentrated on composing their own music and planning their stage act. Whitaker told website All Things If in 2012:

> Frank had a wonderfully brilliant mind for staging and coming up with wacky stuff. We all would feed it. 'Let's have clowns jump out. Oh, yeah! Clowns! Clowns would be great!' It would fill in for our lack of vocals. We flirted with a couple of vocalists early on in Happy the Man, but they didn't work out. We knew our musical side was much stronger … It was image-evoking music, so it made sense to have slide shows and movies going on, as well as theatrics with dancers coming out occasionally. We would push the envelope. We didn't care.

An example was 'Death's Crown', a 45-minute piece written by Wyatt that had actors, sets and dancers, with a light show produced by a three-man crew, performed around 1974. Rehearsal recordings were eventually released in 1999.

However, early gigs suggested their music was an acquired taste that didn't necessarily go down well with some irritable US audiences. They supported blues band Hot Tuna and, on more than one occasion, were advised not to play in case they were torn apart by the impatient crowd. Whitaker recalls one performance on Long Island that lasted just 45 seconds before the 10,000-strong audience started throwing beer bottles at the band and demanding the headliners.

Things got better when they moved to Washington, DC. Happy the Man pretty much became the house band at The Cellar Door, a dark, arty venue on M Street, where they would play every month. Then two things happened in quick succession to put the band on the road to … well, not fame and fortune exactly, but at least the chance to record and release a debut album.

The first was a summons by Arista Records to audition for Clive Davis, already a legend in the music business. President of Columbia Records for six years, he had snapped up some of the biggest US acts of the 1960s and 1970s, including Janis Joplin, Santana, Bruce Springsteen, Chicago, Aerosmith, Billy Joel and Blood, Sweat & Tears. Quitting in 1973, he formed Arista Records and built up another impressive stable of artists. His head of A&R, Rick Chertoff, had seen HTM and was raving about them, so they went to New York to perform for the head honcho himself.

According to Whitaker, Davis sat in the front row, hands behind his head, legs out straight and eyes closed, while the band ran through their 45-minute set. When they finished, he didn't even clap. But the first words out of his mouth were the ones quoted at the beginning of this piece.

Of course, saying they would be signed and actually being signed are two different things. So, the second surprise of the year helped move things along. Bassist Rick had been sending tapes of the band to friends who worked as road crew members for Genesis. When Peter Gabriel was looking for musicians for his first solo album, his management contacted The Cellar Door and said: 'Peter wants to talk to you.' Whitaker told the website:

Peter came in, met us and sat down at the piano. He said, 'Let me play you a little bit of what I'm working on', and he closed his eyes, played a few chords, sang one or two lines, and then just stopped still with his eyes closed. I remember us in Happy the Man standing around, kind of nudging each other. We're thinking, 'What? Are we supposed to say something? What's he doing?' Then, out of nowhere, he just started singing again. It seemed the stuff was so new for him that he was trying to think of where it would go next. It was the embryonic stage of the music, and we proceeded – over the next seven and a half hours – to work with him extensively on two of the songs. He used a lot of the arrangements we – especially Kit and me – came up with for two of the tunes on that first record.

Initially, Gabriel wanted just Whitaker and Watkins for his album, but Stan said no, it's all or nothing. The band were also worried about prioritising Gabriel's project when the Arista signing was in the air. They insisted that, on a live tour, Happy the Man would open the shows and then become Gabriel's backing band. In the end, after weeks of negotiations, the Gabriel deal fell through. Whitaker said: 'If I have any regrets at all in my life (though I've tried to live life with no regrets), that's the only one I can think of … But Peter's wanting us so bad actually helped kick Arista in the ass to sign us quicker, so it was a blessing in that way.'

Kit Watkins has his own theory of why Arista wanted HTM. In a 1993 interview with Innerviews website, he revealed: 'They were trying to get us to do the soundtrack to *Star Wars*, which, of course, would have been a joke because we weren't writing orchestral music like John Williams was. At the time, we didn't even know what the movie was. We heard about it a year before it was out.'

With Arista fully on board, it was time to choose a producer. HTM wanted Ken Scott, who had previously worked on one of their favourite albums, *Birds Of Fire* by the Mahavishnu Orchestra, and whose credits included engineering for The Beatles, Pink Floyd and Procol Harum, and producing David Bowie, Supertramp and Elton John. It was a match made in heaven – Happy the Man and Scott became so close that they even shared a jacuzzi together. Whitaker told All Things If:

It was glorious working with Ken Scott. He was a living legend as a producer … He had stories like crazy. He was a storyteller, so we'd just sit and listen. It was part of his British personality. He would come into the studio every day with a scent of, what was it … not B.O. but some kind of scotch. He had an affinity for J&B scotch. He would come in every day with a fresh bottle and plop it down. By the end of the day, he would have gone through that whole bottle. I don't know how he could drink that much; it was his poison of choice, but he was such a wonderful, gifted engineer/producer to work with – it was like going to school. We learned so much making those two records and heard so many wonderful stories about The Beatles, Elton, Ziggy and Jimi. He had great 'war' stories, as we liked to call them.

It's probably fair to say that Happy the Man did not require a huge amount of producing. Yes, the music they composed was difficult and challenging, but they were talented players with a dedicated work ethic, rehearsing for eight to ten hours a day, so everything was embedded in their heads and hands. They viewed themselves as an orchestra rather than as a typical prog band and prioritised melody in a bid to be 'different'.

Their debut album pretty much reflected their stage show at the time – tracks such as 'Stumpy Meets The Firecracker In Stencil Forest', 'Mr Mirror's Reflection On Dreams' and 'New York Dreams Suite' were in their set back in

1975, while most of the remaining tunes were being played live through 1976. In fact, the only track that took shape in the studio rather than as part of the live set was 'Carousel'… about which, more later.

The band had three different writers in Whitaker, Wyatt and Watkins. As the guitarist, Whitaker's songwriting tended more towards rock. He also felt proggers took themselves too seriously, so he would give his complicated compositions amusing titles to add a touch of humour. He told me: 'I always had little cartoons going in my head and I would channel that.' He was the least prolific of the trio, writing just three tracks across the band's first two Arista albums and contributing to a fourth, and would painstakingly piece things together from fragments of melodies.

Wyatt, on the other hand, was able to sit down at the piano and compose wild, complicated music right off the bat – he would play what the band dubbed 'Frank chords' because they would be unlike anything they had ever heard before and certainly weren't guitar-friendly. He was the more orchestral writer and also penned the lyrics for the two vocal tracks on the debut album.

Finally, Watkins was just as brilliant but in a different way – he liked to write in odd time signatures, particularly in 5/4. Whitaker told me: 'I thought his sense of melody was wonderful; it was all very cinematic stuff.' As the main ivory-tickler in the band, Watkins's work was understandably heavy on the keyboards, frequently alternating gentle washes of sound with faster, more dramatic interludes.

A prime example of his work is the surprisingly laidback opener 'Starborne', in which layers of keyboards move sedately through minor sixth chords, accompanied by Kennell's pointillistic bass, ending on dramatic orchestral chords. Whitaker is also in there, matching the keyboard chords with a 12-string guitar. Whitaker admits it was a strange way to open the record, but producer Scott liked it and Watkins had a lot of influence on the running order. Whitaker told me: 'I didn't care for it back then when we did it, but now I love it – Kit plays this beautiful, subtle Moog melody on that song. It's just so subdued; every note is so lyrical and so perfect.'

It is followed by Whitaker's first songwriting credit on the album, the faster, upbeat and tricksy 'Stumpy…', a track that many thought should have been the opener. Meaty guitar notes and pounding chords greet the listener before lightning-fast guitar riffs, doubled by sax, leap all over the place. Whitaker seems to channel a bit of *Relayer*-era Steve Howe in his guitar lead, while the entire effect reminds me of Frank Zappa's 'Regyptian Strut' from his *Läther* collection.

There are strange time signatures ahoy, but don't ask the writer what they are. He told me:

I had a little cartoon in my head of a little dwarf-like creature, who was Stumpy, and he was running through the Stencil Forest. I mean, I smoked a lot of pot back then, so that might have had a little bit to do with it. So, I was following this cartoon in my head and as soon as I finished one part, my Muse would give me the next section. So, it came together very organically. I wanted it to be very happy and very up, and it was sometimes challenging to perform that song, but it was a good one … I had no idea what time signatures I even had going on in that song until some more technically inclined musicians came up and told me, you're in five and a half here, and six here. I said, really?

There is also a fascinating story behind his second track on the album, the equally sprightly and unpredictable 'Knee Bitten Nymphs In Limbo'. He said:

I went to high school in Frankfurt in Germany, which is how I got to see all these amazing bands way before they hit the States, and in high school, we had a thing called 'knee biting' – we would be out on the grass on a break from class or after school, and there was a girl who invented knee biting where you would literally bite the other person's knee. We discovered it was a very sensual thing. So, that was the initial impression I wanted to put in the song.

Fast, riffy and with excellent opportunities for the keyboard wizards to do their stuff, 'Knee Bitten…' is quintessential Happy the Man. But the record company didn't want an album of instrumentals – in fact, they demanded to know if there were some vocal numbers coming down the line. Arista were saying no songs, no signee.

So, there are two vocals on the album, both performed by Whitaker, who had sung before in his high school choir. Both are fairly gentle, minor key ballads but with melodies that defy expectations, moving sinuously over sublime chords and shifting keys. Watkins's 'Upon The Rainbow (Befrost)' was particularly challenging for Whitaker to sing because the top note of G# was above his range, requiring Scott to do some jiggery-pokery with the tape speed. 'On Time As A Helix Of Precious Laughs' started off in 1976 almost as an exercise in shifting keyboard arpeggios before a dramatic interlude of soaring electric guitar and an insistent ticking beat.

Lyrically, both songs sport dense, difficult lyrics that take a lot of deciphering, and Wyatt was clearly inspired by Peter Hammill of Van der Graaf Generator. Here's a line from 'Upon The Rainbow (Befrost)': 'He laughs and climbs in colours and threes/The sun holds his hand to guide him/Sing, all singing/'Listen to the sound, little man/The map is all inside you". 'On Time…' is perhaps a little more decipherable – there's a woman growing old and filling her time with precious laughs, which is not a bad way to age. It may well be inspired by a 1969 science-fiction short story by Samuel R Delany, 'Time Considered As A Helix Of Semi-Precious Stones', which charts the rise of a criminal. Sadly, Wyatt is no longer around to confirm for us – he died in 2023 from kidney cancer.

His other compositions include 'Carousel', which was originally part of a much longer piece called 'I Carve The Chariot On The Carousel'. Producer Scott didn't like any of it except the sinister piano arpeggio ending, so they took that piece and repeated it over and over again, with the band adding additional keyboards and guitar over the top.

Watkins's remaining contributions included the pretty 'Hidden Moods', with Wyatt on flute and Whitaker on acoustic guitar, and the classically-inspired 'Mr Mirror's Reflections On Dreams', the longest track on the album at nearly nine minutes. The closer, Frank Wyatt's 'New York Dreams Suite', dates back to 1974 and tries to encapsulate the beauty and madness of the city that never sleeps in music that veers wildly from gentle keyboards to a full band rock-out.

Happy the Man's debut album was released with barely a parp, let alone a fanfare – Whitaker thinks there was one full-page ad in *Billboard* magazine and that was it – and failed to make much, if any, impact in the States. It might have been a different matter if the band had been able to tour in Europe, for this was music that probably appealed more to adventurous European tastes. But it wasn't to be, and Arista dropped the band on the eve of the release of their follow-up, *Crafty Hands*.

However, that spirited 1977 debut has since become a bit of a cult album, a 'lost' prog masterpiece that, in the words of Allmusic, 'combines a number of diverse influences in a distinctive manner, and their music is as complex and meticulously arranged as any prog album one cares to mention'. This is unashamed prog composed and played by musical geniuses who ignored the changing musical scene and fearlessly did their own thing.

Hawkwind – Quark, Strangeness And Charm

Personnel:
Dave Brock: guitar, synthesisers, sound effects, vocals
Robert Calvert: vocals, spoken word, percussion, morse
Simon House: keyboards, violin, anvil, vocals
Adrian Shaw: bass guitar, vocals
Simon King: drums, percussion
Recorded at Rockfield Studios, Wales, in February 1977
Producer: Hawkwind
Engineer: Dave Charles, assisted by Robert Calvert
Label: Charisma Records (UK) and Sire Records (US)
Release date: 17 June 1977
Chart places: UK: 30
Cover design: Hipgnosis
Tracks: 'Spirit Of The Age' (Robert Calvert, Dave Brock), 'Damnation Alley' (Calvert, Brock, Simon House), 'Fable Of A Failed Race' (Calvert, Brock), 'Quark, Strangeness And Charm' (Calvert, Brock), 'Hassan I Sahba' (Calvert, Paul Rudolph), 'The Forge Of Vulcan' (House), 'Days Of The Underground' (Calvert, Brock), 'Iron Dream' (Simon King)

The Story So Far...

The band was formed in 1969 by David Anthony Brock from Middlesex and Mick Slattery, both members of London psychedelic band Famous Cure. They met bassist John Harrison and gained drummer Terry Ollis through a music mag ad. Brock's friend Nik Turner and Michael Davies helped out as roadies but soon became band members. They were signed to Liberty Records after playing a 20-minute jam at a talent night in Notting Hill. The band name came from Turner's nickname for his habits of clearing his throat and farting. Slattery quit and was replaced by Huw Lloyd-Langton on lead guitar. Debut album *Hawkwind* (1970) was well-received, reaching number 75 in the UK and labelled 'tremendous' by *Melody Maker*. Harrison quit over the band's drug use, followed by Lloyd-Langton, who'd experienced a bad LSD trip. The follow-up, *In Search Of Space* (1971), saw the addition of Dave Anderson from Amon Duul II on bass and Del Dettmar on synthesiser, while Robert Newton Calvert was an occasional member as lyricist, performance poet and singer. The album reached number 18 in the UK. More lineup changes ensued: Anderson was replaced by Ian 'Lemmy' Kilmister and Ollis was replaced by Simon King. A live charity gig at the Roundhouse in aid of Greasy Truckers saw the release of hit single 'Silver Machine'. The third album, *Doremi Fasol Latido* (1972), reached number 14 in the UK. Live album *Space Ritual* (1973) did even better, hitting number eight. The departure of Davies allowed Simon House to join on keyboards for 1974's *Hall Of The Mountain Grill*. Second drummer Alan Powell joined for *Warrior At The Edge Of Time* (1975), after which Lemmy was sacked for trying to smuggle amphetamines from the US into Canada. He was replaced on bass by Paul Rudolph. Calvert became full-time lead vocalist for *Astounding Sounds, Amazing Music* (1976).

The Album

In the past, I have been somewhat dismissive of Hawkwind. Remove the burbling synth, the sci-fi lyrics and the naked dancer, I said, and they were little more than a three-chord thrash band, not fit to sniff the same pot fumes as Yes, Genesis and the rest. But I have also suggested you can view Hawkwind as early punk, channelling raw energy rather than any noticeable musical ability, so by 1977, they fitted very nicely into the current sonic landscape.

They also fought each other – a lot. They took copious amounts of drugs, they got arrested, they had mental breakdowns and they sacked each other constantly. In fact, I would say Hawkwind were the only band in this book to have more lineups than Yes. Believe me, that's saying something.

You would have expected them to have become a footnote in prog history. Yet, by hook or by crook, they have survived across the decades, releasing their 37th album, *There Is No Space For Us*, in 2025, and they sound exactly the same as they did in the 1970s. Not bad for a band that, according to Lemmy, made a 'black fucking nightmare of noise.'

Listen to that single, 'Silver Machine', probably the only Hawkwind track that most people have heard. The verse is a four-chord thrash with no subtlety whatsoever – it slams into your head with the delicacy of a triphammer. Oh, and there's a fifth chord in the chorus – that's about two more than you usually get from Hawkwind. The lyrics are vaguely sci-fi but punkishly simplistic: 'Do you want to ride? See yourself going by/The other side of the sky/I got a silver machine'. Replace them with lyrics about gobbing on life, and you could be listening to the Sex Pistols.

Perhaps that was the secret of their success – instead of trying to follow current trends, like Gentle Giant, they did their own thing, stayed true to their own ideals and waited for the trends to coincide with them. Briefly.

Ah, I'm being harsh, I know. You've got to admire them for their single-minded dedication to their art. Like a rocket ship heading for the stars, nothing would be allowed to knock them off course, not even the occasional musician who failed to understand the mission statement, and there were a few of those. In fact, Hawkwind almost broke up at the end of 1976 as they went into the studio to record a standalone single, 'Back On The Streets'. First, Nik Turner was kicked out because he kept playing his saxophone at maximum volume over everyone else. Then, the band decided they didn't need two drummers – believe me, no band does except for King Crimson, which at one time had three – so it was goodbye Alan Powell. The remaining members recorded the single – composed by Paul Rudolph and Bob Calvert – which was released in January 1977.

Here's what the *New Musical Express* said at the time: 'Cranked-out basic chords designed to make your eardrums bleed, lyrics that are unintelligible apart from the chanted title-chorus and the rhythm section playing like they enjoy feeling those blisters squish against their instruments.' Today, it doesn't sound nearly as brutal as the review suggests, but, boy, is it mindless nonsense. Don't worry. I've listened to it, so you don't have to.

Then came another split, a major one this time that threatened to destroy the band. As they rehearsed in the bucolic surroundings of Rockfield Studios in Wales, Dave Brock and Robert Calvert decided that bass player Rudolph was trying to turn them into a funky soul band. In a 1977 interview with fanzine *Penetration 13*, Brock claimed:

Rudolph wanted to play really funky soul music, which really pissed me off and I contemplated leaving, ya know. I was pissed off with it and we got involved with a different management, which was everything I hated, ya know. It was evolving into a real music business scene, and there were all these undercurrents in the band, little fuckin' cliques, and I thought, fuck it … and then we said, ahh fuck it, we'll just split Hawkwind. Then, we thought, why should we fuckin' split and leave Rudolph and company in power? All these things had been going on without me realising it; you think nothing like this goes on and it happens.

Rudolph's recollection, detailed in Ian Abrahams' book *Sonic Assassins*, was: 'Apparently, some band members felt my attitude was not 'band-like' and I had the opportunity of apologising for something or leaving. I chose the latter, not fully understanding the situation.'

Eventually, Brock, Calvert and the two Simons were left with the band name and a string of live dates to fulfil. So, the hunt was on for a new bassist. They turned to someone they knew – Londoner Adrian 'Ade' Shaw, who had supported Hawkwind with his band Muscle Memory during the *Space Ritual* tour. Shaw had turned down the job once before when Lemmy was acting the maggot but filled in on a few dates when the maggot went missing.

By the time he arrived at Rockfield Studios in Wales, most of the tracks for *Quark, Strangeness And Charm* had been completed without the basslines – Shaw's job was to overdub his instrument. However, he also got a chance to contribute to the songwriting, even if he didn't get a credit. In Abrahams' book, he praised the collective spirit of the band during that time. He said:

The songwriting was pretty fair back then. If you had something worth considering, it was considered … [The Brock and Calvert combination] seemed a very creative partnership – they worked well together. Calvert added a lyrical sophistication that Brock never had on his own, and Calvert's lack of expertise was helped by working with Brock.

The album, with a cover by design gurus Hipgnosis showing the inside of Battersea Power Station – a second appearance for the plant on a prog album in 1977 – was released in June at the height of the punk explosion. Opener 'Spirit Of The Age' hits the listener with a blast of random electronic noise and garbled voices before chopping guitar chords (owing not a little to King Crimson's 'Larks Tongues In Aspic Part 1') introduce a driving two-chord riff (F# and E, if you want to try it at home) that stays the same throughout the entire seven-minute length. The ludicrous lyrics tell of someone's desire to have their loved one deep-frozen, but 'your father refused to sign the forms'. Calvert was responsible for the rhythmic electronic pulse throughout the song that repeats the Morse Code for SOS.

The nine-minute epic 'Damnation Alley' is inspired by a 1969 science-fiction novel of the same name by Roger Zelazny – it's about a criminal's suicide vision transporting a plague vaccine across post-apocalyptic America. Calvert's lyrics tell of 'driving through the burning hoop of doom in an eight-wheeled anti-radiation tomb' across an America where there is 'no more Arizona now Phoenix is fried, Oklahoma City, what a pity it's gone, Louisiana Delta where the Mississippi's dried up, no more Chattanooga, Cherokee, Lexington', all set against the usual heads-down, no-nonsense driving beat that Hawkwind do so well, and so frequently.

Side one closes with 'Fable Of A Failed Race', another two-chord wonder (B and A, chord fans) but taken at a slower pace, made up mostly of a short verse about beings arriving as seeds to populate a planet, followed by a drawn-out guitar solo.

Title track 'Quark, Strangeness And Charm' adds a third chord to the musical stew but repeats the same sequence over and over again. The lyrics suggest that Albert Einstein was unable to get laid because he didn't know about quark, strangeness and charm – and they are right. Not necessarily about his sex life, but certainly about quarks – elementary particles that weren't discovered until 1968, 13 years after Einstein's death. There are six types – or flavors (note the US spelling) – of quark: up, down, top, bottom, charm and strange, the latter four only produced in high-energy collisions.

Departed bassman Rudolph gets a writing credit for the Middle Eastern-sounding 'Hassan I Sahba', which mixes legends about the 11th-century founder of the Order of the Assassins with references to Black September and petro-dollars. 'The Forge Of Vulcan' is a powerful, doomy instrumental with House playing Phantom of the Opera-style organ chords and hitting an anvil.

'Days Of The Underground' is a self-referential song about the early years of Hawkwind, asking, 'Whatever happened to those chromium heroes? Are there none of them still left around?'. Finally, 'Iron Dream' is an instrumental by drummer Harris loosely based on Gustav Holst's 'Mars' from the Planets Suite. The title comes from another post-apocalyptic story, *The Iron Dream* by Norman Spinrad.

The new Hawkwind lineup was unveiled at the Roundhouse on 27 February, with support from Lemmy's new band Motörhead – named after the last track he composed for Hawkwind – followed by tours of Germany, the

Netherlands, France and the UK. The album was hailed as the work of a rejuvenated band after the disappointment of its predecessor. *Sounds* said Calvert 'pulls out all the stops, his poetical-lyrical contributions working particularly well', and *Melody Maker* was surprised to discover 'the band have developed a real sense of humour.'

Commercially, *Quark, Strangeness And Charm* was not as successful as some of Hawkwind's earlier – and, indeed, later – albums. However, contemporary reviewers such as Allmusic still praise its 'concise lyricism and accessible melodies'. Indeed, I'll leave the last word to Allmusic, who call the album 'one of their most endearingly enduring, charming, strange, and, if not quark, then certainly quirky.'

They Also Served...

801 – Listen Now

This was the only studio album by a short-lived prog 'supergroup' featuring Roxy Music guitarist Manzanera, Canterbury Scene bassist Bill McCormick and a host of celebrity friends, including Lol Creme, Kevin Godley, Eddie Jobson, Francis Monkman and Dave Mattacks of Fairport Convention. The album is melodic pop prog.

Aksak Maboul – Onze Danses Pour Combattre La Migraine

Translated in English as *Eleven Dances For Fighting Migraines*, there are, er, 17 tracks here that encompass strange electronic drumbeats overlaid with random keyboard flourishes, atonal woodwind duets, mysterious plinky-plonky piano melodies and nightclub sax. File under avant-garde, as in 'I avant-garde a clue what's going on here'.

Daevid Allen – Now Is The Happiest Time Of Your Life

Former Gong founder's second solo album after leaving the band is a spacey, mostly acoustic affair, assisted by Spanish musicians. If you like Allen's brand of child-like whimsy (and I do), then this is one of his best solo efforts.

Barclay James Harvest – Gone To Earth

Derided as the poor man's Moody Blues, BJH recorded a song for this release with that very same title, an amusing pastiche of the Moodies' 'Nights In White Satin' that reportedly angered Justin Heyward. *Gone To Earth* is a very pleasant, tuneful album – one of my favourites of theirs – but it's soft rock, not prog.

Birth Control – Increase

This features muscular, almost funky, hard rock from a West Berlin band. Is it prog? Earlier albums were, but by 1977, the band were succumbing to some unfortunate commercial influences, including disco. However, I'll give full marks for the title of the eight-minute closer, 'Seems My Bike's Riding Me'.

Tim Blake – Crystal Machine

Another former Gongster, the band's keyboard player, who left around the same time as Daevid Allen, presented his first solo album – a trippy, spacey, electronic ambient soundscape – in 1977.

Brand X – Moroccan Roll

The second album by Genesis drummer Phil Collins's side project melds jazz fusion with Eastern scales and is worth a listen, although only after you have heard the superior debut *Unorthodox Behaviour* (1976) and 1978's *Masques*.

Caravan – Better by Far

Along with Soft Machine, Caravan were one of the founders of the Canterbury Scene but steadily moved away from their progressive roots as leader Pye Hastings steered them in a more commercial direction. Their eighth studio album bears little resemblance to their early 1970s classics but contains two bona fide bangers in 'The Last Unicorn' and 'Nightmare'.

Circus – Movin' On

This five-piece from Basel, Switzerland, offered up raunchy prog, channelling Gentle Giant, Van der Graaf Generator and Jethro Tull despite sparing use of electric guitar or keyboards. Instead, the soundscape is dominated by saxophones, flutes, bass pedals and jazz drumming.

Colosseum II – Electric Savage & Wardance

The original Colosseum, formed by drummer Jon Hiseman, were a thumping good progressive blues/jazz/rock band. The second incarnation was more jazz-fusion but still entertaining, if commercially less successful. The two albums released in 1977 are excellent examples of the genre, graced by the talents of the late ex-Thin Lizzy guitarist Gary Moore.

Dixie Dregs – Free Fall

This US band mixed funk, bluegrass, metal and Mahavishnu-style jazz in a rich prog stew led by uber-talented future Deep Purple guitarist Steve Morse. This was the first album released under the name and is probably the best. Although, the subsequent three are damn fine, too.

Earth And Fire – Gate To Infinity

Formed in the Netherlands in 1970, Earth and Fire served up very nice symphonic prog – all Mellotron and organ – until they went right down the pan with this: their disco-oriented fifth album. Heat in microwave and use as a plant pot.

Eloy – Ocean

An album that frequently turns up in lists of the best albums of 1977 – but not in mine, as I find it too dull and derivative – this is a concept album with four lengthy tracks about the rise and fall of Atlantis, so its prog credentials are unarguable. Unfortunately, it's also musically forgettable. It's very big in Germany, though.

England – Garden Shed

You've probably never heard of them, which is a shame because their 1977 debut is a fine progressive album described by *Melody Maker* as 'Yes in Toyland' and is notable for keyboardist Robert Webb playing a Mellotron that had been deliberately sawn in half. Sadly, even a full Mellotron wouldn't have been enough to stop the album from sinking without a trace under the punk bombardment.

The Enid – Aerie Faerie Nonsense

The Enid were one of the few prog bands that numbered punks as fans, despite the music – romantic orchestral suites crossed with rock instruments – being the absolute antithesis of punk. This, their second album, is described by some fans as their masterpiece, although it was unavailable for many years until re-recorded in the 1980s.

Ethos – Open Up

This US four-piece was formed in 1973. This, their second and final album, is an intriguing mix of Lizard-era King Crimson, a light take on Yes and Kansas overlaid with melodic pop sensibilities.

Far East Family Band – Tenkujin

Regarded as the first Japanese progressive rock band (under the name Far Out), their fourth and final album is their least successful, mainly because of the departure of keyboard player Kitaro. Check out the earlier albums for some unique Japanese progressive psychedelia.

Finch – Galleons Of Passion

To the Netherlands again for a sort of sub-Focus band (complete with flute). They made three albums of very pleasant melodic prog, heavy on the keyboards.

Forgas – Cocktail

This debut album by French drummer Patrick Forgas is inspired by Soft Machine and Robert Wyatt. Funky, jazzy and unpredictable, *Cocktail* is mostly instrumental – the 20-minute-long side two track 'My Trip' tells you all you need to know.

Gong – Gazeuse

Not the Daevid Allen-led band, with its Pothead Pixies and Flying Teapots, but the less interesting instrumental version led by drummer and percussionist Pierre Moerlen. It is notable for featuring guitar genius Allan Holdsworth and whimsical Gong sax blower Didier Malherbe in the lineup, but they are not enough to stop *Gazeuse* from being wholly forgettable.

Grobschnitt – Rockpommel's Land

A concept album about a daydreamer called Ernie and his fairytale adventures with big bird Maraboo in a city where laughter is banned, *Rockpommel's Land* is surprisingly gentle and melodic for a German prog band and owes plenty to the likes of Genesis and Yes. Regarded as the band's most important work, it can drag at times – particularly in the 19-minute title track – but it's definitely worth your attention.

Gryphon – Treason

Gryphon were a medieval folk group from London who combined modern electric guitars and keyboards with ye olde instruments such as crumhorns. Fifth release *Treason* was their most rock-oriented album but heralded the band's demise as they threw in the towel in the face of the punk onslaught. *Midnight Mushrumps* (1974) is their best offering.

Heldon – Interface

I know people who insist this was the best progressive rock album of 1977. It may be, but only if you like disturbing industrial soundscapes overlaid with unhinged guitar solos. The band were led by French guitarist Richard Pinhas, who was influenced by Robert Fripp and Brian Eno. An acquired taste that I haven't acquired.

Iceberg – Sentiments

You wouldn't guess from the sound that Iceberg were Spanish, formed in Barcelona in 1974. Their four albums contain excellent instrumental jazz fusion with fast and furious keyboard and guitar interplay a la the Mahavishnu Orchestra. *Sentiments* is a fine example of their work.

Il Baricentro – Trusciant

On offer here is some Italian jazz-rock clearly inspired by Weather Report, with added Latin rhythms. This, their second and last album, is a lovely listen from start to finish.

Kansas – Point Of Know Return

The US band, led by keyboard player Steve Walsh, can claim to be prog thanks to their earlier albums, but by 1977, they were peddling unmemorable pop-rock songs. It worked, though – *Point Of Know Return* was their most successful album in the US.

Kayak – Starlight Dancer

Dutch band Kayak's most prog albums were their first three, released between 1972 and 1975. By *Starlight Dancer*, they were following the route of many prog bands down the pop-rock route, so don't bother with it.

Kraan – Wiederhoren

This is the sixth album by the tuneful Krautrock band. The first five albums are great, but this one isn't. It's worth hunting out, though, just to laugh at the cover, showing the musicians looking like a deranged boy band.

La Locanda Delle Fate – Forse Le Lucciole Non Si Amano Piu

I'm a big fan of Italian prog and this is a fine but overlooked debut release by a short-lived band that broke up soon after. Based mostly on piano, keyboard strings and acoustic guitar, it sounds a bit like an Italian Renaissance (the band, not the historical era) with some excellent instrumental playing. The title translates into English as Maybe Fireflies Don't Love Each Other Any More.

Le Orme – Storio O Leggenda

Long-lasting Italian band Le Orme (formed in 1969 and still going strong) sound a bit like early Renaissance – all dreamy keyboards and acoustic guitars. Their best period was the early 1970s, so this 1977 release is not essential – in fact, it's a bit dull.

Maneige – Ni Vent…Ni Nouvelle

This jazzy prog six-piece can be described as a cross between early Frank Zappa and Pink Floyd, a fascinating mix of keyboards, saxophone, electric guitar and marimba. This is their third album and is definitely worth listening to.

Modry Efekt – Svitanie

This Czech band had to change its name from Blue Effect on the orders of the government (it was too English) and embraced instrumental jazz-rock because it was politically safer. This resulted in some excellent albums featuring tight, dramatic and expressive musicianship, particularly from leader and guitarist Radim Hladik. Svitanie is an excellent example of what Modry Efekt could do – listen to it and you'll be wondering why you have never heard of this band before.

Patrick Moraz – Out In The Sun

Recorded and released after he was booted out of Yes, Moraz's upbeat second solo album is drenched in Brazilian and Latin rhythms. But is it prog? It certainly sounds nothing like Yes.

Pekka Pohjola – The Mathematician's Air Display

Jussi Pekka Pohjola was a bass player in Finnish prog band Wigwam before embarking on a solo career incorporating Frank Zappa-influenced jazz fusion. His third album was co-produced by Mike Oldfield, who also plays guitar, and has been released under various titles in different parts of the world, often credited to Oldfield and his sister Sally, who provides vocals.

Potemkine – Triton

On offer here is some sparse, jazzy instrumental prog with Magma overtones from France. Excellent bass playing from Doudou Duboisson drives percussive piano and sparing use of guitar.

Premiata Forneria Marconi – Jet Lag

An Italian band (their name means Award-winning Marconi Bakery, for some reason), PFM formed in 1970 and are still in existence as I write these words with my very prog quill pen. Their earlier albums are the best, but *Jet Lag* is worth a listen for its dive into jazz fusion.

Procol Harum – Something Magic

Side one is quite listenable, but side two – a 19-minute suite in which Gary Brooker recites a Keith Reid poem over classical-style piano and orchestra – is a crime against music.

Pulsar – Halloween

Despite opening with a clumsy attempt to hum the saccharine Irish lament 'Danny Boy', the French band's third album contains two epic tracks dominated by Mellotron, guitars and flute, heavily influenced by Pink Floyd and King Crimson.

Quantum Jump – Barracuda

This second album by funky Canterbury-influenced band led by Rupert Hine suffers from the loss of guitar wizard Mark Warner. The debut album, the year before, is better and includes the hilarious hit single 'The Lone Ranger'.

Renaissance – Novella

Sandwiched between the artistic triumphs of *Scheherazade And Other Stories* (1975) and *A Song For All Seasons* (1978), *Novella* was a lacklustre and formulaic addition to the band's catalogue.

Ripaille – La Vieille Que L'on Brula

This French band combine gentle, melodic jazz fusion with folkie sounds, thanks to the addition of crumhorn, accordion and violin. This was their only album – their record label went bust soon after.

Schicke Fuhrs Frohling – Sunburst

Collectively known as SFF, the trio of Eduard Schicke, Gerd Fuhrs and Heinz Frohling combine intricate drums, synth and guitar interplay on a superb collection of spacey jazz-rock instrumentals. *Sunburst* is an album that should be much better known than it is and is a worthy addition to your prog collection.

Starcastle – Fountains Of Light

This US band channelled Yes perhaps a bit too much, failing to establish a clear musical identity for themselves. The singer sounds a bit too much like Jon Anderson, but the vocal harmonies are very well done. They released a second album in 1977, *Citadel*, but it's rubbish.

Supertramp – Even In The Quietest Moments

The English rock band led by Roger Hodgson and Rick Davies were moving steadily away from prog to pop, achieving huge commercial success as a result. So, their fifth album contains little that we would recognise as prog except for the 11-minute closing epic 'Fool's Overture', which combines a random sound collage with pseudo-orchestral string backing.

Tangerine Dream – Encore

Yes, I know I said no live albums. But I've made an exception for Tangerine Dream because this is a double album consisting of four brand-new, improvised tracks recorded on a tour. Personally, it all sounds the same to me, but I'm told by those who like this stuff that it's a cracker. Oh, and the band had a UK top-40 album the same year with the soundtrack to a film called *Sorcerer*.

Univers Zero – Univers Zero [aka 1313]

Those of you who speak Kobaian, the language invented by Magma, will know that Zeuhl is the name given to a particularly French musical genre that combines jazz-fusion and symphonic prog with what today we would call a goth approach. Belgian band Univers Zero were cut from the same cloth – they played dark, dense and challenging instrumental music designed to pummel the listener into submission. Their debut is a strong, powerful album that will appeal to any fans of the aforementioned Magma (who didn't release a studio album in 1977, otherwise they would definitely be in this book). The album was later remixed and re-released as 1313, which was its catalogue number.

Utopia – Ra

Genre-hopper Todd Rundgren released nine albums under the name of his progressive rock outfit. *Ra*, the third release, is a turgid, lumbering affair that could almost be a parody if it had even an ounce of humour in it. Unfortunately, Rundgren takes it all too seriously and misses the mark by a mile.

Rick Wakeman – Criminal Record

Recorded after *Going For The One*, Wakeman's sixth solo album is inspired by all things illegal, such as the Birdman of Alcatraz and the Chamber of Horrors. Musically, it's a 1977 version of his *The Six Wives Of Henry VIII*, full of very entertaining musical portraits. Dare I say this one has been criminally overlooked?

Where Prog Went Next

Punk didn't kill prog. In fact, by 1979, the first wave of punk had almost run out of phlegm as bands realised that three chords and a lot of snarling were not creatively satisfying. By the early 1980s, the popular musical landscape had splintered into various offshoots, including new wave, ska, the mod revival, synthpop and sophisticated hard pop. Some punk bands even went prog – listen to 'Golden Brown' by The Stranglers and tell me if that isn't channelling classic Caravan!

We have already noted at the beginning of the book that some of the prog bands of 1977 didn't survive the decade. So, it was goodbye Gentle Giant and Emerson, Lake & Palmer (apart from the occasional ill-advised comeback), and farewell Happy the Man (although they released comeback albums and singles).

However, many of the groups in these pages continued to make great music into the 1980s and beyond. Roger Waters used his unfortunate *Animals* touring experience to create *The Wall*, a sprawling double LP epic about the alienation of the poor millionaire rock star that gave Pink Floyd their first hit single since 1968 in 'Another Brick In The Wall', which topped the charts in 14 countries. Unfortunately, internal divisions ripped the band apart soon afterwards, sending it on a four-year hiatus after the truly dreadful *The Final Cut* before David Gilmour resurrected the name for three more studio albums.

Yes also had a torrid time after *Going For The One*. *Tormato* in 1978 was a bit of a disaster, heralding a split that saw three-fifths of the band join forces with The Buggles before South African guitarist Trevor Rabin gave them their biggest single hit in 'Owner Of A Lonely Heart' in 1983. Since then, the band have continued releasing albums, some good, some not so good, including *Mirror To The Sky* in 2023. Thanks to splits and deaths, the current lineup has no-one from the *Going For The One* years except Steve Howe.

Jethro Tull continued through the 1980s and 1990s, hitting some high points with 1982's *Broadsword And The Beast* and 1987's award-winning *Crest Of A Knave* and some low points with the electronic album *Under Wraps* in 1984. They split in 2011 but were recently resurrected by Ian Anderson, releasing three more albums. They are not essential.

Styx went on to even greater success with 1981's *Paradise Theater* and are still touring and releasing albums but without Dennis DeYoung. Anthony Phillips has beavered away in almost total obscurity, having released nearly 40 albums to date, while his former bandmate Peter Gabriel is now recognised as a major British musical and technological innovator, with a number-one album, *i/o*, in 2023.

The Alan Parsons Project went on to even greater commercial success with their tuneful concept albums, eventually breaking up in 1990. Lol Creme and Kevin Godley put the disaster of *Consequences* behind them and embarked on a series of quirky, intelligent pop albums before concentrating on music videos.

Goblin continued scoring movies until 2001. Since then, there have been several live comebacks with the result that there appear to be no fewer than three different Goblin bands doing the rounds, along with a reformed Cherry Five. Also still making music is Steve Hillage, who in 1989 formed the electronic dance music band System 7, releasing 14 albums over the last 30 years.

Rush are no longer a going concern – drummer Neil Peart sadly died in 2020 – but they had a good long run, arguably reaching their peak in 1981 with the *Moving Pictures* album. Some of their 1980s synth-drenched stuff is a bit forgettable, but they redeemed themselves with 2012's *Clockwork Angels*, a brilliant return to form.

Van der Graaf Generator took an extended break between 1978 and 2005, but since then, they have been gigging and releasing new albums fairly regularly, although they last toured in 2022 and there is no word of any future plans. All is quiet in the Camel camp, too, after Andy Latimer cancelled the 2023 tour dates to have back surgery. His band released nine further studio albums after *Rain Dances*, including the well-received *Nude* (1981) and *Harbour Of Tears* (1996).

As for John Greaves and Brian Eno, both are still working and playing and sporadically releasing their idiosyncratic albums to a select but devoted audience.

Of course, no musical genre can survive just on the old established acts – it needs regular injections of new blood. A second wave of prog came in the early 1980s with bands such as Marillion, Pendragon and IQ, while a third wave hit us all in the 1990s, spearheaded by the Flower Kings, Spock's Beard and Porcupine Tree.

Today, the popular musical landscape is dominated by solo artists – in fact, in 2023, only four groups got into the UK top 100 singles. Many pin the blame on social media, which is geared towards promoting individuals. But drill down and you'll find many musical genres co-existing very nicely indeed – including our old friend prog.

Bands such as Big Big Train, The Tangent, Public Service Broadcasting, King Gizzard and the Lizard Wizard, Opeth and Sigur Rós – and solo artists including Steven Wilson, Neal Morse and Tim Bowness – are making albums and selling out tours. They may not be soaring around on their own personalised jets or trundling across the US with a convoy of pantechnicons and a symphony orchestra, but they are managing to make enough money to survive thanks to their ability to build up a loyal following through social media.

Of course, the fanbase for these bands consists mostly of old blokes like me with enough spare cash to buy the overpriced tickets and the box sets that trundle endlessly out of the pressing plants, thus helping to keep veteran musicians such as Steve Hackett, David Gilmour and Focus on the road. Once we all pop our clogs, who knows what future prog will have?

Until then, hoorah for the capes and codpieces, the endless keyboard solos, the guitar pyrotechnics and the impenetrable lyrical nonsense that make prog so irresistible.

Also available from Sonicbond

On Track series
AC/DC – Chris Sutton 978-1-78952-307-2
Allman Brothers Band – Andrew Wild 978-1-78952-252-5
Tori Amos – Lisa Torem 978-1-78952-142-9
Aphex Twin – Beau Waddell 978-1-78952-267-9
Asia – Peter Braidis 978-1-78952-099-6
Badfinger – Robert Day-Webb 978-1-878952-176-4
Barclay James Harvest – Keith and Monica Domone 978-1-78952-067-5
Beck – Arthur Lizie 978-1-78952-258-7
The Beat, General Public, Fine Young Cannibals – Steve Parry 978-1-78952-274-7
The Beatles 1962-1996 – Alberto Bravin and Andrew Wild 978-1-78952-355-3
The Beatles Solo 1969-1980 – Andrew Wild 978-1-78952-030-9
Blue Oyster Cult – Jacob Holm-Lupo 978-1-78952-007-1
Blur – Matt Bishop 978-178952-164-1
Marc Bolan and T.Rex – Peter Gallagher 978-1-78952-124-5
David Bowie 1964 to 1982 – Carl Ewens 978-1-78952-324-9
David Bowie 1963 to 2016 – Don Klees 978-1-78952-351-5
Kate Bush – Bill Thomas 978-1-78952-097-2
The Byrds – Andy McArthur 978-1-78952-280-8
Camel – Hamish Kuzminski 978-1-78952-040-8
Captain Beefheart – Opher Goodwin 978-1-78952-235-8
Caravan – Andy Boot 978-1-78952-127-6
Cardiacs – Eric Benac 978-1-78952-131-3
Wendy Carlos – Mark Marrington 978-1-78952-331-7
The Carpenters – Paul Tornbohm 978-1-78952-301-0
Nick Cave and The Bad Seeds – Dominic Sanderson 978-1-78952-240-2
Eric Clapton Solo – Andrew Wild 978-1-78952-141-2
The Clash (revised edition) – Nick Assirati 978-1-78952-325-6
Elvis Costello and The Attractions – Georg Purvis 978-1-78952-129-0
Crosby, Stills and Nash – Andrew Wild 978-1-78952-039-2
Creedence Clearwater Revival – Tony Thompson 978-1-78952-237-2
Crowded House – Jon Magidsohn 978-1-78952-292-1
The Damned – Morgan Brown 978-1-78952-136-8
David Bowie 1964 to 1982 – Carl Ewens 978-1-78952-324-9
David Bowie 1964 to 1982 – Carl Ewens 978-1-78952-324-9
Deep Purple and Rainbow 1968-79 – Steve Pilkington 978-1-78952-002-6
Deep Purple from 1984 – Phil Kafcaloudes 978-1-78952-354-6
Depeche Mode – Brian J. Robb 978-1-78952-277-8
Dire Straits – Andrew Wild 978-1-78952-044-6
The Divine Comedy – Alan Draper 978-1-78952-308-9
The Doors – Tony Thompson 978-1-78952-137-5
Dream Theater – Jordan Blum 978-1-78952-050-7
Bob Dylan 1962-1970 – Opher Goodwin 978-1-78952-275-2
Eagles – John Van der Kiste 978-1-78952-260-0
Earth, Wind and Fire – Bud Wilkins 978-1-78952-272-3
Electric Light Orchestra – Barry Delve 978-1-78952-152-8
Emerson Lake and Palmer – Mike Goode 978-1-78952-000-2
Fairport Convention – Kevan Furbank 978-1-78952-051-4
Peter Gabriel – Graeme Scarfe 978-1-78952-138-2
Genesis – Stuart MacFarlane 978-1-78952-005-7
Gentle Giant – Gary Steel 978-1-78952-058-3
Gong – Kevan Furbank 978-1-78952-082-8
Green Day – William E. Spevack 978-1-78952-261-7
Steve Hackett – Geoffrey Feakes 978-1-78952-098-9
Hall and Oates – Ian Abrahams 978-1-78952-167-2
Peter Hammill – Richard Rees Jones 978-1-78952-163-4
Roy Harper – Opher Goodwin 978-1-78952-130-6
Hawkwind (new edition) – Duncan Harris 978-1-78952-290-7
Jimi Hendrix – Emma Stott 978-1-78952-175-7

Also available from Sonicbond

The Hollies – Andrew Darlington 978-1-78952-159-7
Horslips – Richard James 978-1-78952-263-1
The Human League and The Sheffield Scene – Andrew Darlington 978-1-78952-186-3
Humble Pie –Robert Day-Webb 978-1-78952-2761
Ian Hunter – G. Mick Smith 978-1-78952-304-1
The Incredible String Band – Tim Moon 978-1-78952-107-8
INXS – Manny Grillo 978-1-78952-302-7
Iron Maiden – Steve Pilkington 978-1-78952-061-3
Joe Jackson – Richard James 978-1-78952-189-4
The Jam – Stan Jeffries 978-1-78952-299-0
Jefferson Airplane – Richard Butterworth 978-1-78952-143-6
Jethro Tull – Jordan Blum 978-1-78952-016-3
J. Geils Band – James Romag 978-1-78952-332-4
Elton John in the 1970s – Peter Kearns 978-1-78952-034-7
Billy Joel – Lisa Torem 978-1-78952-183-2
Journey – Doug Thornton 978-1-78952-337-9
Judas Priest – John Tucker 978-1-78952-018-7
Kansas – Kevin Cummings 978-1-78952-057-6
Killing Joke – Nic Ransome 978-1-78952-273-0
The Kinks – Martin Hutchinson 978-1-78952-172-6
Korn – Matt Karpe 978-1-78952-153-5
Led Zeppelin – Steve Pilkington 978-1-78952-151-1
Level 42 – Matt Philips 978-1-78952-102-3
Little Feat – Georg Purvis – 978-1-78952-168-9
Magnum – Matthew Taylor – 978-1-78952-286-0
Aimee Mann – Jez Rowden 978-1-78952-036-1
Ralph McTell – Paul O. Jenkins 978-1-78952-294-5
Metallica – Barry Wood 978-1-78952-269-3
Joni Mitchell – Peter Kearns 978-1-78952-081-1
The Moody Blues – Geoffrey Feakes 978-1-78952-042-2
Motorhead – Duncan Harris 978-1-78952-173-3
Nektar – Scott Meze – 978-1-78952-257-0
New Order – Dennis Remmer – 978-1-78952-249-5
Nightwish – Simon McMurdo – 978-1-78952-270-9
Nirvana – William E. Spevack 978-1-78952-318-8
Laura Nyro – Philip Ward 978-1-78952-182-5
Oasis – Andrew Rooney 978-1-78952-300-3
Phil Ochs – Opher Goodwin 978-1-78952-326-3
Mike Oldfield – Ryan Yard 978-1-78952-060-6
Opeth – Jordan Blum 978-1-78-952-166-5
Pearl Jam – Ben L. Connor 978-1-78952-188-7
Tom Petty – Richard James 978-1-78952-128-3
Pink Floyd – Richard Butterworth 978-1-78952-242-6
The Police – Pete Braidis 978-1-78952-158-0
Porcupine Tree (Revised Edition) – Nick Holmes 978-1-78952-346-1
Procol Harum – Scott Meze 978-1-78952-315-7
Queen – Andrew Wild 978-1-78952-003-3
Radiohead – William Allen 978-1-78952-149-8
Gerry Rafferty – John Van der Kiste 978-1-78952-349-2
Rancid – Paul Matts 978-1-78952-187-0
Lou Reed 1972-1986 – Ethan Roy 978-1-78952-283-9
Renaissance – David Detmer 978-1-78952-062-0
REO Speedwagon – Jim Romag 978-1-78952-262-4
The Rolling Stones 1963-80 – Steve Pilkington 978-1-78952-017-0
Linda Ronstadt 1969-1989 – Daryl O. Lawrence 987-1-78952-293-8
Roxy Music – Michael Kulikowski 978-1-78952-335-5
Rush 1973 to 1982 – Richard James 978-1-78952-338-6
Sensational Alex Harvey Band – Peter Gallagher 978-1-7952-289-1
The Small Faces and The Faces – Andrew Darlington 978-1-78952-316-4

The Smashing Pumpkins – Matt Karpe 978-1-7952-291-4
The Smiths and Morrissey – Tommy Gunnarsson 978-1-78952-140-5
Soft Machine – Scott Meze 978-1078952-271-6
Sparks 1969-1979 – Chris Sutton 978-1-78952-279-2
Spirit – Rev. Keith A. Gordon – 978-1-78952- 248-8
Stackridge – Alan Draper 978-1-78952-232-7
Status Quo the Frantic Four Years – Richard James 978-1-78952-160-3
Steely Dan – Jez Rowden 978-1-78952-043-9
The Stranglers – Martin Hutchinson 978-1-78952-323-2
Talk Talk – Gary Steel 978-1-78952-284-6
Talking Heads – David Starkey 978-178952-353-9
Tears For Fears – Paul Clark – 978-178952-238-9
Thin Lizzy – Graeme Stroud 978-1-78952-064-4
Tool – Matt Karpe 978-1-78952-234-1
Toto – Jacob Holm-Lupo 978-1-78952-019-4
U2 – Eoghan Lyng 978-1-78952-078-1
UFO – Richard James 978-1-78952-073-6
Ultravox – Brian J. Robb 978-1-78952-330-0
Van Der Graaf Generator – Dan Coffey 978-1-78952-031-6
Van Halen – Morgan Brown – 9781-78952-256-3
Suzanne Vega – Lisa Torem 978-1-78952-281-5
Jack White And The White Stripes – Ben L. Connor 978-1-78952-303-4
The Who – Geoffrey Feakes 978-1-78952-076-7
Roy Wood and the Move – James R Turner 978-1-78952-008-8
Yes (new edition) – Stephen Lambe 978-1-78952-282-2
Neil Young 1963 to 1970 – Oper Goodwin 978-1-78952-298-3
Frank Zappa 1966 to 1979 – Eric Benac 978-1-78952-033-0
Warren Zevon – Peter Gallagher 978-1-78952-170-2
The Zombies – Emma Stott 978-1-78952-297-6
10CC – Peter Kearns 978-1-78952-054-5

Decades Series
The Bee Gees in the 1960s – Andrew Mon Hughes et al 978-1-78952-148-1
The Bee Gees in the 1970s – Andrew Mon Hughes et al 978-1-78952-179-5
Black Sabbath in the 1970s – Chris Sutton 978-1-78952-171-9
Britpop – Peter Richard Adams and Matt Pooler 978-1-78952-169-6
Phil Collins in the 1980s – Andrew Wild 978-1-78952-185-6
Alice Cooper in the 1970s – Chris Sutton 978-1-78952-104-7
Alice Cooper in the 1980s – Chris Sutton 978-1-78952-259-4
Curved Air in the 1970s – Laura Shenton 978-1-78952-069-9
Donovan in the 1960s – Jeff Fitzgerald 978-1-78952-233-4
Bob Dylan in the 1980s – Don Klees 978-1-78952-157-3
Brian Eno in the 1970s – Gary Parsons 978-1-78952-239-6
Faith No More in the 1990s – Matt Karpe 978-1-78952-250-1
Fleetwood Mac in the 1970s – Andrew Wild 978-1-78952-105-4
Fleetwood Mac in the 1980s – Don Klees 978-178952-254-9
Focus in the 1970s – Stephen Lambe 978-1-78952-079-8
Free and Bad Company in the 1970s – John Van der Kiste 978-1-78952-178-8
Genesis in the 1970s – Bill Thomas 978178952-146-7
George Harrison in the 1970s – Eoghan Lyng 978-1-78952-174-0
Kiss in the 1970s – Peter Gallagher 978-1-78952-246-4
Manfred Mann's Earth Band in the 1970s – John Van der Kiste 978178952-243-3
Marillion in the 1980s – Nathaniel Webb 978-1-78952-065-1
Van Morrison in the 1970s – Peter Childs – 978-1-78952-241-9
Mott the Hoople & Ian Hunter in the 1970s – John Van der Kiste 978-1-78-952-162-7
Pink Floyd In The 1970s – Georg Purvis 978-1-78952-072-9
Suzi Quatro in the 1970s – Darren Johnson 978-1-78952-236-5
Queen in the 1970s – James Griffiths 978-1-78952-265-5
Roxy Music in the 1970s – Dave Thompson 978-1-78952-180-1

Also available from Sonicbond

Slade in the 1970s – Darren Johnson 978-1-78952-268-6
Status Quo in the 1980s – Greg Harper 978-1-78952-244-0
Tangerine Dream in the 1970s – Stephen Palmer 978-1-78952-161-0
The Sweet in the 1970s – Darren Johnson 978-1-78952-139-9
Uriah Heep in the 1970s – Steve Pilkington 978-1-78952-103-0
Van der Graaf Generator in the 1970s – Steve Pilkington 978-1-78952-245-7
Rick Wakeman in the 1970s – Geoffrey Feakes 978-1-78952-264-8
Yes in the 1980s – Stephen Lambe with David Watkinson 978-1-78952-125-2

Rock Classics Series
90125 by Yes – Stephen Lambe 978-1-78952-329-4
Bat Out Of Hell by Meatloaf – Geoffrey Feakes 978-1-78952-320-1
Bringing It All Back Home by Bob Dylan – Opher Goodwin 978-1-78952-314-0
Californication by Red Hot Chili Peppers - Matt Karpe 978-1-78952-348-5
Crime Of The Century by Supertramp – Steve Pilkington 978-1-78952-327-0
The Dreaming by Kate Bush – Peter Kearns 978-1-78952-341-6
Let It Bleed by The Rolling Stones – John Van der Kiste 978-1-78952-309-6
Pawn Hearts by Van Der Graaf Generator – Paolo Carnelli 978-1-78952-357-7
Purple Rain by Prince – Matt Karpe 978-1-78952-322-5
The White Album by The Beatles – Opher Goodwin 978-1-78952-333-1

On Screen Series
Carry On… – Stephen Lambe 978-1-78952-004-0
David Cronenberg – Patrick Chapman 978-1-78952-071-2
Doctor Who: The David Tennant Years – Jamie Hailstone 978-1-78952-066-8
James Bond – Andrew Wild 978-1-78952-010-1
Monty Python – Steve Pilkington 978-1-78952-047-7
Seinfeld Seasons 1 to 5 – Stephen Lambe 978-1-78952-012-5

Other Books
1967: A Year In Psychedelic Rock 978-1-78952-155-9
1970: A Year In Rock – John Van der Kiste 978-1-78952-147-4
1972: The Year Progressive Rock Ruled The World – Kevan Furbank 978-1-78952-288-4
1973: The Golden Year of Progressive Rock 978-1-78952-165-8
Eric Clapton Sessions – Andrew Wild 978-1-78952-177-1
Dark Horse Records – Aaron Badgley 978-1-78952-287-7
Derek Taylor: For Your Radioactive Children – Andrew Darlington 978-1-78952-038-5
Ghosts – Journeys To Post-Pop – Matthew Restall 978-1-78952-334-8
The Golden Age of Easy Listening – Derek Taylor 978-1-78952-285-3
The Golden Road: The Recording History of The Grateful Dead – John Kilbride 978-1-78952-156-6
Hoggin' The Page – Groudhogs The Classic Years – Martyn Hanson 978-1-78952-343-0
Iggy and The Stooges On Stage 1967-1974 – Per Nilsen 978-1-78952-101-6
Jon Anderson and the Warriors – the Road to Yes – David Watkinson 978-1-78952-059-0
Magic: The David Paton Story – David Paton 978-1-78952-266-2
Misty: The Music of Johnny Mathis – Jakob Baekgaard 978-1-78952-247-1
Musical Guide To Red By King Crimson – Andrew Keeling 978-1-78952-321-8
Nu Metal: A Definitive Guide – Matt Karpe 978-1-78952-063-7
Philip Lynott – Renegade – Alan Byrne 978-1-78952-339-3
Remembering Live Aid – Andrew Wild 978-1-78952-328-7
Thank You For The Days - Fans Of The Kinks Share 60 Years of Stories – Ed. Chris Kocher 978-1-78952-342-3
The Sonicbond On Track Sampler – 978-1-78952-190-0
The Sonicbond Progressive Rock Sampler (Ebook only) – 978-1-78952-056-9
Tommy Bolin: In and Out of Deep Purple – Laura Shenton 978-1-78952-070-5
Maximum Darkness – Deke Leonard 978-1-78952-048-4
The Twang Dynasty – Deke Leonard 978-1-78952-049-1

and many more to come!